First World War
and Army of Occupation
War Diary
France, Belgium and Germany

46 DIVISION
Headquarters, Branches and Services
Commander Royal Engineers
19 August 1916 - 14 June 1919

WO95/2672/1

The Naval & Military Press Ltd
www.nmarchive.com
Published in association with The National Archives

Published by

The Naval & Military Press Ltd

Unit 10 Ridgewood Industrial Park,
Uckfield, East Sussex,
TN22 5QE England
Tel: +44 (0) 1825 749494

www.naval-military-press.com
www.nmarchive.com

This diary has been reprinted in facsimile from the original. Any imperfections are inevitably reproduced and the quality may fall short of modern type and cartographic standards.

© Crown Copyright
Images reproduced by permission of The National Archives, London, England, 2015.

Contents

Document type	Place/Title	Date From	Date To
Heading	WO95/2672/1 Commander Royal Engineers.		
Heading	Division Engineers R.E. 16 June 1919		
War Diary	Bavincourt	19/08/1916	30/10/1916
War Diary	Mezerolles	31/10/1916	01/11/1916
War Diary	St. Riquier	02/11/1916	30/11/1916
Miscellaneous	Operation Order by Brig-General. C.V. Wingfield-Stratford. C.M.G.	10/11/1916	10/11/1916
Miscellaneous	Operation Order by Brig-General. C.V. Wingfield-Stratford. C.M.G. C.H.E. 46th Division.	20/11/1916	20/11/1916
War Diary	Lucheux Sheet 51e T.16.d.	01/12/1916	07/12/1916
War Diary	Henu Sheet 57d D.19.a	08/12/1916	31/12/1916
War Diary	Henu	01/01/1917	20/02/1917
War Diary	Gouv	21/02/1917	28/02/1917
Miscellaneous	O.C. 465th Field Coy. R.E. Headqrs, 46th Division (for information).	17/02/1917	17/02/1917
Miscellaneous	O.C. 466th Field Coy. R.E. O.C. 468th Field Coy. R.E. Headqrs, 46th Division. (for information).	17/02/1917	17/02/1917
War Diary	Henu	01/03/1917	17/03/1917
War Diary	La Haie Ferme	18/03/1917	21/03/1917
War Diary	Couin	22/03/1917	23/03/1917
War Diary	Dury	24/03/1917	28/03/1917
War Diary	Norrent Fontes	28/03/1917	31/03/1917
Operation(al) Order(s)	C.R.E's 58th Division Operation Order No. 6	01/03/1917	01/03/1917
Operation(al) Order(s)	C.R.E's 58th Division Operation Order No. 7	02/03/1917	02/03/1917
Miscellaneous	O.C. 466th Field Co R.E.	04/03/1917	04/03/1917
Miscellaneous	Operation Order by Brigadier-General C.V. Wingfield-Stratford C.M.G. C.R.E. 46th Division	06/03/1917	06/03/1917
Miscellaneous	C Form (Duplicate). Messages And Signals.		
Miscellaneous	Operation Order by Brigadier-General C.V. Wingfield-Stratford C.M.G. C.R.E. 38th Division	06/03/1917	06/03/1917
Operation(al) Order(s)	C.R.E's 58th Division Operation Order No. 9	06/03/1917	06/03/1917
Miscellaneous	O.C. 465th Field Coy. R.E.	06/03/1917	06/03/1917
Operation(al) Order(s)	Operation Order No. 1. by Brig-General. C.V. Wingfield-Stratford., C.M.G. C.R.E., 46th Division.	10/03/1917	10/03/1917
Miscellaneous	A Form. Messages And Signals.		
Operation(al) Order(s)	46th Division Order No. 146	13/03/1917	13/03/1917
Operation(al) Order(s)	Operation Order No 4. by Brigadier-General C.V. Wingfield-Stratford C.M.G. C.R.E. 46th Division.	16/03/1917	16/03/1917
Miscellaneous	O.C. 468th Field Coy. R.E.	18/03/1917	18/03/1917
Operation(al) Order(s)	Operation Order No. 3 by Brigadier-General C.V. Wingfield-Stratford. C.M.G. C.R.E. 46th Division.	16/03/1917	16/03/1917
Miscellaneous	O.C. 465th Field Coy. R.E.	17/03/1917	17/03/1917
Operation(al) Order(s)	46th Division Order No. 149	17/03/1917	17/03/1917
Miscellaneous	Entrainment Programme. for Move of 46th Division less Artillery.	27/03/1917	27/03/1917
Miscellaneous	Table "D" Move Of 46th (North Midland) Division (Less Artillery).		
Miscellaneous	46th Division No. Q745	25/03/1917	25/03/1917
War Diary	Norrent Fontes	01/04/1917	12/04/1917
War Diary	Busnes	13/04/1917	16/04/1917

War Diary	Labuissiere	17/04/1917	19/04/1917
War Diary	Sains en Gohelle	20/04/1917	30/04/1917
Miscellaneous	O.C. 465th Field Co R.E.	06/04/1917	06/04/1917
Miscellaneous	46th Division. 2639/2/G.	07/04/1917	07/04/1917
Miscellaneous	A Form. Messages And Signals.		
Miscellaneous	46th Division 2639/2/G, C.R.E. 46th Div. E. 485	07/04/1917	07/04/1917
Miscellaneous	Operation Order No. 5. issued by Brig-Genl, C.V. Wingfield-Stratford., C.M.G.	10/04/1917	10/04/1917
Miscellaneous	Operation Order No. 6. issued by Brig-General C.V. Wingfield-Stratford., C.M.G. Commanding Royal Engineers	10/04/1917	10/04/1917
Miscellaneous	Operation Order No. 7. issued by Brig-General C.V. Wingfield-Stratford., C.M.G. C.R.E. 46th Division	12/04/1917	12/04/1917
Operation(al) Order(s)	Operation Order 8. by Brigadier-General C.V. Wingfield-Stratford C.M.G. C.R.E. 46th Division	13/04/1917	13/04/1917
Operation(al) Order(s)	Operation Order No. 8.A. by Brig-Genl C.V. Wingfield-Stratford C.M.G. C.R.E. 46th Division	14/04/1917	14/04/1917
Operation(al) Order(s)	Operation Order No. 9. by Brig-Genl C.V. Wingfield-Stratford C.M.G. C.R.E. 46th Division	14/04/1917	14/04/1917
Operation(al) Order(s)	Operation Order No. 10 By Brig-Genl C.V. Wingfield-Stratford C.M.G. C.R.E. 46th Division	15/04/1917	15/04/1917
Operation(al) Order(s)	Operation Order No. 11 by Brig-Genl C.V. Wingfield-Stratford C.M.G. C.R.E. 46th Division	17/04/1917	17/04/1917
Operation(al) Order(s)	Operation Order No. 12 By Brig-General C.V. Wingfield-Stratford C.M.G. C.R.E. 46th Division	18/04/1917	18/04/1917
Miscellaneous	O.C. 465 Field Coy	20/04/1917	20/04/1917
Miscellaneous	CRE 46th Division	28/04/1917	28/04/1917
Operation(al) Order(s)	46th Division Order No. 167	23/04/1917	23/04/1917
Operation(al) Order(s)	46th Division Order No. 170	27/04/1917	27/04/1917
Operation(al) Order(s)	46th Division Order No. 171	30/04/1917	30/04/1917
War Diary	Sains en Gohelle	01/03/1917	31/03/1917
Miscellaneous	O.C. 468th Field Co R.E.	01/05/1917	01/05/1917
Miscellaneous	O.C. 468th Field Co R.E.	02/05/1917	02/05/1917
Operation(al) Order(s)	46th Division Order No 172	04/05/1917	04/05/1917
Operation(al) Order(s)	46th Division Order No 173	10/05/1917	10/05/1917
Miscellaneous	46th Division.	11/05/1917	11/05/1917
Operation(al) Order(s)	Operation Order No. 14. by Brig-Genl. C.V. Wingfield Stratford. C.M.G. C.R.E. 46th Division	14/05/1917	14/05/1917
Miscellaneous	O.C. 465th Field Co. R.E.	14/05/1917	14/05/1917
Operation(al) Order(s)	Operation Order No. 15. by Brig-Genl. C.V. Wingfield-Stratford C.M.G. C.R.E., 46th Division.	14/05/1917	14/05/1917
Operation(al) Order(s)	46th Division Order No 175	15/05/1917	15/05/1917
Operation(al) Order(s)	46th Division Order No 176	15/05/1917	15/05/1917
Operation(al) Order(s)	Addendum To 46th Division Order No. 175	16/05/1917	16/05/1917
Miscellaneous	Reference Order No. 175 of the 15th., Para. 8	17/05/1917	17/05/1917
Miscellaneous	46th Division wire begins.	18/05/1917	18/05/1917
Miscellaneous	A Form. Messages And Signals.		
Operation(al) Order(s)	46th Division Order No. 177	18/05/1917	18/05/1917
Operation(al) Order(s)	46th Division Order No. 178	22/05/1917	22/05/1917
Operation(al) Order(s)	46th Division Order No. 179	24/05/1917	24/05/1917
Miscellaneous	Headquarters, 139th Infantry Brigade.	29/05/1917	29/05/1917
War Diary	Sains en Gohelle	01/06/1917	30/06/1917
Miscellaneous	Reference 46th Divisional Order No. 182 And Amendment.	07/06/1917	07/06/1917
Operation(al) Order(s)	46th Division Order No. 189	12/06/1917	12/06/1917
Operation(al) Order(s)	46th Division Order No. 190	12/06/1917	12/06/1917

Type	Description	Start	End
Miscellaneous	Orders By Brigadier-General C.V. Wingfield-Stratford. C.M.G. C.R.E. 46th. Division	15/06/1917	15/06/1917
Miscellaneous	C.R.E. 46th Division.	15/06/1917	15/06/1917
Operation(al) Order(s)	Operation Order No. 22 By Brig-Genl. C.V. Wingfield-Stratford. C.M.G. C.R.E. 46th Division.	15/06/1917	15/06/1917
Miscellaneous	Orders By Brig-General C.V. Wingfield-Stratford C.M.G. C.R.E. 46th Division.	16/06/1917	16/06/1917
Operation(al) Order(s)	46th Division Order No. 195	18/06/1917	18/06/1917
Operation(al) Order(s)	46th Division Order No. 196	18/06/1917	18/06/1917
Miscellaneous	46th Division. C. 703	18/06/1917	18/06/1917
Miscellaneous	46th Division G. 723	19/06/1917	19/06/1917
Operation(al) Order(s)	46th Division Order No 198	22/06/1917	22/06/1917
Operation(al) Order(s)	46th Division Order No 200	23/06/1917	23/06/1917
Operation(al) Order(s)	Operation Order No. 23. By Brig-Genl. C.V. Wingfield-Stratford C.M.G. C.R.E. 46th Division.	23/06/1917	23/06/1917
Miscellaneous	A Form. Messages And Signals.		
Operation(al) Order(s)	46th Division Order No. 201	24/06/1917	24/06/1917
Operation(al) Order(s)	Operation Order No 24. By Brig-Genl. C.V. Wingfield-Stratford C.M.G. C.R.E. 46th Division.	24/06/1917	24/06/1917
Operation(al) Order(s)	Operation Order No 25. By Brig-Genl. C.V. Wingfield-Stratford C.M.G. C.R.E. 46th Division.	24/06/1917	24/06/1917
Miscellaneous	A Form. Messages And Signals.		
Miscellaneous	46th Division. G. 695	28/06/1917	28/06/1917
Operation(al) Order(s)	46th Division Order No. 210	29/06/1917	29/06/1917
Operation(al) Order(s)	Operation Order No 26. By Brig-Genl & C.V. Wingfield-Stratford C.M.G. C.R.E. 46th Division	30/06/1917	30/06/1917
War Diary	Sains en Gohelle	01/07/1917	03/07/1917
War Diary	La Comte	04/07/1917	23/07/1917
War Diary	Sailly La Bourse	24/07/1917	31/07/1917
Operation(al) Order(s)	Operation Order No 28 By Brig-Genl C.V. Wingfield-Stratford C.M.G. 46th Division.	02/07/1917	02/07/1917
Miscellaneous	March Table July 2nd. & 3rd.		
Operation(al) Order(s)	Operation Order No 29 By Brig-General C.V. Wingfield-Stratford C.M.G. C.R.E. 46th Division	20/07/1917	20/07/1917
Operation(al) Order(s)	Operation Order No 30 By Brig-General C.V. Wingfield-Stratford C.M.G. C.R.E. 46th Division.	29/07/1917	29/07/1917
Miscellaneous	Ref: C.R.E. Operation Order No 30	30/07/1917	30/07/1917
War Diary	Sailly La Bourse	01/08/1917	31/08/1917
Operation(al) Order(s)	Operation Order No 31 By Brig-General C.V. Wingfield-Stratford C.M.G. C.R.E. 46th Division	10/08/1917	10/08/1917
Operation(al) Order(s)	Operation Order No 32 By Brigadier-General C.V. Wingfield-Stratford C.M.G. C.R.E. 46th Division.	11/08/1917	11/08/1917
Operation(al) Order(s)	Operation Order No 33 By Brig-General C.V. Wingfield-Stratford C.M.G.	19/08/1917	19/08/1917
Operation(al) Order(s)	Operation Order No 34 By Brig-General C.V. Wingfield-Stratford C.M.G.	21/08/1917	21/08/1917
War Diary	Sailly La Bourse	01/09/1917	30/09/1917
Operation(al) Order(s)	46th Divisional Warning Order No. 14	16/09/1917	16/09/1917
Operation(al) Order(s)	Operation Order No. 35 By. Major L.J. Coussmaker M.C. Commanding Royal Engineers 46th Division.	18/09/1917	18/09/1917
War Diary	Sailly La Bourse	01/10/1917	31/10/1917
Miscellaneous	Cancel my 2489/162/G dated 27th instant.	29/10/1917	29/10/1917
War Diary	Sailly La Bourse	01/11/1917	30/11/1917
Operation(al) Order(s)	46th Division Order No 260	07/11/1917	07/11/1917
Operation(al) Order(s)	46th Division Warning Order No 267	23/11/1917	23/11/1917
Miscellaneous	O.C. 468th Field Co R.E.	24/11/1917	24/11/1917

Miscellaneous	Orders By Major R.K.A. Macaulay D.S.O., R.E., A/C.R.E., 25th Division.	25/11/1917	25/11/1917
Operation(al) Order(s)	C.R.E. Order No. 34	25/11/1917	25/11/1917
Miscellaneous	O.C. 468th Field Co R.E.	25/11/1917	25/11/1917
Miscellaneous	O.C. 468th Field Co R.E.	26/11/1917	26/11/1917
Miscellaneous	G.S. 46th Headquarters G.	25/11/1917	25/11/1917
Miscellaneous	C.R.E. 46th Division.	25/11/1917	25/11/1917
Miscellaneous	Handing Over Statement Hill 70 Section	00/11/1917	00/11/1917
War Diary	Sailly La Bourse	01/12/1917	22/01/1918
War Diary	Busnes	23/01/1918	31/01/1918
Miscellaneous	O.C. 46th Divisional Train. S.S.O. 46th Division.	15/01/1918	15/01/1918
Operation(al) Order(s)	46th Division Warning Order No 274	06/01/1918	06/01/1918
Miscellaneous	46th. Division. No. A2510/491	12/01/1918	12/01/1918
Miscellaneous	O.C. 465 Field Co R.E. Reference Operation Order No. 40	18/01/1918	18/01/1918
Miscellaneous			
Miscellaneous	O.C. 465 Field Co R.E.	20/01/1918	20/01/1918
Miscellaneous	Marching In State.	22/01/1918	22/01/1918
Miscellaneous	C.R.E. 46th Divn. Marching in State.	24/01/1918	24/01/1918
Miscellaneous	C.R.E. 46th Divn. Reference Operation Order No. 40	24/01/1918	24/01/1918
War Diary	Busnes	01/02/1918	08/02/1918
War Diary	Bomy	09/02/1918	28/02/1918
Miscellaneous	O.C. 465th Field Co R.E.	04/02/1918	04/02/1918
Miscellaneous	P.A. Moves.	12/02/1918	12/02/1918
Miscellaneous	C.R.E. 46th Division	13/02/1918	13/02/1918
Miscellaneous	Warning Order O.C. 466 Field Co R.E.	24/02/1918	24/02/1918
Miscellaneous	O.C. 466 Field Co R.E.	25/02/1918	25/02/1918
Operation(al) Order(s)	O.C. 465 Field Co R.E. 46th Divisional Warning Order No. 276.A.	25/02/1918	25/02/1918
Operation(al) Order(s)	46th Division Warning Order No. 276.A.	25/02/1918	25/02/1918
Miscellaneous	O.C. 465 Field Co R.E.	25/02/1918	25/02/1918
Miscellaneous	G. 209/11. C.R.A.	25/02/1918	25/02/1918
Miscellaneous	March Table-Issued With 46th Division Order No. G 209/11		
Miscellaneous	March Table-Issued With 46th Division Order No		
Operation(al) Order(s)	Operation Order No 41. By Brig-General C.V. Wingfield-Stratford, C.B., C.M.G. C.R.E. 46th Division.	28/02/1918	28/02/1918
Operation(al) Order(s)	46th Division Order No 276.B.	28/02/1918	28/02/1918
Miscellaneous	Grouping Table 137th Infantry Brigade. Group. Appendix A		
Miscellaneous	Accomodation Table Appendix B		
Miscellaneous	March Table.		
Miscellaneous	Messages And Signals.		
Miscellaneous	From O.C. 468th Field Coy R.E. to CRE 46th Division.	26/02/1918	26/02/1918
Miscellaneous	A Form Messages And Signals.		
Miscellaneous	C.R.E. 46th. Division. Reference Your E.59 dated 28-2-18	28/02/1918	28/02/1918
War Diary	Bomy	01/03/1918	02/03/1918
War Diary	Touquieres	03/03/1918	28/03/1918
War Diary	Braquemont	29/03/1918	31/03/1918
Miscellaneous	O.C. 465 Field Co R.E.	01/03/1918	01/03/1918
Operation(al) Order(s)	46th Division Order No 276.C	01/03/1918	01/03/1918
Miscellaneous	March Table Issued With 46th Division Order No 276.c.		
Miscellaneous	419 Field Co. R.E. 134 Infantry Bde.	02/03/1918	02/03/1918

Miscellaneous	Movement Table.		
Miscellaneous	Messages And Signals.		
Miscellaneous	C.R.E. 46th Division.	01/03/1918	01/03/1918
Miscellaneous	From O.C. To C.R.E. 46th Division.	01/03/1918	01/03/1918
Miscellaneous	From O.C Marching In State.	02/03/1918	02/03/1918
Miscellaneous	Messages And Signals.		
Miscellaneous	Form Messages And Signals.		
Miscellaneous	C Form. Messages And Signals.		
Miscellaneous	A Form. Messages And Signals.		
Miscellaneous	C.R.E. 46th Divn.	27/03/1918	27/03/1918
Miscellaneous	C.R.E. 46th Division. Marching in State.	28/03/1918	28/03/1918
Miscellaneous	C Form Messages And Signals.		
Miscellaneous	A Form. Messages And Signals.		
Heading	46th (North Midland) Divisional Engineers C.R.E. 46th Division April 1918		
War Diary	Braquemont	01/04/1918	12/04/1918
War Diary	Brvay	13/04/1918	23/04/1918
War Diary	Gosnay	24/04/1918	31/05/1918
Operation(al) Order(s)	Operation Order No 50 By Lieut Col E.J. Walthew. M.C. C.R.E. 46th Division. App I	04/05/1918	04/05/1918
Operation(al) Order(s)	Operation Order No 51 By Lieut Colonel E.J. Walthew. M.C. C.R.E. 46th Division App II	09/05/1918	09/05/1918
Operation(al) Order(s)	Operation Order No 52 By Lieut Col. E.J. Walthew. M.C. C.R.E. 46th Division App III	12/05/1918	12/05/1918
Operation(al) Order(s)	Operation Order No 53 By Lieut Col. E.J. Walthew. M.C. C.R.E. 46th Division App IV	17/05/1918	17/05/1918
Operation(al) Order(s)	Operation Order No 54 By Lieut Col. E.J. Walthew. M.C. C.R.E. 46th Division App V	21/05/1918	21/05/1918
Operation(al) Order(s)	Operation Order No 55 By Major W.D. Zeller. M.C. A/C.R.E. 46th Division. App VI	24/05/1918	24/05/1918
Operation(al) Order(s)	Operation Order No 56 By Major W.D. Zeller. M.C. A/C.R.E. 46th Division. App VII	28/05/1918	28/05/1918
War Diary	Gosnay	01/06/1918	25/06/1918
Operation(al) Order(s)	Operation Order No 57 By Lieut Colonel H.T. Mcrshead. D.S.O.C.R.E. 46th Division. App I	02/06/1918	02/06/1918
Operation(al) Order(s)	46th Divisional R.E. Order No. 59. by Lieut-Col. H.T. Morshead. D.S.O., R.E. Commanding Royal Engineers.	06/06/1916	06/06/1916
Operation(al) Order(s)	46th Divisional R.E. Order No. 60 by Lieut Colonel T.H. Morshead. D.S.O.C.R.E. 46th Division App III	10/06/1918	10/06/1918
Operation(al) Order(s)	46th Divisional R.E. Order No 61 By Lieut Col. H.T. Morshead. D.S.O. R.E. Commanding Royal Engineers 46th Division App IV		
Miscellaneous	137th Infantry Brigade. App V	16/06/1918	16/06/1918
War Diary	Gosnay	06/07/1918	30/07/1918
War Diary	Gosnay	09/07/1918	12/07/1918
Operation(al) Order(s)	46th Division R.E. Order No 62 By Lieut Col. H.T. Morshead. D.S.O. R.E. Commanding Royal Engineers 46th Division App I	04/07/1918	04/07/1918
War Diary	Gosnay E 25a 74	01/08/1918	25/08/1918
War Diary	Gosnay E 25a 74	12/08/1918	12/08/1918
Operation(al) Order(s)	46th Division R.E. Order No 62/A By Major H.M. Fordham. M.C. A/C.R.E. 46th Division.	03/08/1918	03/08/1918
Operation(al) Order(s)	46th Division R.E. Order No 64. By Lieut Colonel, H.T. Morshead. D.S.O. C.R.E. 46th Division.	25/08/1918	25/08/1918
Miscellaneous	B8 A,B		
War Diary	Gosnay (near Hesdigneul Bethune Sheet E 25a 74)	01/09/1918	08/09/1918

War Diary	Beaucourt Sur L'Hallue (10th N.E. of Amiens)	18/09/1918	18/09/1918
War Diary	Cauvigny Farm nr Tertry	19/09/1918	19/09/1918
War Diary	Vraignes	21/09/1918	30/09/1918
Miscellaneous	O.C. 465th Field Co R.E. Warning Order. App I	04/09/1918	04/09/1918
Operation(al) Order(s)	46th Divisional Royal Engineer Order No 65 By Lieut-Col. H.T. Morshead D.S.O. C.R.E. 46th Division	05/09/1918	05/09/1918
Operation(al) Order(s)	46th Divisional Royal Engineer Order No 66 By Lieut Colonel H.T. Morshead D.S.O. C.R.E. 46th Division App II	20/09/1918	20/09/1918
Miscellaneous			
Operation(al) Order(s)	46th Divisional R.E. Order No 67 By Major W.H. Hardman. M.C. A/C.R.E. 46th Divn. App III	27/09/1918	27/09/1918
Miscellaneous	Work For Field Companies & Pioneer Battalion On "Z" Day & Following.		
Miscellaneous	46th Division App III	29/09/1918	29/09/1918
Miscellaneous	O.C. 465 Field Co R.E. App IV	02/10/1918	02/10/1918
Miscellaneous	Instructions For Field Companies & Pioneers in amplification of "Outline Of Work"		
War Diary	Bellenglise	01/10/1918	09/10/1918
War Diary	Fresnoy La Grand	10/10/1918	31/10/1918
Miscellaneous	Report on R.E. Work During Operations Of 29th September Appx I	29/10/1918	29/10/1918
Heading	List of Casualties for period 29th September to 7th October.		
Operation(al) Order(s)	46th Divisional R.E. Order No 68 By Lieut Colonel W. Garforth. D.S.O. M.C. A/C.R.E. 46th Division. Appendix II	02/10/1918	02/10/1918
Miscellaneous	Account Of The Part Taken By The 46th Division In The Battle Of Bellenglise On The 29th September, 1918. Appendix II	07/10/1918	07/10/1918
Miscellaneous	Account Of The Part Taken By The 46th Division In The Battle Of Ralicourt, On The 3rd Oct, 18. Appendix III	03/10/1918	03/10/1918
Operation(al) Order(s)	46th Divisional R.E. Order No 71. By Lieut Colonel, W. Garforth. D.S.O., M.C. C.R.E. 46th Division. App IV	16/10/1918	16/10/1918
Operation(al) Order(s)	46th Divisional R.E. Order No 70 By Lieut Colonel, W. Garforth. D.S.O., M.C. C.R.E. 46th Division. App V	16/10/1918	16/10/1918
Miscellaneous	Operation Order by C.R.E. 46th Division. In accordance with O.O. 108., dated 27/10/1918	27/10/1918	27/10/1918
War Diary	Molain	04/11/1918	04/11/1918
War Diary	Arbre De Guise	05/11/1918	05/11/1918
War Diary	Prisches	06/11/1918	10/11/1918
War Diary	Sains Du Nord	11/11/1918	11/11/1918
War Diary	Landrecies	14/11/1918	14/11/1918
Operation(al) Order(s)	46th Divisional Engineer Order No 73 By Lieut-Col. W. Garforth. D.S.O., M.C. Commanding Royal Engineers 46th Division.	02/11/1918	02/11/1918
Miscellaneous	46th Division Operation "E" R.E. and Pioneer Instructions.	02/11/1918	02/11/1918
War Diary	Landrecies	01/12/1918	01/12/1918
War Diary	Preux-au.Bois	12/12/1918	12/12/1918
Operation(al) Order(s)	46th Divisional R.E. Order No 75 By Lieut Colonel H.T. Morshead. D.S.O. C.R.E. 46th Division. App I	08/12/1918	08/12/1918
War Diary	Preux Au Bois	31/01/1919	27/02/1919
War Diary	Inchy-Beaumont	28/02/1919	31/03/1919

War Diary		09/03/1919	26/03/1919
War Diary	Inchy Beaumont	01/04/1919	30/04/1919
War Diary		02/04/1919	28/04/1919
War Diary	Caudry	01/05/1919	22/06/1919
War Diary	Caudry	14/06/1919	14/06/1919

WO95/2672/1
Commander Royal Engineers

DIVISION
ENGINEERS

R. E.

16 ~~MAY 1919~~
JUNE 1919

DIVISION
ENGINEERS

Sheet 2.

CRE 46' Div

Army Form C. 2118

WAR DIARY
INTELLIGENCE SUMMARY
(Erase heading not required.)

Place	Date	Hour	Summary of Events and Information	Remarks and references to Appendices
BAVINCOURT	May 19th 1916	—	Front L'TCE 1/c 1st TCE at POMMIER - afternoon work on communication	
	20th	—	Intention to front line trace - effect of Sormans after heavy rain - My 1st day - took over Capt Hedges in hospital No 20.	
	21st	—	took W. BERLES to see M.I." Monuments - saw much of old S. line (old line)	
			Went round old 'line from RENFREW Along front to BIENVILLERS with O.C. 1st Monmouths so far as his line trace (in centre) & then with O.C. 1/7 Argylls to his portion - Capt Hedges died of wounds.	
	22	—	Inspected 139' Bde front line trench & strong points with Bt 2/L 137th L aftern'n inspected trench in LANARK & LLANDAFF trenches - Capt Hedges buried 1/2	
	23rd	—	Went to see trench in 138' Bde area - adj to BRETENCOURT to make report on trench scheme to front line	
	24th	—	Went Portuits work on in morning RENFREW lane to Be. l. with O.C. Monmouths in afternoon -	

WAR DIARY
INTELLIGENCE SUMMARY
(Erase heading not required.)

Army Form C. 2118

Place	Date	Hour	Summary of Events and Information	Remarks and references to Appendices
BAVINCOURT.	25/8/16	—	Major B. McGRATH came to H.Q. & was seen by G.O.C. 46 Div. — went to see O. 1/2 p.m. C.R.E. re Dugout plans — Adj. to SOMBRAIN to hire an Enquiry & to BRETENCOURT re Watch scheme —	
	26/8.	—	Inspected work in 139th Sector — progress is much not — and inspected Sit- for O.P. approved by C.R.A. near BURNT FARM. — Lieut TAPPER joined the Unit. Posted to 1/1 H.F.M.	
	27/8	—	Inspected work in 138th Brigade. & to see the drainage works STONEYGATE St - Communication Trench — went with C.R.E. & alternoon round BIENVILLERS defences to BAILLEULMONT to see the new M.G.	
	28/8	—	Went to visit works in new defence div." with C.R.E. & G.S.1. — afternoon went to BIENVILLERS & met Lt. 1st movements at C. 1/. Hst-all & explained in Vil- the work required to the same & made arrangements for working parties & took over (ammunition)	
	29/8.	—	Afternoon inspected work done by PIONEER Bn — STRONG point - RENFREW & B. FARMBURO my hrst day.	
	30/. Aug	—	Went to BIENVILLERS & inspected works (trenches) on divisional line to defence of Village & PAS. & to C.E. & MONDICOURT Etree and new hutting from Batteries - my hrst day.	

Army Form C. 2118

WAR DIARY
or
INTELLIGENCE SUMMARY
(Erase heading not required.)

Instructions regarding War Diaries and Intelligence Summaries are contained in F. S. Regs., Part II. and the Staff Manual respectively. Title Pages will be prepared in manuscript.

Place	Date	Hour	Summary of Events and Information	Remarks and references to Appendices
BAIZIEUX	31/8/16	—	Prohibited works in progress BIENVILLERS defences - also drainage in progress on communication trenches 138.1St. - M.G. fire emplac.' by BEAPLES tram line - 2 works referred for transport 137t Bde. - Saw O.C.1/2 + took him on at his HQ. - & Saw O.C. 1st Monmouths. —	

Cing.Vier.OverAind NG
O.i/c 48th Dis.

WAR DIARY
or
INTELLIGENCE SUMMARY

Army Form C. 2118

CRE 46th Div²

Place	Date	Hour	Summary of Events and Information	Remarks and references to Appendices
BAVINCOURT	1/9/16		Inspected works in progress 139th Bde Sectn - also work on Strongpoints STANDOUT	
	2/9/16		LANARK x RENFREW - Front line trenches 130-5 - and dug outs 137 Bde F. Sectn. Went to BIENVILLERS & inspected work in new div¹ line also on STONEYGATE F. Sectn & NAKED St. - returned to BERLES	
	3/9/16		Inspected BIENVILLERS defences - new div¹ line -	
	4/9/16		Went to BERLES & saw OC MONMOUTHS & went round works being carried out by his men - RENFREW, H.D. x A. Strong points. Arty k PAS - DOUIENS - S¹ POL & TINQUES for engines. 3rd F¹ NE and his	
	5/9/16		went round works in progress on div¹ line - Saw OC ½ horse standing.	
	6/9/16		reconnoitred CE JK Corps around Re-work 139 p. Bde area - dugs outs - Strong points & div¹ line from BELLACOURT k LANARK	
	7/9/16		Went to BIENVILLERS & inspected div¹ line defences. Work on STONEYGATE St. 88 gr CROSS St. and dug outs - inspected div line & horse standing in progress.	
	8/9/16		Saw OC ½ F¹ NE & MG 137 Bde & went round front of 137 Bde trenches with G O C - inspected work FARNBORO LANE new support trenches 104. 105 - new scouts pk - 11mms NORTH St. - inspected work on horse standing ¾ F¹ NE M F¹ NE	
	9/9/16		inspected BIENVILLERS defences. - Saw Monmouths at work in 88 St - inspected deep dug NAKEDT	

WAR DIARY
or
INTELLIGENCE SUMMARY

(Erase heading not required.)

Army Form C. 2118

CRE 46 div

Place	Date	Hour	Summary of Events and Information	Remarks and references to Appendices
BAVINCOURT	10/9/16		Went to BERLES & inspected work on div: line - A Stg point to RENFREW - went W. of ST CLEMENTS & selected site to have standing ex for 4'' MORTAR in LA HERLIETTE. Accompanied G.O.C. & inspected dug outs & O.P.s in 139th section. Lt. 2/L MORE came with us	
	11/9/16		Inspected div: defences BIENVILLERS - and BERLES defences from RENFREW to Be.1 with OC Monmouths	
	12/9/16		Went to BERLES with interpreter & arranged for purchase of material from derelict houses to be in repair - Saw engine working 2 saws commenced work - Cie. was arranged for pulling road in repair Stb. for advance -	
	14/9/16		Took Maj Phillips RE from SME Chatham round & further of line - & showed him O.P.s - T.M. emplacements, front line trenches, dug outs intended sentry posts & ? Inspected R.E. works 138 Bde section - BIENVILLERS div: line - work on 88 ST & STONEYGATE - Dug outs CROSS ST. & return by NAKED ST & inspected part of BERLES, MONCHY road	
	16/9/16		Inspected works on div: line from RENFREW to Be.A. with OC Monmouths. also went to inspect work on LANARK & LLANDAFF - Park St to long front line trenches & LLANDAFF communication trench.	
	17/9/16		Inspected works on new work standing 1/1 & 2/1 3rd MORE.	
	18/9/16		Inspected BIENVILLERS div: line defences by SMOKE [Smith?] behind hedge round RE works to 138th sector & Monmouths round by MONCHY behind lostering hill cross roads front line trenches 78 - 88 & around SERJEANTS house & SHELL ST. - Worked on account & writing	

CRE 46th Div

Army Form C. 2118

WAR DIARY or INTELLIGENCE SUMMARY

Place	Date	Hour	Summary of Events and Information	Remarks and references to Appendices
BAVINCOURT	19/9/16	-	Inspected works in progress at BERLES & afterwards work on Be.A. and FARNBURO LANE - FISH LANE Support - NORTH ST. with O/C. MONMOUTHS. Went three experiments by 1/1 Btn R.E. with by Stokes Jack in front trench. 8" trench 30' long in 1/2 hour	
	20/9/16	-	Inspected div line 139th section with G.S.I. -	
	21/9/16	-	Inspected BIENVILLERS defences - work in STONEYGATE and 88 trench - Inspected trench lines 2/1 & 1/1 L.O. - saw O.C. 1/1 & 1/2 2nd R.E. - O.C. Monmouths & M.G. 137th Bde	
	22/9/16	-	Went with C.E. 7th Corps to make arrangements concerning Div. Watersupply at RETENCOURT with Corps Supply - went round R.E. work 139th section with O.C. 1/1 1st R.E. - went on with the Monmouths to inspect works in LEANDAR & LANARK.	
	23/9/16	-	Went to BIENVILLERS & inspected old line - also work in STONEYGATE 88 trench - NARED ST. Dugouts - new revetting 98 & 99 trenches trench line 9.3 - 103. - Gave instructions to Will of a. about new buildings round BERLES. MONCHY - O.C.1/1 & 2/ CLEMENTS accompanied me.	
	24/9	-	Office work	
	25/9		C.R.E. work on trunk lever - hey LOUSSMAKER ended as C.R.E.	
	26/9		Reply to 137th Bde H.Q. Spec Ind whether Pork in hand from 104 - 141 also dug outs & Communication trenches	

WAR DIARY
or
INTELLIGENCE SUMMARY

(Erase heading not required.)

Army Form C. 2118

CRE 46th Div

Place	Date	Hour	Summary of Events and Information	Remarks and references to Appendices
BAVINCOURT	27/9/16	—	Inspected BIENVILLERS & BERLES defences as far as Bn Sr. Had R.O. & 'BERLES'	
	28/9		& had a talk with Major to show And. at GASTINEAU & HOUVETTE & M.G. emplacts. Man with C.E. ? Corps & inspected Divl line from GASTINEAU to STONEGATE with hut planter, arranged BIENVILLERS	
	29/9		Mr to Monmouth & BERLES & had with them to point out positions wanted yesterday - inwards trench wanted such - a BC defence & 10 men	
	30/9		Went with Brigade Major 137th around trenches N of b - Got with & communicated intended 137' meters. Saw officer in OTLR at Berles, & instructed have standings for H.TMs.	

Clayton Churchill
Lt.Col. 46th Div.

HQrs. R.E. 46. Div.

Army Form C. 2118

WAR DIARY
or
INTELLIGENCE SUMMARY
(Erase heading not required.)

Vol 3

Place	Date	Hour	Summary of Events and Information	Remarks and references to Appendices
BAVINCOURT	1/10/16	—	Went to BIENVILLERS & inspected defence work with Q.S.1	
	2/10/16	—	Office work & wrote in to see 1/2 p. Cne.	
	3/10/16	—	Saw C.E. XII Corps re increasing facilities for watering horses — went to BERLES & inspected BERLES defences	
	4/10	—	To BIENVILLERS & inspected B; defences — sited M.G. emplacement in SWANKEY ST & gave St James instructions to commence work.	
	5/10	—	The returns 10 P.M.	
	6/10	—	Went with May Commander to BIENVILLERS to see B; defences & work in progress.	
	7/10	—	Inspected site of tram line to PONT ST. to GASTINEAU with R.M. 137 & O.C. 1/2 inspected site of work ALOUETTE. GASTINEAU & M.G. emplmt. — & work in progress RENFREW trench.	
	8/10	—	Inspected Bn. work with O.C. MONMOUTHS — Hants starting up & Klainville — QUARRY wks. Gave order re: reconnoitering RANSART QUARRY — & KLAINVILLE — QUARRY wks.	
	9/10	—	Went round R.E. work in progress 139 Bde. sector with O.C. 2/1. R.E. Co & also went in/shells string point in RIDGE ROAD.	
	10/10	—	Went to POMPIER & went on with O.C. 1/1. to see work in progress trench lines — inspected work in progress in Bi defences — & new work in STUMPY ST.	
	11/10	—	Went EMERIES & inspected work on RIDGE rd. & inspect. done previous night inspected work in RENFREW trench in progress went to P.A.T. & WCCR re work for C.E. who were waiting in line.	
	12/10	—	Went to see O.C. 1/1 to Cope re allocation to plan in proposed new posts in shelled works in supper RIDGE Rd. B.E. works.	

H.Q. 46' Div. R.E.

2

Army Form C. 2118

WAR DIARY
or
INTELLIGENCE SUMMARY
(Erase heading not required.)

Place	Date	Hour	Summary of Events and Information	Remarks and references to Appendices
BAVINCOURT	13.10.16	—	Inspected R.E. work in progress 139" & 137" Bde sector	
	14.10	—	Rode to P.A.D. & inspected route SOUASTRE to SAILLY & reported on bad state. Rode with G.O.C. & inspected work on new protected saps, put in front trenches. 139". Recce also work being done by Dug out party. Visited a new work old sunken road & gave instructions for commencement of work. — Met director of Mines at conference at H.Q.	
	15.10	—	Went to BIENVILLERS with tunnelling officer & fixed site for latrine pits — inspected R.E. work at BERLES & went to see R.E. 137 Bde	
	16.10	—	Went with G.S.3 mud obs. line — & afterwards with R.O.C.	
	17.10	—	Went with R.O.C. to GASTINEAU & ALOUETTE & made examination of cases M.C. enquiry into.	
	18.10	—	Inspected horse lines 1/1 F.Cie. & made fresh arrangements to provide a workshop 1/1 F.Cie — went to BERLES to see what being done by pioneer B".	
	19.10	—	Went with O.C. 1/1. & showed him with O.C. 2/1. new protected sentry posts being carried on by O.C. 2/1. — Sent to BERLES to report on damage done by enemy shelling, & wd of a F.W. point.	
	20.10	—	annual return	
	21.10	—	Obs. — an officer sent in and to T.M. school to obs. horse line near AUTH[?]ua	
	22.10	—	Went to BERLES with G.S.I. & inspected work RIDGE Rd. attained work of pioneers with O.C. which mine, that wd. was to be taken away to mine & pt & dugout. HINTON Cuins is not in order shortly.	
	23.10	—	Report sent to H.Q. re program of R.E. work. Saty' kinetiy are	

WAR DIARY or INTELLIGENCE SUMMARY

Army Form C. 2118

H.Q. 46th div

Place	Date	Hour	Summary of Events and Information	Remarks and references to Appendices
BAVINCOURT	23/10	—	Inspected water by PIONEER Bn. adj. handing over 7th dvn	
	24.10	—	went with G.S.O.3 & O.C. 2/1st wks. Bn. trenches. O.A.O. & Brig. mtd. 139 sections	
	25.10	—	to BIENVILLERS with Adj. & inspected trucks & made arrangements to concentrate them at BERLES for carrying "GINGER BEER" In trenches - instructed w.k.s. on horse and in formation - CRE 30th div came to take over	
	26.10	—	with CRE 30th div. inspected R.E. work & progress RIDGE Rd. & to BERLES & BIENVILLERS to see train line arrangements for taking cylinders - were working satisfactorily. Inc dug. & a wood dump of billets to Ballon being up	
	27.10	—	with CRE 30th div round part of div. line - & made arrangements for billeting some of the sections with 46th div. R.E. - Adj. handing over to 30th div Adj.	
	28.10	—	with CRE 30th rounds div' lines & shown Push form FARNBORO LANE & STARFISH. had Adj. handing over to other Adj. (30A)	
	29.10	—	handing over to CRE 30' div & with him round head q. 139th Rd to Saulty	
	30.10	—	46th R.E. Co's left line & marched to billets in a fresh area 1/1 GRENAY 1/2 LUCHEUX 2/1 WARLUZEL With CRE 30 to LA HERLIERE to see horse lines & 1/1 & 2/1 Fs handing over & packing up	
MEZEROLLES	31.10	—	Left BAVINCOURT 6 a.m. arrived MEZEROLLES 3 p.m. about 20 miles march Capt. Spendour left to join 39th div. 2 Lt. Hunter both up studies of Adj.	A.Martin

HQ RE 46th DIV

HQ RE
46th Div.
Vol 4

Army Form C. 2118

WAR DIARY
or
INTELLIGENCE SUMMARY
(Erase heading not required.)

Place	Date	Hour	Summary of Events and Information	Remarks and references to Appendices
PROVEN-L GAPPES MEZEROLLES ST RIQUET	Nov 1st	—	Head Qrs fm PITCHEM. Lt. GRAND & Lt. Lee up to Offrs. m̅ess in the m̅orn̅g.	
	2nd		Left MEZEROLLES 8 a.m for ST RIQUET & found office there in afternoon	
	3rd		2º C.R.E arrived Neuf Moulin and made billeting arrangements for 1st & arranged for their supply to hence at ST RIQUET	
	4th		Went to see 1st in billets - Sent to St Riquet to MONCOURT for training purposes & arranged for drains.	
	5th		Church service with 1st - went over training area with 2d/c - selected site for new heck	
	6th		Training & rehearsed for G.O.C's inspection in afternoon - finished items for monoliths	
	7th		Inspection brigades one/weather - had with G.O.C. & invited 2d/c to luncheon	
	8th		1st changed billets & marched to CANCHY. Went with 1st to see billets	
	9th		Second training at CANCHY - Capt. Miller & Lt. BRAM arrived from base	
	10th		Went to see a new billeting area in p.m. at GRAND LAVIERS & new huts French & a new site near there on SOMME for harboring. Went to see training being done by French — drilling - bayonet fighting & musketry. H.Q. training attached	

1875 Wt. W593/826 1,000,000 4/15 J.B.C. & A. A.D.S.S./Forms/C. 2118.

HQ R.E. 40th Div
HQ RE
40th Div

Army Form C. 2118

Instructions regarding War Diaries and Intelligence Summaries are contained in F.S. Regs., Part II. and the Staff Manual respectively. Title Pages will be prepared in manuscript.

WAR DIARY
or
INTELLIGENCE SUMMARY
(Erase heading not required.)

Place	Date	Hour	Summary of Events and Information	Remarks and references to Appendices
Camp RIPLEY	Nov 11	—	Went here to settle down in new area — Satisfactory march & was settled quickly without hitch.	
	12		Church parade at 3 P.M. continued — Saw O.C. re programme of work to be carried out — Putting kentons down to the cinema & laying out stores	
	13		Pontoons. Selected site for ramps	
	14		Pontoons. See left & at practice — musketry on new camp	
	15		Pontoons & musketry practice	
	16			
	17		Inspection of pontoon by G.O.C. in afternoon — Pontooning in morning	
	18		Pontoon competition between 3 Pontoon Bridges arranged & held. A very good performance resulting in a tie between 1/2 & 2/1 Cos. Snow — sleet & high wind.	
	19		No rest day	
	20		Had to see O.C. re G.R. LAVIERS — preparing to move tomorrow.	Special order dated
	21		Thursfield to march to St. ROUEN	

HQ 4th RE 46th Div

WAR DIARY
or
INTELLIGENCE SUMMARY
(Erase heading not required.)

Army Form C. 2118

Instructions regarding War Diaries and Intelligence Summaries are contained in F.S. Regs., Part II. and the Staff Manual respectively. Title Pages will be prepared in manuscript.

Place	Date	Hour	Summary of Events and Information	Remarks and references to Appendices
ST RIQUIER	Nov 22nd		1/1 & 2/1 Fd. Coy marched to MAIZICOURT & LE PESTEL RIBEAUCOURT	
	23rd		Hqrs RE marched to OUTREBOIS — 2/1 Fd. RE continues their march	
	24th		9th Fd. Coy see P.B. 139th Bde & 1/1 Fd. at RAMSART	
	25th		HQrs RE marches to LUCHEUX	
	26th		Went to HALLOY to see work done by RE. Then on in movement to huts	
	27th		Went to HAUT. VISÉE & saw 1/1 (?) Fd. & to LUCHEUX & saw 1/1 Coy Fd.	
	28th		Went to see C.R.E. 49th Divn at HENU & his workshops — In afternoon went to see C.E. 7th Corps	
	29th		Went with 9 Staff 46th to inspect army sites for increased billetting	
	30th		continued this work — & made report	

(signed) P. .... Lt Col RE
6/XII/18
CRE 46th Divn

OPERATION ORDER
by
Brig-General.C.V.WINGFIELD-STRATFORD.C.M.G.

November 10th. 1916.

1. The 3 Field Companies will march from CANCHY to Gd.LAVIERS on 11-11-16.

2. The starting point will be where the road to LAMOTTE crosses the Main Road to CANCHY. Companies will leave here at 8-50 a.m. in the following order, 1/1st Co., 1/2nd Co., 2/1st Co., under the command of Major.B.McCraith.

3. The following route will be followed: CANCHY, LAMOTTE, BULEUX, HAUTVILLERS, BUIGNY, to Gd.LAVIERS.

4. Billetting parties and guides should be sent on ahead to mark billets and guide Companies in.

5. All billets, latrines, horse lines etc., will be left clean before moving off.

6. Report completion of move.

Chas. A. Hunter

2/Lieut & Adjutant.R.E.
for C.R.E. 46th Division.

1 copy to each Field Coy.
1 copy to Headqrs 46th Divn.
1 copy to War Diary.

OPERATION ORDER
by
Brig-General.C.V.WINGFIELD-STRATFORD.,C.M.G.
C.R.E. 48th DIVISION.

November 20th, 1916.

1. The 3 Field Companies.R.E. will move from GRAND LAVIERS to St. RIQUIER to-morrow, 21-11-16.

2. The Companies will move in order of seniority, the head of the column leaving the 1/1st Field Coys Mess at 10-30 a.m.

3. Companies will march through ABBEVILLE to St. RIQUIER.

4. Billetting parties and guides from each Company will meet M.ARNAL at the C.R.E's Mess at 9-30 a.m., 21-11-16.

5. All billets, latrines and horse lines will be left clean.

2/Lieut & Adjutant.R.E.
for C.R.E. 48th Division.

Army Form C. 2118

CRE 46 Div

Vol 4

WAR DIARY
or
INTELLIGENCE SUMMARY
(Erase heading not required.)

Instructions regarding War Diaries and Intelligence Summaries are contained in F. S. Regs., Part II. and the Staff Manual respectively. Title Pages will be prepared in manuscript.

Place	Date	Hour	Summary of Events and Information	Remarks and references to Appendices
LUCHEUX Sheet 57e T.16.d	1/12/16		Went with S.O. RE III Army re Water Supply. toured the proposed sites for Horse standings re Water supply arrangements. Submitted report to C.E. VII Corps with Map.	
	2/12/16		Went with S.O. RA to inspect sites for R.F.A. Bdes and D.A.C. Horse standings. Attended conference at Div'l H.Q.	
	3/12/16		Went with C.R.E., Adj. 49th D'n to show them sites for Horse standings & hutments	
	4/12/16		One section of each Field Coy moves up to line & is attached to Field Coys of 49th D'n in taking over	
	5/12/16		Reviewing sections of Field Coys now into line & relieve Field Coys of 49th D'n	
	6/12/16		HQ. RE move to HENU. Adj goes to SOUASTRE and BIENVILLERS to inspect Field Coy billets.	
	7/12/16		C.R.E. laid up sick. Saw OC 1/2 Field Coy re Water	
HENU Sheet 57d D.19.a.	8/12/16		Adj visits Coys in BIENVILLERS	
	9/12/16		One section 1/2 Field Coy arrived HQ from BIENVILLERS	
	12/12/16		1/2 Field Coy sections in BIENVILLERS move to GAUDIENPRE prior to Bombardment	
	13/12/16		Bombardment of German line at MONCHY	
	14/12/16		1/2 Field Coy sections in GAUDIENPRE return to BIENVILLERS	
	15/12/16		G.S.O.1. went round Div'l line with OC's Field Coys to point out work requiring to be done.	

Army Form C. 2118

WAR DIARY
or
INTELLIGENCE SUMMARY
(Erase heading not required.)

CRE 46 Div.

Place	Date	Hour	Summary of Events and Information	Remarks and references to Appendices
HENU Sheet 57d D.19.a.	16/12/16		Saw OC Monmouths, GS re work	
	17/12/16		Major Zeebi OC 2/1 Field Coy returned from leave	
	18/12/16		Capt. Miles & L. Clements 1/1 Field Coy went to ST POL to inspect III Army T.H. Railway	
	20/12/16		C.R.E (Brig. Gen. C.U Wingfield-Stratford CHG) proceeds to England on 7 months sick leave Duties taken over by Major L.J. Crossmake RE O/C 1/2 Field Coy.	
	21/12/16		Rode over to SHULTY with Capt Russ & arranged joint workshop for 1/2, 2/1 Field Coys. Saw AA QMG re moving huts from HENU to ST AMAND. Went to D" HQ Saw Col Thorpe.	
	22/12/16		Hitried to BIENVILLERS with Col Thorpe inspected D" line Posts. Went up NAKED ST & met Bdier 137 who took us along 92 Fu trench	
	23/12/16		Rode to BIENVILLERS with OC 2/1 Coy inspected all posts in 9th line in his sector visited by CRE 3rd Line on tour from ENGLAND	
	24/12/16		Rode to BIENVILLERS & went round trenches with Lt Hud. Thompson. Inspected Bn	
	25/12/16		Met OC 1/1 Field Coy in SOUASTRE at 11.30 am & rode to FONQUEVILLERS inspected C/Ts LINCOLN LANE, ST MARTINS LANE, GOOCH ST & made arrangements for MONMOUTHS to commence work on them next day.	
	26/12/16		Took CRE 3rd line to GAUDIENPRE to see Coy workshop. Bdier 137 Bde came to see me at HENU in the afternoon. Adj to England on leave Duties taken over by Capt Miles 1/1 Field	

Army Form C. 2118

CRE 46 Div

WAR DIARY
or
INTELLIGENCE SUMMARY
(Erase heading not required.)

Instructions regarding War Diaries and Intelligence Summaries are contained in F.S. Regs., Part II. and the Staff Manual respectively. Title Pages will be prepared in manuscript.

Place	Date	Hour	Summary of Events and Information	Remarks and references to Appendices
HENU Sheet 57d. D.19.a	27/12/16		Bad frost, stay in under H.O. orders. G.O.C came to billets, gave instructions for a ticket office, pitch to be erected at Whizz-Bangs Rooms SOUASTRE. Also seating for Cinema at ST AMAND. Col Thorpe saw me about extra lorries for transport of stones.	
	28/12/16		Cleared up arrears of office work	
	29/12/16		— do — — do —	
	30/12/16		Rode over to POMMIER, saw B'dier 137 Bde, went on to BIENVILLERS & gave instructions to O.C 1/2 Field Coy re draining SHELL S' and paths to front line under water.	
	31/12/16		Rode to ST AMAND. and inspected work on Cinema & Huts. Went on to BIENVILLERS saw O.C 1/2 Field Coy, from there to HQ 137 Bde.	

F.J. Faussnekin Major
for C.R.E
46th Div

Secret

C.R.E. 46th div

Army Form C. 2118

WAR DIARY
or
INTELLIGENCE SUMMARY
(Erase heading not required.)

Vol 6

Place	Date	Hour	Summary of Events and Information	Remarks and references to Appendices
HENU	1st Jan 1917		Went round Hinchy Z section with Bt. Major 137th Bde — Saw G.S.O. 2 & printing work over & went to walk in front line & O.T.s.	
	2nd		Inspected works round Henu	
	3rd		Sent R.E. & truck to SOUASTRE & saw O.C. 1/1 & works	
	4th		Inspected work FONQUEVILLERS with O.C. 1/1 & dug'l line	
	5th		Inspected work with O.C. 1/1 to BIENVILLERS — & went on NAKED BF & drew strong points B.1. & 2 — Saw G.S.O. re work on Div'l line	
	6th		Rode FAUQUEMBERGUES & inspected work of 2/1 C.F.C. on div line & R.O.P & went to SAULTY & inspected work at saw mill — & afterward to Div school	
	7th		Inspected work on St Martin's Lane & Quack St dug outs & T.M. emplacements	
	8th		With O.C. 1/1 & went on B.R.1 & support line X section	
	9th		Inspected work at HENU — & to GAUDIEMPRE to see O.C. 1/1	
	10th		To ABBEVILLE in motor to purchase iron	

C.R.E. 46th Div Secret Army Form C. 2118

WAR DIARY
or
INTELLIGENCE SUMMARY
(Erase heading not required.)

Place	Date	Hour	Summary of Events and Information	Remarks and references to Appendices
HENU	11th Jany 19.17		Went with R.E. to div Lane & sited block for breaking & strip gate — also sight winch & scale which was full of water & arranged for getting rid of it.	
	12th	"	Inspected Laundry at PK5 & saw mill at SAULTY with Capt. MILLER	
	13th	"	Composite Fg of 3 off. and 180 Sappers under Capt. Rouse left for work under O.C. Railways R.E. at NANQUETIN, HALLOY & DOULENS — went to ST AMAND with A.A. & P.M.G. to advise re constructional work there	
	14th	"	Inspected trenches Z sector with O.C. 1/2 — also saw Br. Head (Pt. NAKED) St. Gt. and the relaying of 92 fire trench.	
	15th	"	To AMIENS to get wine & found good supply.	
	16th	"	A large scale map to show all trenches in Divisional area commencing	
	17th	"	Showed C.E. XVIII Corps round the line	
	18th	"	Went to trenches with OC. 1/2 & inspected work in support line Z sector	
	19th	"	Bgd MINGFIELD — STRATFORD returns — Saw D.D.E — workshops & went over papers with Major COUSSMAKER —	

"C.R.E. 46 Div" Secret   Army Form C. 2118

WAR DIARY
or
INTELLIGENCE SUMMARY
(Erase heading not required.)

Instructions regarding War Diaries and Intelligence Summaries are contained in F. S. Regs., Part II. and the Staff Manual respectively. Title Pages will be prepared in manuscript.

Place	Date	Hour	Summary of Events and Information	Remarks and references to Appendices
HEND	Jan' 20th		Went to SOUASTRE with Adj' & Saw O.C. Monmouths & Lillers, Chimps & Firths A/1/3rd F-RE - Maj Coussmaker went round div'l line with G.O.C. & CE	
	21st		Commenced hutment for Co/m R.A. Office work	
	22nd		Went with Maj Coussmaker & inspected the drainage operation on W/F work at Z Section - Saw work in progress Lillers wood Lane, Saw G.O.C. at work	
	23rd		Went round part of X Section with O.C. 1/1, & reported on Martins Lane M.T. front line, arranged for broken trench elements. - Saw Sharp Posts and T.M. tramway. - Reported in roads div fonts area & pro pro of work in month	
	24		Conference of CRE's at CE. G office	
	25th		Went round 2 section with O.C. 1/2 F.S.T.M.R.E. —	
	26th		Went round div' line Y section with O.C. 2/1 - to ST AMAND in afternoon with Adj	
	27th		Went with G.S.1 & inspected work in front line X section - Div' line & Sharp Posts & Gendarmerie —	

C.R.E. 46th div — Secret

Army Form C. 2118

WAR DIARY
or
INTELLIGENCE SUMMARY
(Erase heading not required.)

Place	Date	Hour	Summary of Events and Information	Remarks and references to Appendices
HENU	Jan 28th 1917		Inspected STONEGATE & CROSS St Trenches — saw O.E. 2/1 1st/1st R.E. Work very difficult owing to frozen ground.	
	29th		Inspected Div' line & Jectr gene instruction re alterations K.M. G. an Maer! No 3 S.P. — inspected trench tramway.	
	30th		Went to SOUASTRE & saw 139, 139 Bdes — also O.E. 1/1 1st R.E. BIENVILLERS & saw O.E. 2/1. — In afternoon to SOUASTRE & saw O.C. Monmouths. re work	
	31st		Went to BIENVILLERS with Ady! & inspected Div' line Y sectr, Then to stony P.R. & sectr & 1/— 2/1 1st R.E. at BIVOUAC — VILLERS — saw 139, 139 Bdes — went to see C.E. very hard frost with high strong wind since 18th. Found my hand in slightly thermometer registered 26° of frost - refilled at MAIRIE, PAS.	

Chief Christopher Fowler Kt?
CBE 4th Army

WAR DIARY
or
INTELLIGENCE SUMMARY
(Erase heading not required.)

Army Form C. 2118

N.O. R.E.
46 Div
Vol 7

Place	Date	Hour	Summary of Events and Information	Remarks and references to Appendices
Henu	Feb 1st	—	Went round part of the line with Cmpy Commander & Lyt 46th Divn — It was decided to put in small elephant shelters for men in front line trenches — 504 2nd C.R.E. S8th Divn allotted for instruction — 1 section attached 2nd 2/o & 1 section Lonsdale kitro	
	2nd "	"	Saw in structure to Lt Marshall & Clements regards the laying out of trenches in operation of operation — in which hours 1/o 2nd P.R.E. - Adj both O.C. of 2nd C.R.E. to line.	
	3rd "	"	Went to see trenches at Malloy — met C.E. at GAUDIEMPRE re huts for Div. Wkshp.	
	4th "	"	Explained reorganization of work to C.R.E. S8th Divn — both him in afternoon to SOUASTRE — Saw O.C. 1st Monmouths & O.C. 1/1 ArC. RE.	
	5th "	"	Accompanied Corps Commander & G.O.C. 46th around part of the line — Adjt went with C.R.A. trench O.P. re "THORPE ST" — C.R.E. S8th Divn arrived for instruction	
	6th "	"	Went to AVESNES & saw M.S. 139 Bde — also O.C. 1/1 2nd RE & O.C. Monmouth. Went to HALLOY to see work in trenches.	
	7th "	"	Accompanied Corps Commander round part of the line — Saw Lt Clements re work contemplated for a raid — C.E. present.	

WAR DIARY or INTELLIGENCE SUMMARY

Army Form C. 2118

HQ R.E. 16 Div?

Place	Date	Hour	Summary of Events and Information	Remarks and references to Appendices
HENU	Feb. 8th 1917	9h	Went to Training Ground HALLOY with G.I. & saw R.E. Officers engaged there - Inspected trenches - C.R.E. 58' Left.	
			Went round Div'l line from BERLES to FONQUEVILLERS with G.S.I. & Brig. Gen. 137 - decided to hasten some of the M.G. works - also arranged to commence pioneer work to revise - ARRAS -	
	10h		Went with D.Y.[?] to see work in Training Ground at HALLOY - went to SAVY to see work at Saw Mills - & to see O.C. 1/2 9th T. R.E. -	
	11th		Went to Berles to C. in C. Commander & afterwards with staff to see works & new D.P.'s in THORPE ST. - & wiring in SIXTH ST. & MILL ST. - Inspected works in old line FONQUEVILLERS.	
	12h		Went to ARRAS with C.E. XVIII Corps & saw 5ith Aug. 01.6 in advanced Billets & arranged for erecting same - saw O.E. del Pioneer	
	13th		Went to ARRAS with G.S.2 & saw O.E. Monuments Off & R.E. Off - saw Billets & Sites proposed for additional shel/into - went round part of the line at ARRAS - Attended conference at HQr in evening.	

1875 Wt. W593/826 1,000,000 4/15 J.B.C. & A. A.D.S.S./Forms/C. 2118.

Army Form C. 2118

3

HQ RE
46 Div

WAR DIARY
or
INTELLIGENCE SUMMARY
(Erase heading not required.)

Instructions regarding War Diaries and Intelligence Summaries are contained in F. S. Regs., Part II. and the Staff Manual respectively. Title Pages will be prepared in manuscript.

Place	Date	Hour	Summary of Events and Information	Remarks and references to Appendices
HENU	Feb 14 1917		prepared report of work to be done in new area - saw O.C. 2/1 9th FCE Adjt 96t CRE arrived	
	9/1/15		went to ARRAS & saw work in progress in Railway Embankment - selected site for new dug out & met G.S.I. re unrevisited trenches in new area	
	16th		Adjt to ARRAS with G.S.3 - made arrangements with CRE 9th Corps for new dumps - to Marshall Cerve & with CRE & G.S.I. arranged for marking out trenches in (new) new Sus. St. LEGER - saw C.E. XVIII Corps & O.C. 1/c of work	
	17th		went to FONQUEVILLERS & saw work in GOOCH ST & Stony Bob	
	18th		saw C.E. at PAS & O.C. Monmouths at SOUASTRE - went to believe in "Q2S" & saw O.C. 1/1 9th FCE	
	19th		saw CRE with Major McGrath - office work & clearing up the lines	
	20th		went to GOVY - very cold day for march & no transport (lorry) available. 001 own to hand & stock of march. 465 & 466 9th FCE marched to Sus. St. LEGER 466 & 468 9th Cos. to DOSSEUR	

Army Form C. 2118

HQ RE 46 Div

WAR DIARY
or
INTELLIGENCE SUMMARY
(Erase heading not required.)

Instructions regarding War Diaries and Intelligence Summaries are contained in F. S. Regs., Part II. and the Staff Manual respectively. Title Pages will be prepared in manuscript.

Place	Date	Hour	Summary of Events and Information	Remarks and references to Appendices
GOUY	21. Febry 1917		Went to see C.E. at FOSSEUX & INS ST LEGER – 466 PTMC & 468 MF went to ARRAS – also PIONEER BN – went to see RE dump at La HERLIERE – adjutant to ARRAS to see Co billets	
	22		Went with G.S.I. to ARRAS & found line to see work & the line – O.C. 466 & 468 accompanied us – Saw O.R. reconnaissance of opp land work well covered – Weather very muddy.	
	23		Saw CE 9th Corps at FOSSEUX & CRE 30th div at BERNAVILLE – ARRAS & saw O.Cs 466 & 468 PTs – Ditch R.E. dump. Arranged with CRE 30th div for Army men's church at LADRET – Reconnoitred ARRAS BOULENS road & ACHICOURT DAINVILLE road.	
	24		Minutes &c & hours of 466 & 468 at SIMONCOURT.	
	25		Went to ARRAS – saw O.Cs 466 & 468 PTs & inspected works – HOPE ST & GREEN ST – & reconnoitred road for additional clay with	
	26		Saw CE 7th Corps at FOSSEUX – went to inspect work in trenches at INS ST LEGER – adjt to ARRAS	

WAR DIARY
or
INTELLIGENCE SUMMARY
(Erase heading not required.)

Army Form C. 2118

Place	Date	Hour	Summary of Events and Information	Remarks and references to Appendices
GOUY	27 Sept 1917		Lieut KARRAN & Serjt OC Pioneers & 2/Lt ? work in progress and CE ? Culp ? examine bridge over railway - which requires strengthening & later been notified - went to CHURCH to look at work required for shot school & later ST LEGER to look at work required for wired trenches.	
	28		Orders received to 465, 466, 468 not true to move to MARTINCOURT. - HQ P. held in readiness tomorrow to move.	

C. Hughson Stratford RS
O/C 46 Div

① War Diary

O.C. 465th Field Coy.R.E.
Headqrs, 46th Division (for information).

In accordance with 46th Divisional Order No.128 your Company will move to the SUS ST LEGER area on February 20th, via GAUDIEMPRE and COUTURELLE. Billets will be arranged for by the 139th Infantry Brigade. Orders for the march will be issued by the 139th Infantry Brigade.

An Officer of the 504th Field Coy.R.E. (58th Div) will take over all maps, papers &c, on the 18th. Arrangements should be made with this officer for the taking over of the forward billets and dumps when your Company moves out.

The sapper of your Company working with the 141st Army Troops Coy.R.E., will return to his unit on returning from leave.

All billets, horse standings, latrines &c, will be cleaned and inspected before moving off.

17:2:17.

Lieut & Adjutant.R.E.
for C.R.E. 46th Division.

War Diary

O.C. 466th Field Coy.R.E.
 "   468th   "   "
Headqrs, 46th Division. (for information).

      The 466th and 468th Field Companies will move to FOSSEUX on February 20th via SOLERNEAU and BAVINCOURT.

      The 468th Company will follow immediately behind the 466th Company, the head of the column leaving the junction of the HUMBERCAMPS amd WARLINCOURT HALTE roads at 8 a.m.

      An Officer of the 504th Field Coy.R.E. (58th Div) will take over all maps, papers&c, on Sunday the 18th February.

      An advance party of the 504th Company will take over the forward billets and dumps at BIENVILLERS and BERLES early in the afternoon of the 18th.

      The personnel of the 468th Company at present working the pumping engines at EHNU and WARLINCOURT will be relieved on the 18th inst., ny the 141st Army Troops Coy.R.E.

      Men employed at the SAULTY saw mill will not be relieved.

      Further details of billeting at FOSSEUX will be sent.

      All billets, Horse standings and latrines will be cleaned and inspected before moving off.

17:2:17.
                                              Lieut & Adjutant.R.E.
                                          for C.R.E. 46th Division.

WAR DIARY or INTELLIGENCE SUMMARY

Army Form C. 2118.

HQ'rs R.E. 46th Div.

Place	Date	Hour	Summary of Events and Information	Remarks and references to Appendices
HENU	March 1st		Arrived from GOUY & HENU saw C.E. XVII Corps about roads & stores & discussed priority of work with F.I. - 2nd LT R.E. showed their billets & new area.	
"	2nd		Went to FONQUEVILLERS & GOMMECOURT to see work required - Held a conference of O.C.'s, Pioneers & O.C. 1st Monmouths (pioneers) to explain work to be carried out -	
"	3rd		Went from Divisional Hd to new dumps to be made & for the increasing of road to GOMMECOURT when it crossed NO MANS LAND. July laid out tracks & made arrangements for dump walk & screening at night - Went with G.O.C. 137 DIV Millers & 139 orderlies trenches opposite MONCHY - & returned by BERLES & reported to R.G.E.	
"	4th		Went to FONQUEVILLERS & GOMMECOURT with R.E. 465 to fix & 139 trench 463 walk gun em[placement].	
"	5th		Went to GOMMECOURT with C.E. XVII Corps & inspected work & made discussion - Issue of tramway - Held conference of C.R.E.'s & explained situation & work to be done - Road through GOMMECOURT made fit for horse traffic.	
"	6th		Work on roads & tram lines in GOMMECOURT continued. Made tramway from O.O. attack from HEDOTERNE through German wire to NAMELESS Farm	
"	7th		Work on advanced roads & tram lines continued - Inspected work in progress round ground through GOMMECOURT - Conference at H.Qrs of XVII Corps. 5.04 pm - returned to XVIII Corps.	

Army Form C. 2118.

WAR DIARY
or
INTELLIGENCE SUMMARY.
(Erase heading not required.)

HQrs 46th Div: RE

Instructions regarding War Diaries and Intelligence Summaries are contained in F. S. Regs, Part II. and the Staff Manual respectively. Title pages will be prepared in manuscript.

Place	Date	Hour	Summary of Events and Information	Remarks and references to Appendices
Henu	8th March 1917		in preparing advanced orders — & carrying in to PIGEON WOOD — Inspected work in progress	2
	9th		went to FONQUEVILLERS, ROSSIGNOL WOOD — BIEZ WOOD & RATTENER farm & inspected work on roads & tram line. Lt Marshall & Graves laying out intended line for tracking attack — commenced road GOMMECOURT to NAMELESS farm	
	10h		work on advanced roads continued — inspected same & laying out tracks continued	
	11th		went with O.C. 465 to inspect work going on, on GOMMECOURT & CRUCIFIX? Whynots road by ROSSIGNOL WD to BUCQUOY & thence by HEBUTERNE & whynots road by 466 2/Lt R.E. in their way there — but own to work O.O.!	
			saw O.C. monmouths & 466 2/Lt R.E. at BAYENCOURT attacks	
	12h		of which went to BAYENCOURT — then to O.E. 465 the went to see O.C. 466 2/Lt R.E. at BAYENCOURT. & him to AMIENS to buy tape — road through GOMMECOURT to NAMELESS farm opened to traffic	CRE no attacks
	13h		went to FONQUEVILLERS & saw O.Cs 465 & 466 'F' 2/Lt R.E. & made arrangements for night for attack. — 6 RE's 466 to attached to 137h B. to ammund tubes — 3000x of knife little for Infantry advance — 48 lbs of stores taken by tramway to BIEZ WOOD & unloaded —	

HQ 1st R.E. 46th Div.

Army Form C. 2118.

WAR DIARY
or
INTELLIGENCE SUMMARY.
(Erase heading not required.)

Instructions regarding War Diaries and Intelligence Summaries are contained in F. S. Regs., Part II. and the Staff Manual respectively. Title pages will be prepared in manuscript.

3

Place	Date	Hour	Summary of Events and Information	Remarks and references to Appendices
HENU	14th March		Saw duck walk laid out to GOMMECOURT from SOUASTRE road & arrived FONQUEVILLERS. Inspected advanced roads from GOMMECOURT with O.C. 466 1st/RE	
	15th		Inspected advanced road work with Adjt & new duck walk – Saw O.C. 465 & 466 1st/RE.	
	16th		Saw O.C. 466 1st/RE at BAYENCOURT & then went to FONQUEVILLERS. Inspected advanced road to CRUCIFIX & ROSSIGNOL – & thence to R/E 2 GOMMECOURT & inspected work & tram line to GOMMECOURT – Saw Gen.	
	17th		With RATTENBY & returned to BAYENCOURT & with O.C. 466 1st/RE went to HEBUTERNE and rode to BAYENCOURT & with O.C. 466 1st/RE went to HEBUTERNE and made reconnaissance of HEBUTERNE – CRUCIFIX road with a view to making up road – muddy state	
LA HAIE FERME	18th		Adv'd HQrs. HQrs occupies at LA HAIE FERME – rode from HENU in morning – rode to HANNESCAMP & inspected work to ESSARTS. BUQUOY road – Saw O.Cs. 466 & 468 1st/Cos. 468 taking 465 Cos. at FONQUEVILLERS	O.O. 4
	19th		Inspected work on FONQUEVILLERS – GOMMECOURT – CRUCIFIX. ROSSIGNOL & BUQUOY – ESSARTS – HANNESCAMP – FONQUEVILLERS – Saw O.C. 137 1st/B de M 46th 1st/RE	

Army Form C. 2118.

H. Qrs 46th div R.E.

WAR DIARY
or
INTELLIGENCE SUMMARY.

Place	Date	Hour	Summary of Events and Information	Remarks and references to Appendices
LA HAIE FERME	March 20th	—	Inspected works in advanced zones — visited 468 T. Coy at RATTENOY farm — returned by BUQUOY & ESSARTS.	
	21st	—	Moved to RATTENOY farm — 466 to FONQUEVILLERS & 465 to BAYENCOURT — visited 466 & new HQrs. Inspected work in advanced zones — & saw O.C. 468 Coy at work in PUSSIEUX — BUQUOY road — & views Villers to BAYENCOURT. — 465 to COURCELLES. — Inspected 137th R.E. at work on ESSART — BUQUOY road.	
COUIN	22nd	—	Div HQrs moved to COUIN — Inspected work in HANNESCAMP — BUQUOY road. Saw OCs 466 & 137th R.E. & HANNESCAMP — FONQUEVILLERS road.	
	23rd	—	RE Units moved to new billets.	
DURY	24th	—	Div. HQrs. moved from COUIN to DURY by march route. Companies moved to SALEUX near AMIENS area.	
	25th	—	Resting & cleaning up.	

HQ gp R.E. 46th div.

WAR DIARY
or
INTELLIGENCE SUMMARY.

Army Form C. 2118.

Place	Date	Hour	Summary of Events and Information	Remarks and references to Appendices
DURY	26 March		} status clearing up – R.E. Companies entrains on 28th to LILLERS	5
	27th			
	28th			
NORRENT FONTES	29th		Entrains at SALEUX for LILLERS – arrives 11.30 p.m. Detrains L.a.m 30/3	
"	30		Companies cleaning up & inspecting kits –	
"	31		Interview with 9/Lt 46 div & 9/Lt 2nd Corps to the different Brigades where Corps Commander saw all officers – lunch with 2nd Corps C.E. 2nd Corps & afterwards to 1st Army Branch at LILLERS.	

L. Hartfield Strathorn
Maj Genl
CRE 46 div

SECRET.   COPY NO. 2

C.R.E's 58th Division OPERATION ORDER NO.6

                                              1st March.1917.

Reference:- Map sheet LENS 11. 1/100,000
SS--

1.   The 504th Field Co.R.E. will be relieved on March 1st,
by 465th Field Co.R.E. The relief will not take place till
the evening. After relief, the 504th Field Co.R.E. will
return to SOUASTRE for the night, and on the 2nd March will
move to HUMBERCAMP.
Time and route to be detailed by O.C. 504th Field Co.R.E.

2.   Headquarters, 58th Divisional Engineers will move from
HENU to BAVINCOURT on March 1st.
Move at 9-30 a.m.
Route:- GAUDIEMPRE - BARLINCOURT HALTE.

3. Hutmensberg.
                                          J H Chapman
                                              Captain R.E.
                                     for Lieut. Colonel R.E.
                                           C.R.E. 58th Division.

Copy No.1 to 504th Field Co.R.E. issued to Signals at 12-25 a.m.

Issued to Signals by D.R.L.S.
        at 5 p.m.

Copies to:-
    Copy No. 2 to C.R.E. 46th Division
      "   "   3 " O.C. 465th Field Co.R.E.
      "   "   4 " Headquarters, 58th Division "G"
      "   "   5 " Headquarters, 58th Division "A & Q"
      "   "   6 " Chief Engineer, XVlll Corps.
      "   "   7 " O.C. 58th Divisional Signal Co.R.E.
      "   "   8 " Headquarters, 138th Infantry Brigade.
      "   "   9 " Headquarters, 173rd Infantry Brigade.
      "   " 10 " O.C. Divisional Train.
      "   " 11 " S.S.O.
      "   " 12 " O.C. Divisional Supply Column.
      "   " 13 " D.A.D.O.S.
      "   " 14 " A.D.M.S.
      "   " 15 " A.D.V.S.
      "   " 16 " A.P.M.
      "   " 17 " File
      "   " 18 " War Diary.
      "   " 19 " War Diary.

SECRET.   Copy No 4

C.R.E.'s 58th DIVISION OPERATION ORDER NO.7

2nd March.1917.

Reference Map LENS Sheet 11. 1/100,000.

1. The 504th Field Co.R.E. will remain at SOUASTRE under the orders of the 46th Division.

2. Acknowledge.

S.H. Chapman
Captain R.E.
for Lieut. Colonel R.E.
C.R.E. 58th Division

Issued to Signals by D.R.L.S. at 4 p.m.
Copies to:-
```
Copy No. 1  to  O.C. 504th Field Co.R.E.
  "    "  2  "   Headquarters, 46th Division. "G"
  "    "  3  "   Headquarters, 46th Division. "A & Q"
  "    "  4  "   C.R.E. 46th Division.
  "    "  5  "   Headquarters, 58th Division. "G"
  "    "  6  "   Headquarters, 58th Division. "A & Q"
  "    "  7  "   Chief Engineer, XVlll Corps.
  "    "  8  "   O.C. 58th Divisional Signal Coy.R.E.
  "    "  9  "   Headquarters, 173rd Infantry Brigade.
  "    " 10  "   O.C. 58th Divisional Train.
  "    " 11  "   S.S.O.
  "    " 12  "   O.C. 58th Divisional Supply Column.
  "    " 13  "   D.A.D.O.S.
  "    " 14  "   A.D.M.S.
  "    " 15  "   A.D.V.S.
  "    " 16  "   A.P.M.
  "    " 17  "   File
  "    " 18  "   War Diary
  "    " 19  "   War Diary.
```

O.C.466th Field Co R.E.

In accordance with 46th Division Order No 133 your Company will move to BIENVILLERS to-morrow 5/3/17 and will be under the order of the C.R.E.

Time of move etc. will be arranged by you.

Transport will remain at POMMIER. Report completion of move to this office. ACKNOWLEDGE.

Lieut & Adjutant R.E.
for C.R.E.46th Division

4/3/17.

OPERATION ORDER
by
Brigadier-General C.V.WINGFIELD - STRATFORD C.M.G.
C.R.E. 46th Division
****

March 6th 1917.

1. The 504th Field Coy R.E.,58th Division, will move as follows to-morrow the 7:3:17, leaving SOUASTRE at 10 a.m.

2. Two Sections to HUMBERCAMPS via ST AMAND.
Two Sections to POMMIER via ST AMAND
Transport to LARBERT via ST AMAND, HUMBERCAMPS & LA BAZEQUE.

3. All stores drawn from Dump will be handed over to O.C. 465th Field Co R.E., at SOUASTRE.

4. The billets vacated by the 504th Field Coy.R.E., will be taken over by the O.C.468th Field Co R.E., who will send representatives of his Company to report to ~~you~~ O.C. 504 Coy at 9 a.m. 7:3:17.

5. All billets, horse standings, latrines Etc. will be left clean and inspected before moving off.

6. ACKNOWLEDGE.

Chas A Heaton
Lieut & Adjutant R.E.
for C.R.E.46th Division.

6:3:17.

Copies to :-

O.C.504th Field Co R.E.
C.R.E.58th Division
Headquarters 46th Division
O.C.465th Field Co R.E.
O.C.468th Field Co R.E.
O.C.Divisional Train.
File.
War Dairy.

"C" Form (Duplicate).
MESSAGES AND SIGNALS.

Army Form C. 2123.
(In books of 50's in duplicate.)

Handed in at 4.H **Office** 6.10 p.m. **Received** 6.4 p.m.

TO CRE 46 Division

Sender's Number: G433 **Day of Month:** 6

504 field Coy should move tomorrow as follows aaa headqrs and 2 sections to HUMBERCAMP aaa 2 sections to POMMIER aaa transport to LARBRET aaa CRE 46 Division is kindly issuing necessary orders aaa this cancels G419 of todays date aaa addsd CRE 46 repld CRE and Q 58 Divn

FROM PLACE & TIME: 58 Division 6 pm

OPERATION ORDER
by
Brigadier-General C.V. WINGFIELD - STRATFORD C.M.G.
C.R.E. 46th Division

March 6th 1917.

1. The 504th Field Coy R.E., 46th Division, will move as follows to-morrow the 7:3:17, leaving SOUASTRE at 10 a.m.

2. Two Sections to HUMBERCAMPS via ST AMAND.
Two Sections to POMMIER via ST AMAND
Transport to LARBERT via ST AMAND, HUMBERCAMPS & LA BAZEQUE.

3. All stores drawn from Dump will be handed over to O.C. 465th Field Co R.E., at SOUASTRE.

4. The billets vacated by the 504th Field Coy.R.E., will be taken over by the O.C. 468th Field Co R.E., who will send representatives of his Company to report to OC 504 Cy at 9 a.m. 7:3:17.

5. All billets, horse standings, latrines Etc. will be left clean and inspected before moving off.

6. ACKNOWLEDGE.

6:3:17.

Chas. A. Hutton
Lieut & Adjutant R.E.
for C.R.E. 46th Division.

Copies to :-

O.C. 504th Field Co R.E.
C.R.E. 58th Division
Headquarters 46th Division
O.C. 465th Field Co R.E.
O.C. 468th Field Co R.E.
O.C. Divisional Train.
File. ✓
War Diary.

SECRET.   Copy No. 2

C.R.E's 58th DIVISION OPERATION ORDER No.9

                                            6th March, 1917.

Reference - Map Sheet LENS 11. 1/100,000.
----

1. MOVE. The 504th Field Co.y R.E. will move from SOUASTRE
to BAILLEULMONT tomorrow, 7th instant, under orders of the
C.R.E. 46th Division.

2. Acknowledge.

                                        S/W Chapman
                                        Captain R.E.
                                    for Lieut. Colonel R.E.
                                        C.R.E. 58th Division.

Issued to Signals at 4 p.m.

    Copies to:-
    Copy No. 1 to O.C. 504th Field Co.R.E.
     "   " 2 " C.R.E. 46th Division.
     "   " 3 " Headquarters, 58th Division. "G"
     "   " 4 " Headquarters, 58th Division. "A & Q"
     "   " 5 " Headquarters, 173rd Infantry Brigade.
     "   " 6 " Chief Engineer, XVIII Corps.
     "   " 7 " O.C. 503rd Field Co.R.E.
     "   " 8 " O.C. 511th Field Co.R.E.
     "   " 9 " O.C. Signals.
     "   "10 " O.C. Divl. Train.
     "   "11 " S.S.O.
     "   "12 " O.C. Div. Supply Col.
     "   "13 " D.A.D.O.S.
     "   "14 " A.D.M.S.
     "   "15 " A.D.V.S.
     "   "16 " A.P.M.
     "   "17 " File
     "   "18 " War Diary
     "   "19 " War Diary.

O.C. 465th Field Coy.R.E.

    Please arrange to move your horses in the standings at present occupied by the 504th Field Coy.R.E., at 10 a.m. to-morrow the 7:3:17.

    The billets of the 504th Coy and the standings at present occupied by you will be taken over at 10 a.m. to-morrow by the 468th Field Coy.R.E.

    The standings and any billets vacated by you will be left clean.

6:3:17.

Lieut & Adjutant.R.E.
for C.R.E., 46th Division.

Copy No. 4

OPERATION ORDER No.1.
by
Brig-General.C.V.WINGFIELD-STRATFORD., C.M.G.
C.R.E., 46th Division.

March. 10th, 1917.

1. The 466th Field Coy.R.E., will move to HEBUTERNE to-morrow the 11:3:1917, leaving BIENVILLERS at 9.15 a.m., and marching via SOUASTRE and SAILLY.

2. Billeting parties will be sent on ahead and report to the Town Major, HEBUTERNE at 11 a.m.

3. All billets, horse lines, latrines &c., will be left clean before moving off.

4. ACKNOWLEDGE.

Chas A Hinton

Lieut & Adjutant.R.E.
for C.R.E. 46th Division.

Copy No.1. to O.C. 466th Field Co.R.E.
,, 2. to Headquarters "G" 46th Div.
,, 3. to File.
,, 4. to War Diary.

"A" Form.
MESSAGES AND SIGNALS.

Army Form C.2121 (in pads of 100).

TO	ELF	LADAS	O.C. Signals.
	SEFTON	7th Division	A.A. & Q.M.G.
	MEMOIR	5th Corps.	CRE

Sender's Number: G.193. Day of Month: 13

AAA

Reference Divisional Order No. 145 dated 13th March, 1917, if BUCQUOY is not occupied the green and brown lines are to be taken tonight AAA Heavy artillery will bombard these lines for half an hour at a time to be notified later AAA 137th Infantry Brigade will be prepared to capture its 1st objective after the conclusion of the heavy artillery bombardment under a field artillery barrage to be put down on the green line and subsequently shifted to form a standing barrage to cover the occupation and consolidation of the objective AAA The G.O.C. 137th Brigade will detail two battalions for the operation and to take over the posts on the BIEZ GRABEN at present occupied by 139th Brigade AAA A third battalion will be held in reserve at ROSSIGNOL WOOD and the fourth will be retained in billets at half an hours notice AAA 139th Infantry Brigade will cooperate in prolonging the left flank of the 137th Brigade from RETTEMOY GRABEN as far east as F.26.a.0.1 where touch with 137th Brigade will be established, or if opportunity offers ro prolong the line of 137th Brigade along BUCQUOY GRABEN and LANDSTURM GRABEN to our present line AAA Addressed ELF

From: SEFTOn, MEMOIR and LADAS reptd 5th Corps an 7th Division, O.C. Signals and A.A. Q.M.G.

Place: 46th Division

Time: 2.45 pm.

sd/ R.G. Stone Capt-

SECRET.   Copy No. 7

40th Division Order No. 146.

13th March, 1917.

Reference G.193 dated 13th instant.

1. Bombardment by Heavy Artillery will be from 10 p.m. to 10.30 p.m.

    Field artillery barrage commences at 11.45 p.m. lifts off German 1st line at 11.54 p.m. and moves back at the rate of 100 yards in 2 minutes to GREEN and BROWN objectives, when it becomes a protective barrage until 1 a.m. It will then lift clear to allow strong battle patrols to push forward in the case of 7th Division to DIERVILLE FARM and in the case of 40th Division to HILL 155.

    In the case of no opposition the posts detailed in 40th Division Order No. 145 dated 13th March 'Plan of Attack' paras. 3 and 4, will be established and touch gained with 7th Division at DIERVILLE FARM.

2. Acknowledge.

                                             Major.,
                                   General Staff, 40th Division.

Issued at 3.20 p.m.

To recipients of G.193.

(margin note: 11.51 p.m.)

Copy No 1

OPERATION ORDER No 4.
by
Brigadier-General C.V.Wingfield-Stratford C.M.G.
C.R.E. 46th Division.

March 16th 1917.

1. Operation Order No.2.is cancelled.

2. The 468th.Field Co.R.E. will relieve the 465th Field Company R.E.,on the 18th instant,taking over their billets in FONQUEVILLERS.

3. The 465th Field Co R.E. will take over the billets vacated by the 468 Field Co R.E. in SOUASTRE.

4. O.C.468th Field Co R.E. will arrange to take over the work to-morrow the 17th instant,prior to relief the following day.

5. Times of relief will be arranged mutually between Os.C. Companies.

6. Completion of relief will be notified to this office.

7. ACKNOWLEDGE.

Chas. A. Hunter.

Lieut & Adjutant R.E.
for C.R.E.46th Division

Copies to:-

O.C.468th Field Co R.E.   No 1
O.C.466th Field Co R.E.   2
O.C.465th Field Co R.E.   3
Headquarters 46th Div."G"   4
     "   "   "Q"   5
O.C.Divisional Train   6
War Diary   7
File.   8

O.C. 468th Field Coy.R.E.

      The following wire has been received from 46th Division:-
"In the event of an advance the 138th Bde with 468th Field Coy
"R.E. and Battery R.F.A. will form the advance guard AAA C.R.A.
"will detail the battery which must be prepared to move at short
"notice AAA A.D.M.S. will detail bearers to accompany advance
"guard AAA Addsd ELF CYLLENE SEFTON MEMIOR LADAS AND BOMBA.

                ****

      Reference above, your Company will be prepared to move
forward with the 138th Inf: Brigade at short notice in the
event of an advance.

    ACKNOWLEDGE.

                                                  Lieut & Adjutant.R.E.
18:3:17.   for C.R.E., 46th Division.

SECRET   Copy No ___6___

OPERATION ORDER No. 3
by
Brigadier-General C.V. Wingfield-Stratford. C.M.G.
C.R.E. 46th Division.

Reference Headqtrs G 263 d/d 15/3/17.   March 16th 1917.
Reference E 305 dated 15/3/1917.

1.   The 468th Field Company R.E. will have a
     section complete with transport held in
     constant readiness to move at short
     notice.

2.   The 468th Field Company to ACHEO RIDGE.

                                Chas. A. Hunton
                                Lieut & Adjutant R.E.
                              for C.R.E. 46th Division

Copies to:-

O.C.465th Field Co R.E.   No 1.
O.C.466th   "   "   No 2
O.C.468th   "   "   No 3
Headquarters "G"   No 4
     "   "G"   No 5
H.Q.138th Brigade   No 6
O.C.Divisional Train   No 7
A.D.M.S.   No 8
War Diary   No 9
File   No 10.

                                        BM 919.

CRE.

Received at 9.10 p.m 16 inst.

G 263 d/15.3.17 was cancelled by wire
at 10.45 am on 16.3.17.

16.3.17.   J Campbell
                                Capt BM 2B

O.C. 465th Field Coy.R.E.
O.C. 466th Field Coy.R.E.
O.C. 468th Field Coy.R.E.

Reference 46th Division Order No. 149, para 7, attached.

The Headquarters of the Field Companies will be situated as follows :-

465th Field Coy.R.E.	SOUASTRE.
466th Field Coy.R.E.	BAYENCOURT.
468th Field Coy.R.E.	FONQUEVILLERS.

Chas A. Hutton

Lieut & Adjutant.R.E.
for C.R.E. 46th Division.

March 17th, 1917.

SECRET.　　　　　　　　　　　　　　　　　　　　　　Copy No.2.

46th DIVISION ORDER No.149

17th March 1917.

1. The enemy's retreat is continuing.

2. The Division will be closed so as to permit of pursuit.

3. The dividing lines for the Division are as follows :-

    Right Boundary.　BUCQUOY - AYETTE road exclusive.

    Left　　,,　　Junction of old front line with
    　　　　　　　HANNESCAMPS - ESSARTS road - F.1.c.0.0.
    　　　　　　　thence N.E. to X.20.a.0.8.

4. The 139th Inf. Brigade will establish a line of posts between the above limits on the line DIERVILLE FARM - HILL 155 - ARTILLERY GRABEN - SCHWARZWALD GRABEN - QUARRY E.18.c. A forward post will be established at LE QUESNOY FARM.

5. The 5th Lincolns will carry out the relief of the 6th North Staffords so as to complete this relief by 9 a.m. 18th.

6. By 9 am. tomorrow Brigades will be disposed of as follows :-

    138th Inf. Brigade.
    　2 battalions holding front DIERVILLE FARM to QUARRY E.18.c.
    　1 battalion North of GOMMECOURT.
    　1　　,,　　GOMMECOURT.

    137th Inf. Brigade.
    　1 battalion GOMMECOURT.
    　1　　,,　　FONQUEVILLERS.
    　1　　,,　　HANNESCAMPS.
    　1　　,,　　BAYENCOURT.

    139th Inf. Brigade.
    　2 battalions SOUASTRE.
    　2　　,,　　ST. AMAND.

7. Field Companies, R.E. will remain with their affiliated Inf. Brigades.

8. Advanced Divisional Headquarters will open at CHAU de la HAIE at 10 a.m. to-morrow 18th March.

9. ACKNOWLEDGE.

　　　　　　　　　　　　　　　　　　　　　G.THORPE, Lieut-Colonl
　　　　　　　　　　　　　　　　　　　General Staff, 46th Division.

ENTRAINMENT PROGRAMME.
FOR
MOVE OF 46th DIVISION less ARTILLERY.

27th - 28th MARCH 1917.

From FIFTH ARMY.　　　　　　　　　　　　　　　　To FIRST ARMY.
　Entraining Stations.　　　　　　　　　　　　　　Regulating Station.
　　"A" SALEUX　　　　　　　　　　　　　　　　　　BERGUETTE
　　"B" BACOUEL

From Stations "A"	"B"	SERIAL NUMBERS	Mobe.	Time of departure entraining Stations	Date	Time of arrival detraining Stations	Date.	Remarks.
(1)	(2)	(3)	(4)	(5)	(6)	(7)	(8)	(9)
1	-	4620,21a,25,26,27	T.70	1:20	27th			
-	2	4630,31a,35,36,37	T.72	3:10	27th			
3	-	4621.	T.74	5:18	27th			
-	4	4631.	T.52	7:00	27th			
5	-	4622.	T.54	9:20	27th			
-	6	4632.	T.56	10:55	27th			
7	-	4622a,77, 82.	T.58	13:13	27th			
-	8	4632a,78,83.	T.60	15:10	27th			
9	-	4623.	T.62	17:20	27th			
-	10	4633.	T.64	19:10	27th			
11	-	4624.	T.66	21:20	27th			
-	12	4634.	T.68	23:10	27th			
13	-	4623a,24a,82,87.	T.70	1:20	28th			
-	14	4633a,34a,88.	T.72	3:10	28th			
15	-	4601,05,90,Wireless Section	T.74	5:18	28th			
-	16	4610,11a,15,16,17.	T.52	7:00	28th			
17	-	4612.	T.54	9:20	28th			
-	18	4611.	T.56.	10:55	28th			
19	-	4612a,76,81.	T.58	13:13	28th			
-	20	4613.	T.60	15:10	28th			
21	-	4604.	T.62	17:20	28th			
-	22	4614.	T.64	19:10	28th			
23	-	4603,04a,06,07,75	T.66	21:20	28th			
-	24	4613a,4614a,86.	T.68	23:10	28th			

Billeting Party of 137th Infantry Brigade entrain on train No.16 from
　　　　　　　　　　　　　　　　　　　　　　　　　　　　　　　　BACOUEL.
Billeting Party of 138th Infantry Brigade entrain on train No.1 from SALEUX.
Billeting Party of 139th Inf. Brigade entrain on train No.2 from BACOUEL.
Military Police Parties on Brigade H.Q. Trains.
Wireless Section on Train No.15 from SALEUX.

TABLE "D".

MOVE OF 46th (NORTH MIDLAND) DIVISION (LESS ARTILLERY).

UNIT.	Serial Number.	Description.
DIVISIONAL UNITS.	4601	Divisional Headquarters.
	4603	H.Q. Divisional Engineers.
	4604	Pioneer Battn less 4604a, (1/1 Mon. Regt.)
	4604a	1 Coy, 1 Cooker & Team & 4 G.S. wagons and Teams of Pioneer Battn (1/1 Mon. Regt.)
	4605	H.Q. & No.1 Section Divisional Signal Coy.
	4606	Cable Section.
	4607	Salvage Coy.
	4608	No.4 Machine Gun Coy. Wireless Section.
137th INFANTRY BDE	4610	Brigade Headquarters.
	4611	1/5 South Staff. Regt. less 4611a.
	4611a	1 Coy, 1 Cooker & Team of 1/5 S.Staff. Regt.
	4612	1/6 South Staff. Regt. less 4612a.
	4612a	1 Coy, 1 Cooker & Team of 1/6 S.Staff. Regt.
	4613	1/5 North Staff. Regt. less 4613a.
	4613a	1 Coy, 1 Cooker & Team of 1/5 N.Staff. Regt.
	4614	1/6 North Staff. Regt. less 4614a.
	4614a	1 Coy, 1 Cooker & Team of 1/6 N.Staff. Regt.
	4615	Section Divisional Signal Coy.
	4616	Brigade Machine Gun Coy.
	4617	Light Trench Mortar Battery.
138th INFANTRY BDE	4620	Brigade Headquarters.
	4621	1/4 Lincoln Regt. less 4621a.
	4621a	1 Coy, 1 Cooker & Team of 1/4 Lincoln Regt.
	4622	1/5 Lincoln Regt. less 4622a.
	4622a	1 Coy, 1 Cooker & Team of 1/5 Lincoln Regt.
	4623	1/4 Leicestershire Regt. less 4623a.
	4623a	1 Coy, 1 Cooker & Team of 1/4 Leicester: Regt.
	4624	1/5 Leicestershire Regt. less 4624a.
	4624a	1 Coy, 1 Cooker & Team of 1/5 Leicester: Regt.
	4625	Section Divisional Signal Coy.
	4626	Brigade Machine Gun Coy.
	4627	Light Trench Mortar Battery.
139th INFANTRY BDE	4630	Brigade Headquarters.
	4631	1/5 Notts. & Derby Regt. less 4631a.
	4631a	1 Coy, 1 Cooker & Team of 1/5 Notts. & Derby Rgt
	4632	1/6 Notts. & Derby Regt. less 4632a.
	4632a	1 Coy, 1 Cooker & Team of 1/6 Notts & Derby Rgt.
	4633	1/7 Notts. & Derby Regt. less 4633a.
	4633a	1 Coy, 1 Cooker & Team of 1/7 Notts & Derby Rgt.
	4634	1/8 Notts. & Derby Regt. less 4634a.
	4634a	1 Coy, 1 Cooker & Team of 1/8 Notts & Derby Rgt.
	4635	Section Divisional Signal Coy.
	4636	Brigade Machine Gun Coy.
	4637	Light Trench Mortar Battery.
DIVISIONAL TRAIN	4675	H.Q. Divisional Train.
	4676	Coy. Divisional Train. No 453
	4677	Coy. Divisional Train. " 452
	4678	Coy. Divisional Train. " 454
DIVISIONAL ENGINEERS	4681	N.Midland Field Coy. R.E. No 466
	4682	N.Midland Field Coy. R.E. " 468
	4683	N.Midland Field Coy. R.E. " 465
MEDICAL UNITS.	4686	N.Midland Field Ambulance. 2nd
	4687	N.Midland Field Ambulance. 3rd
	4688	N.Midland Field Ambulance. 1st.
VETERINARY UNIT.	4690	Mobile Veterinary Section.

SECRET.

C.R.E.

46th. Division.
No. Q45.

(1) /copies of Table 'D' and entrainment tables for the move of the 46th. Division (less Artillery) from Fifth Army to First Army are sent herewith.

(2) Each train consists of :-

One coach for officers, (about 30 seats).
Thirty covered trucks. 40 men or 8 horses.
Seventeen flat trucks. Four axles. (except Pontoons).

(3) Two men will be detailed to each truck of horses.

(4) 138th. Brigade will detail a loading party of one Officer and 50 men to report to R.T.O., SALEUX four hours before departure of first train.
139th. Brigade will detail a loading party of one Officer and 50 men to report to R.T.O., BACOUEL four hours before departure of first train.
The above parties will remain at disposal of R.T.O's until departure of last train, on which they will travel.
A transport Sergeant should be detailed with each party.
Each party will carry two days rations.

(5) Similar parties will be detailed to travel by first train from each Station for unloading at destination. Officers in charge of parties will report to R.T.O., on arrival. These parties will be detailed by 138th. and 139th. Brigades respectively. Each party will carry two days rations.

(6) Each Brigade will send a party to reconnoitre approaches to the Station. Officer in charge to report to R.T.O.,

(7) Officers Commanding Units (or Adjutant) will report personally to R.T.O., on arrival.

(8) Transport of each Unit will report at Station three hours before departure of train. Personnel of each Unit will report at Station one hour before departure of train.

(9) Horses will be watered before entrainment. (Party mentioned in para. 6 to point out watering points).

(10)   Headropes are to be provided. Horses are to be unharnessed, and the harness packed in centre of truck.

(11)   A.P.M. will arrange to police and control the traffic at each Station. Parties for destinations to travel on first trains. Parties at entraining stations leave on last train.

(12)   Supply and Baggage Wagons will entrain with their units, and not with their train company.

(13)   Supplies for following day will be carried in Supply Wagons.
Water Carts will travel empty.

(14)   All Water bottles will be filled before entraining.

W.T.C. Huffam
Captain.
D.A.Q.M.G., 46th. Division.....

March 25th. 1917.

HeadQ. R.E. 46th Div.

HQ RE 46D Army Form C.2118.
Vol 9 11

WAR DIARY
or
INTELLIGENCE SUMMARY.
(Erase heading not required.)

Place	Date	Hour	Summary of Events and Information	Remarks and references to Appendices
NOEUX LES MINES	April 1st 1917		1st overhauling equipment - lot training - reconnaissance & relief schemes.	
	2nd	–	Visited 1st & inspected horses & vehicles. 1st training as infantry.	
	3rd	–	Training as per programme	
	4th	–	do – inoculation of 1st	
	5	–	do	
	6th	–	do – inspected a new billeting area for 466 2nd/1st RE.	
	7th	–	do	
	8th	–	Training	
	9th	–	Divl. march & inspection by Corps Commander 2nd Troops & GOC	
	10th	–	Divisional scheme and proved with Directing Staff	
	11th	–	Training as per programme	
	12th	–	do – Inspected new billeting area for RE near BUSNES	
BUSNES	13th	–	moved to new billets – HQrs BUSNES –	O.O. No 7
	14th	–	465 & 1/1st RE. moved to REBREUVE for work under C.E. 1st Corps, head with G.S.1 & R.S.2 to see model of German trenches at SHARPENBURG afterwards to O.P. at KEMMEL to look at German line - 467 to change billets	OO No 8 OO No 9

HQ R.E. 46th Div

Army Form C. 2118.

WAR DIARY
or
INTELLIGENCE SUMMARY.
(Erase heading not required.)

Place	Date	Hour	Summary of Events and Information	Remarks and references to Appendices
BUSNES	April 15th 1917		Training finished. Have lined (?) held in readiness to move at 6 hr. notice	B.O. 19. 16
	16th		Inspected new billets Divn. were moving to in LABOUVRIERE	
LABOUVRIERE	17th		HQ RE moved to LABOUVRIERE - went with GS to NEUVILLE ST VAAST & walked to VIMY ridge - LA TOLIE ferme & inspected roads when operations were in progress	U-O No 11
	18th		Saw C.E. 170p/n & C.R.E. 24th div - 466 & 468 F Coys changed billets	
	19th		Went to SAINS en GOHELLE with G.S. 2 & saw C.R.E. 24th & went to recce part of area we were to take up - rely looking over sites	O.C. No 12
SAINS en GOHELLE	20th		moved HQs RE to SAINS en GOHELLE with new work from C.R.E. 24th div & went both to see part of area - took over tramways & forward roads.	
	21st		Went with Corps forward roads offr. & tramways officer to inspect roads & gave instructions to 270 & 466 to take over same - inspected work going on R.E. for on forward roads - drawing planked areas - & tramways	
	22		Went to MAROC hewn, shelling with gas shells - several cases of gas poisoning - Co's engaged in roads & tramways & driving off water sectn attacks to each Lor Bdes Brigade for supporting roads	

A5834. Wt. W4973/M687 750,000 8/16 D. D. & L. Ltd. Forms/C.2118/13.

WAR DIARY
or
INTELLIGENCE SUMMARY.
(Erase heading not required.)

Army Form C. 2118.

Head qu. R.E. 46th divr.

Place	Date	Hour	Summary of Events and Information	Remarks and references to Appendices
SAINS en GOHELLE	April 23rd 1917		inspected work in forward area & R.E. divs' dumps.	
	24th		C.E. 1st Corps came in & discussed work to be done. went all the roads with 1 Corps roads officer & see work in progress & make reconnaissance of new roads to be taken in hand.	
	25th		made reconnaissance of div'l. line with O.C. 1st Corps M.G. 46th divn. M.G. Off.	
	26th		continued reconnaissance of new positions accompanied by O.C. 466 & 1st R.E. & div'l M.G. Off.	
	27th		went round position with G.O.C. 46 div. & G.S.1. & O.C. 466 T.M. — & C.O. afterwards.	
	28th		inspected horse lines — office work — & billets	
	29th		went round works in progress on new line & in forward roads — saw O.C. Pioneers.	
	30th		inspected work on forward roads & tramways & new line.	

C.King Frewd Lt Col R.E. CRE 46th

O.C.465th Field Co R.E.
O.C.466th Field Co R.E.
O.C.468th Field Co R.E.

Attached copy of 46th Division Order 155 is forwarded for your information and necessary action.

Orders for the march on 9th will be issued by your Brigade.

6/4/17.

Lieut & Adjutant R.E.
for C.R.E. 46th Division

46th Division.
2639/2/G.

C.R.A.	1/Monmouths.
C.R.E.	Camp Commandant.
Signals.	A.D.M.S.
137th I.B.	A.P.M.
138th I.B.	~~A.D.C., for G.O.C.~~
139th I.B.	A.A.&Q.M.G.
178th M.G. Co.	

Reference Order No. 155.

The interchange of billets between 137th and 138th Inf. Bdes. will take place on 12th April instead of 10th April.

7/4/17.

Lieut-Colonel,
General Staff, 46th Division.

"A" Form.
Army Form C. 2121.

MESSAGES AND SIGNALS.

No. of Message..........

Prefix......... Code......... m. | Words | Charge | This message is on a/c of : | Recd. at..........m.
Office of Origin and Service Instructions. | | | | Date..........
SECRET | Sent | | ....Service. | From..........
| At..........m. | | |
| To | | (Signature of "Franking Officer.") | By..........
| By | | |

TO { 10. R.E.
46th Div.

Sender's Number. | Day of Month. | In reply to Number. |
* R.E. 704 | 7th | E478. | AAA

46th Div.l Order No. 1515 received please

Note with SO 155

From O.C. 468 Fd. Co. R.E.
Place
Time

The above may be forwarded as now corrected.   (Z)

Censor.   Signature of Addressor or person authorised to telegraph in his name.
W.D.W. Major R.E.

225,000. W 14042—M 44. H. W & V., Ld. 12/15.

C.R.E.

46th Division 2639/2/G,
C.R.E. 46th Div. E.485.

Reference order No. 155.
The interchange of billets between 137th and 138th Inf.Bdes. will take place on 12th April instead of 10th April.

7:4:17.

sgd/ G.Thorpe. Lt-Col.
General Staff, 46th Division.

2.

O.C. 465th Field Coy.R.E.
O.C. 466th Field Coy.R.E.
O.C. 468th Field Coy.R.E.

For information reference this office E.478.

Lieut & Adjutant.R.E.
for C.R.E., 46th Division.

8:4:17.

SECRET.

Copy No. 5

O.C. 466th Field Coy.R.E.

OPERATION ORDER No.5.
issued by
Brig-Genl. C.V.WINGFIELD-STRATFORD.,C.M.G.

April 10th, 1917.

1.   The 466th Field Coy.R.E., will move to LA TIRMAND to-morrow, April 11th.

2.   Move will be completed by 12 noon.

3.   All billets, haorse lines, latrines &c., will be left clean before moving off.

4.   ACKNOWLEDGE.

Chas A Ashtin

Lieut & Adjutant.R.E.
for C.R.E. 46th Division.

Copies to :-

O.C. 465th Field Co.R.E.   Copy.No.2.
O.C. 468th Field Co.R.E.   "   No.3.
M.O. 1/c Royal Engineers.   "   No.4.
War Diary.   "   No.5.
Operation Order File.   "   No.6.

O.C.466th Field Co R.E.

4

OPERATION ORDER No 6
by
BRIGADIER-GENERAL C.V.WINGFIELD STRATFORD C.M.G.
Commanding Royal Engineers

Operation Order No 5 is cancelled.   April 10th 1917.

The 466th Field Co R.E. will remain in its present billets.

Copies to :-
O.C.456th Field Co
O.C.468th Field Co
M/O i/c Royal Engineers.
War Diary
O.O.File.

Chas Atkin

Lieut. & Adjutant R.E.
for C.R.E.46th Division.

Copy No 4

OPERATION ORDER No 7.
issued by
BRIGADIER-GENERAL O.V.WINGFIELD-STRATFORD C.M.G.
C.R.E. 46th Division

April 12th.1917

1. Reference 46th Division Order No 157, Companies will move as laid down.

    465th Fld.Co.   to   BUSNETTES
    466th Fld.Co.   "   LA VALLEE
    468th Fld Co.   "   CENES LA VALLEE.

2. A reconnaissance should be made of the new billeting area as early as possible.

3. All billets, horse lines, latrines etc., will be left clean before moving off.

Lieut & Adjutant R.E.
for C.R.E.46th Division

Copies to:-
O.C. 465th Field Co R.E. No 1.
O.C. 466th Field Co R.E. No 2.
O.C. 468th Field Co R.E. No 3.
War Diary   No 4.
Operation Order File   No 5.

OPERATION ORDER 8.   No E 4
by
BRIGADIER-GENERAL C.V.WINGFIELD-STRATFORD C.M.G.
C.R.E.46th Division

April 13th 1917.

O.C.465th Field Co R.E.

1.   The 465th Field Co R.E. will move to REBREUVE (Lens 11) to-morrow 14/4/17 via LOZINGHEM-and BRUAY.

2.   Hour of march will be arranged by O.C.Company so that the Company passes through MARLES LES MINES between 2 and 2-15 p.m.

3.   The Company will be employed for work under orders of C.E.First Army.

4.   All billets,horse lines ect.will be left clean before moving off.

5.   Completion of move to be wired to this office.

6. ACKNOWLEDGE.

Lieut & Adjutant R.E.
for C.R.E.46th Division.

Copies to :-
O.C.466th Field Co R.E.   No.1
O.C.468th   "   "   No 2
War Diary   No 3
O.O.File.   No 4.

OPERATION ORDER No.8.A.   Copy No. 10
by
Brig-Genl. C.V.WINGFIELD-STRATFORD., C.M.G.
C.R.E. 46th Division.
****

O.C. 468th Field Coy.R.E.   April 14th, 1917.

1.   The 468th Field Coy.R.E., will move to BUSNETTES to-day the 14:4:1917, taking over the billets, horse lines &c., of the 465th Field Coy.R.E.

2.   The 465th Field Coy.R.E., will be clear of BUSNETTES by noon.

3.   ACKNOWLEDGE   (468th Field Coy.R.E.)

Copies to.
Headqrs.46th Div."G" No.2
  "   "   "Q"   3
465th Field Coy.R.E.   4
466th   "   "   5
~~468th~~   "   "
Divnl Train.   6
S.S.O.   7
A.D.M.S.   8
A.D.V.S.   9
War Diary   10
File   11

Chas A. Hunton

No 84

OPERATION ORDER No 9.
by
Brig.Genl. C.V.Wingfield-Stratford.C.M.G.
C.R.E. 46th Division.

April 14th 1917

O.C.468th Field Co R.E.

1. The 468th Field Co R.E. will be held in readiness to move at 6 hours notice.

2. ACKNOWLEDGE

Chas. O. Hinton

Lieut & Adjutant R.E.
for C.R.E. 46th Division.

Copies to :-
Headquarters "G" No 2
468th Field Co R.E.   3
War Diary   4
O.O.File.   5

No 54

OPERATION ORDER No.10
By.
Brig-Genl.C.V.Wingfield-Stratford C.M.G.
C.R.E.46th Division

O.C.466th Field Co R.E.   April 15th 1917

1. The 466th Field Co R.E. will be held in readiness to move at 18 Hours notice.

2. 466th Field Co. to ACKNOWLEDGE.

[signature]

Lieut & Adjutant R.E.
for C.R.E.46th Division.

Copies to:-

Headquarters 'G'	No.2
466th Field Co.	No 3
War Diary	No 4
O.O.File	No 5.

War Diary

SECRET   OPERATION ORDER No 11.   No 14
by
Brig-Genl.C.V.Wingfield-Stratford C.M.G.
C.R.E.46th Division.
****

465th Field Co R.E.
466th Field Co R.E.
468th Field Co R.E.

APRIL.17.1917.

1.   The 466th Field Co R.E. and the 468th Field Co.R.E.will move to LES-BREBIS to-morrow 18/4/17 via MARLES-LES-MINES,BRUAY,BARLIN and SAINS-EN-GOHELLE.

2.   Companies to reach LES-BREBIS before 3 p.m.

3.   Billeting parties to report to TOWN MAJOR. LES BREBIS Nr. GRENAY at 11 a.m. 18/4/17.

4.   Each Field Co.(465,466 and 468) will reconnoitre the line on the 19/4/17 with a view to relieving the Field Cos.of the 24th. Division on the 20/4/17,as follows.:-

                                                        Map Ref.Sheet 36C S.W.
465.to reconnoitre line held by 73.Bde.24.Div. Bde.H.Q. M.27.c.6.0.
466   "   "   "   "   17   "   "   "   M.22.b.1.1,
468   "   "   "   "   72   "   "   "   M.3.c.2.2.

5.   Companies will get in touch with the Field Co.working with the above Brigades

6.   2 Sections of each Field Co. will be employed on work in the line with its Brigade.

7.   Remaining 2 Sections will remain at ~~LES BREBIS nr.GRENAY~~ for work under the C.R.E.

8.   Orders for latter work will be issued later

9.   ACKNOWLEDGE.

                                                  Chas.A.Hinton
                                                  Lieut & Adjutant R.E.
Copies to :-   for C.R.E.46th Division
46th Division   "G" No 4
  -do-   "Q" No 5
O.C.Signal Co   No 6
A.D.M.S.   No 7
A.D.V.S.   No 8
46th Divn.Train   No 9
S.S.O.46th Divn.   No 10
M.O.i/c R.E.   No 11
Hoadqtrs."G"24 Divn. No 12
C.R.E.24 Divn.   No 13
War Diary   No 14
O.O.File   No 15.

War Diary

SECRET   Copy No   13.

OPERATION ORDER No 12.
By
Brig-General C.V.Wingfield-Stratford C.M.G.
C.R.E.46th Division.

465th Field Co R.E.   April 18th.1917.
466th Field Co R.E.

1.   The 465th Field Co R.E. will be relieved by the 104th Field Co R.E 24th Division on 19/4/17 at GOUY.

2.   The 465th Field Co R.E. on relief will move to AIX-NOULETTE and take over the back billets of the 129th Field Co R.E.and on 20th. will relieve the 129th Field Co R.E.in the line in according to O.O. No 11.dated 17/4/17.

3.   The 466th Field Co will relieve the 104th Field Co. *in the line* to-morrow 19/4/17.

4.   Time of relief will be arranged between Os C.Field Companies of the two Divisions.

5. *Acknowledge.*

                                                    Chas A Hutton
                                                 Lieut & Adjutant R.E.
Copies to :-   for C.R.E.46th Division
   46th Division H.Q."G"   No 3
        "   H.Q."Q"   No 4
   C.R.E.24th Divn.   No 5
   A.D.M.S.   No 6
   A.D.V.S.   No 7
   Divn.Train   No 8
   S.S.O.46th Divn.   No 9
   O.C.Signal Co.   No 10
   L.C.i/c R.E.   No 11
   468th Fld Co R.E.   No 12
   War Diary   No 13
   O.O.File   No 14

O.C. 465 Field Coy

This is quite alright if you wish.

Chas A Hunt
+adj Ry

20/4/17
Ref above.—

Query (1). Can entire Coy be withdrawn?
 "   (2). Are there sufficient billets in this case?
 "   (3). Will sections of another Coy. require our billets if so. at what time.
      (4) Where are we likely to be required to work + what work if any for a day or two?

HA.

From O.C.

465TH (N.M.) FIELD COY
NO M/1
DATE 20/4/17
R.E.

C.R.E. 46th Division

Ref Your E.463 — wire from Adjt

I am in receipt of above and note that two sections & Hd Qrs can move to BULLY GRENAY.

If you have no objection I would prefer to defer this move till the 30th inst, for the following reasons —

(1) I have several special jobs in hand which will be finished by this latter date, and am anxious to see them completed personally.

(2) The 139 Bde is being relieved by the 137 Bde on the 30th in this sector, and it would be more convenient in this direction also.

Further in view of the above Bde relief would it be possible to take the whole Company out. They have been continuously at work since leaving BUSNETTES on 10/4/17 & Baths & kit renewals are urgently required.

I beg to submit the above suggestion for your approval.

Miller MAJOR R.E.
O.C. 465TH (N.M.) FIELD COY R.E.

P.T.O.

Secret.   Copy No.2.

46th DIVISION ORDER No. 167.

Ref:Map.- LENS, 36c, S.W.1.   23rd April, 1917.
       1/10,000

1. Brigade fronts will be adjusted so as to place the division on a two brigade front, all reliefs to be completed by 4.30 a.m. 25th April.

2. The dividing line between Brigades will be M 20 central to road junction, M 27 b 1 5, thence along road to X roads M 21 d 7 0, to railway at M 22 c 0 1, thence along railway to M 22 d 8 7, due north to railway at 2 PUITS and along railway through FOSSE 9, (roads and railways to southern Brigade).

3. On completion of reliefs the front will be held as follows :-

Southern Sector.-   139th Infantry Brigade.
                    2 battalions holding front.
                    H.Q. and 2 battalions in area
                    allotted within old German lines.

Northern Sector.-   138th Infantry Brigade.
                    2 battalions holding front.
                    2 battalions in area allotted
                    within old German lines.
                    H.Q. as desired either in present
                    138th Bde or 137th Bde Headquarters.

Divisional Reserve. 137th Infantry Brigade.
                    H.Q. and 1 battalion BULLY GRENAY.
                    2 battalions FOSSE 10.
                    1 battalion MARQUEFFLES FARM.

4. The two sections R.E. attached for work to 137th Inf: Bde will revert to work under C.R.E.

5. ACKNOWLEDGE.

                                sgd/ G.THORPE, Lieut-Colonel.
                                General Staff, 46th Division.

                    2.
O.C. 465th Field Coy.R.E.
O.C. 466th Field Coy.R.E.
O.C. 468th Field Coy.R.E.

        The above is forwarded for your information.

                                Lieut & Adjutant.R.E.
24:4:1917.   for C.R.E. 46th Division.

SECRET.   Copy No. 2.

46TH DIVISION ORDER No. 170.

Ref: Map:- LENS, 36c, S.W.1.
1/10,000   27th April 1917.

1. On the night 28th/29th April operations will take place to secure identifications, and to inflict casualties on the enemy.

2. Raids will be carried out by the two brigades in the line in accordance with plans being prepared by infantry brigade commanders. These raids to be completed by 1 a.m. 29th, to allow for subsequent operations.

3. At 2 a.m., 29th April, the following programme will commence :-

(a) 2am to 2.6 am.- Intense rolling barrage by field artillery on front M 30 b 3.2 - M 24 d 2.2 to M 24 d 7.4, and front N.7.b.0.4 - N 7 a 9.6 - N 1 d 1.4. Barrage to lift 100 yards every 2 minutes and cease at 2.6 am.
(b) 2.6 am to 2.10 am.- Bombardment by I Corps H.A and 4.5" howitzers of FOSSE 3, HILL 65 and trenches between these two places, NARWAL Trench and houses East and S.E of this trench.
(c) 2.10 am.- 250 Gas Projectors will be fired into area CITE ST LAURENT and CITE ST EDOUARD, and 50 each on to HILL 65 and FOSSE 3.
  Limits of wind to allow firing of projectors :-
    S.W to N.W for northern projectors.
    S.W to W.N.W for southern projectors.
(d) At 2.10am. 18 pounders will fire for 5 minutes on CONFECTION Trench from the railway to its junction with NABOB ALLEY and on ADJACENT Trench from its junction with ADULT Trench to the Canal.
(e) 2.40 am.- Bombardment by I Corps H.A. and 4.5" howitzers again as in para. (b), 18 pounders turning on to communication trenches, tracks and roads leading up from LENS and CITE ST AUGUSTE, this to continue for 5 minutes.

4. A machine gun barrage will be placed at 2.10 am in front of FOSSE 3 and HILL 65 and the front trenches joining these two places, also in front of NARWAL Trench to prevent enemy getting out of the gas cloud by advancing.

5. All troops in line of fire of projectors and 200 yards to each side will put on their respirators. These to be put on at 2 am and may be removed at 2.20 am.

6. No further carrying in of projectors will take place on night of 28th/29th April.

7. ACKNOWLEDGE.

                                sgd/ G. THORPE, Lt-Col.
                                General Staff, 46th Division.

O.C. 465th Field Coy. R.E.
O.C. 466th Field Coy. R.E.
O.C. 468th Field Coy. R.E.

The above is forwarded for your information and necessary action, please.

SECRET　　　　　　　　　　　　　　　　　　　　　　Copy No 2

46th Division Order No 171

Ref.Map,LENS 36C S.W.1
1/10,000
30th April 1917

1. 46th Division will, on night of 1st/2nd May, take over from 6th Division the front northwards from the present northern limit to M.6.b.9.3.

2. The following readjustment will be made, to be completed by 4 a.m. 2nd May. :-
    137th Infantry Brigade to extend northwards to Railway GRENAY to LENS.

3. 138th Infantry Brigade will take over the new portion of the front, to be completed by 4 a.m. 2nd May.

4. On completion of reliefs the northern divisional boundary will run as follows :-
    (a) Present boundary to road junction M.3.b.05 50- road junction M.3.b.75.62 -SICKLEY ALLEY to M.4. b.28.25 - CORDIALE AVENUE -QUEEN ST-REGENT ST- thence north of QUARRY to old front line at M.6.b. 1.5 to M.6.b.9.3.
    (b) In the event of a forward move this line will be extended to junction of tramline to ~~junction~~ trench at N.1.b.06,93-along tramline to junction with NUNS ALLEY N.2.a.84,50
    All above inclusive to 46th Division (reference paras (a) and (b)
    (c) The boundary between Brigades will be the GRENAY LENS railway to N.13.c.6.9. thence along railway through FOSSE 1 to PUITS 2 (inclusive to southern brigade) billeting areas in LIEVIN will be unchanged

5. Details of reliefs to be arranged between Infantry Brigade Commanders concerned.

6. The C.R.A.46th Division, will arrange the necessary grouping of artillery in accordance with altered dispositions. The 6th Division are leaving the artillery covering the front to be taken over in position.

7. G.O.C.46th Division, will take over command of the new front at 6 a.m.2nd May

Sd/G.THORPE Lieut-Col.
General Staff.46th Division

O.C.466th Field Co R.E.
O.C.468th Field Co R.E.
O.C.468th Field Co R.E.

For your information please.

1/5/17

Lieut.& Adjutant R.E.
for C.R.E 46th Division

WAR DIARY
or
INTELLIGENCE SUMMARY.

Army Form C. 2118.

AIRE 46" div

Place	Date	Hour	Summary of Events and Information	Remarks and references to Appendices
SAINS en GOHELLE	May 1st 1917		CRE. met 2 the Bridging demonstn Tr. at MINX. arranged by C.E. I Corps - Offr. & men from 465, 3rd Fd. & 468 Tp T.R.E. (Chin fud) - met to see OC. Australian Tunnellg Tp. & 173 vt.F.Co. who were camping and work'g on 46' div.	Maj Sefton an Echin from LENS for 36. C.S.N. & LENS 11
	2nd		Bridging continues. Met C.E. I Corps there - making arrangements for reconnaissance in rear of forward advance - Inspected roads to front line area - & up tracks	
	3rd		Inspected M.G. emplacements on div'l line - 468 & Pioneers heavy bridg'g	
	4th		Went to Bridging school at AIRE with O.C. 465 & other officers to see various kinds of bring bridge for use in advance.	
	5th		made a reconnaissance of the rear part of divl hand'd over to 46' div & sited M.G. emplacements.	
	6th			
	7th		office work & went to inspect him from LORETTE ridge.	
	8th		Filling in/to & fittings to Pontoons & trestle wagons. All Co. at work on stamp hinds.	

CRE 46' div - 2

Army Form C. 2118.

WAR DIARY
or
INTELLIGENCE SUMMARY.
(Erase heading not required.)

Place	Date	Hour	Summary of Events and Information	Remarks and references to Appendices
SAINS en GOHELLE	May 9th 1917		Reconnaissance of route to the Dump for dig' line made - ammunition & relief wiring for instruction of Intantry.	
		10h	2 R.E. making machine gun support lines - 1 P.T.R.E. on old line - ex.	
			2 Brigade in front line.	
			Same on top above.	
		12h	Team studied 1/5017 to Riaumont Indsenl work.	
		13h	Wiring obtained	
		14h	Instruction known & shown/shown cellars & making M.G. Pow. emplacets.	OO No 14
			& subtitute points - re-armament of R, in a two Rampase front.	"
		15h	do	
		16h	do. Civil division on work. K.O.C. 466 P.T.R.E.	
		17h	CRE went on to see Major Commander 466 P.T.R.E. as to for CRE	
		18h	& RE Jauntys of Cys & made arrangements to implements wiring	
		19h	with hand with 157 G.S.1 Coys orig.D.1.46 E. & instructed to go to 1 in Bois de	
			RIAUMONT also work being done by 468 P.T.R.E. on LIEVIN-ST PIERRE line	

Army Form C. 2118.

WAR DIARY
or
INTELLIGENCE SUMMARY.
(Erase heading not required.)

3

Place	Date	Hour	Summary of Events and Information	Remarks and references to Appendices
SAINS en GOHELLE	20th May 1917		CIBE went to BULLY GRENAY & mad O.C. 468 T O'RE & went round pits in LIÉVIN - ST PIERRE line - mad O.C. 466 & sited work in BAILLEUL - RIAUMONT line & connect pits in BOIS de RIAUMONT with CRAZY work	
	21st		went with O.C. 465 T.M & + sited 2 O.Ps near HART'S CRATER - & a strong pts near Harrison's crater - 1 Coy commander & CE- 1 Coy in pits.	
	22nd		work in LIÉVIN - ST PIERRE line with OC. 468 T O'RE. Sited a new line through CITÉ de RIAUMONT from ASSIGN. C.T. to ABSALOM C.T. - Inspected dug outs in BOIS de RIAUMONT & CHATEAU (ground) with O.C. 3rd Australian Tunnelling Co.	
	23rd		went with B.G.I. to AMBRES & made arrangement with 138th to Commanr work in CITÉ de RIAUMONT line. 1 Coy Commanr & CE 1 Coy in huts. Work in LIÉVIN ST PIERRE line with O.C. 465 T C.R.E.	
	24th		mornn office work	
	25th		Went to meeor with G.P., inspected Coy hdqrs in sheds CORBSIER sidings & living time prisoners night camps 465 & 468	

Army Form C. 2118.

CRE 46th F.F. R.E.

WAR DIARY
or
INTELLIGENCE SUMMARY.
(Erase heading not required.)

4

Place	Date	Hour	Summary of Events and Information	Remarks and references to Appendices
SAINS en GOHELLE	May 26th 1917		Went to A.D.S. Hqrs. 137 Bde. & saw Brigadier & arranged for 465 F.P.R.E to take on line of resistance - afterwards saw O.C. 468 F.P.R.E	
	27th May		Went to see O.C. 466 F.P.R.E & made arrangements for work to be done in CITÉ de RIAUMONT work.	
	28th		Started new work to CHATEAU - schlts. after dug outs in BOIS de RIAUMONT for Advanced H.Q. - inspected ASSIGN trench.	
	29th		Went to ANGRES with O.C. 468 F.P.R.E. & head to BOIS de RIAUMONT & showed him site for Bde. H.Qr. Saw O.C. 466 F.P.R.E. at work in CITÉ de RIAUMONT	
	30th		Inspected work on ASSIGN & ABSALOM C.T's & new fire trench through CITÉ de RIAUMONT & string points	
	31st		Saw O.C. 466 F.P.R.E. & ———	

S E C R E T & U R G E N T

Office Copy

O.C. 465th Field Co R.E.

1. With reference to 46th Division Order 171 dated 30th April 1917, sent you to-day, please take over from O.C. 509 (London Co) Field Co R.E. the R.E. work in the area being taken over by 138th Brigade.

2. The Headquarters of the 509 Field Co R.E. are at L.36.c.1.8. and C.R.E. 6th Division is arranging for officers to meet you there at 9 a.m. to-morrow the 2nd.inst. to take your officers round.

1st. May 1917.

Brig-General
C.R.E. 46th Division

Office Copy
66171 6701

O.C. 468th Field Co R.E.

    The whole of your Company will be attached to the 138th Brigade for work from today. 2/5/17.

           Chas A Hinton
           Lieut & Adjutant R.E.
2/5/17.   for C.R.E. 46th Division

C O P Y

SECRET   Copy No 2

46th DIVISION ORDER No 172.

Reference Map- LENS 36C. S.W.1. 1/10,000

1.   The 139th Infantry Brigade will relieve the 138th Infantry Brigade in the Northern Sector on the night 6th/7th May. Details to be arranged between Brigade Commanders concerned. Relief to be completed by 4 a.m. 7th May.

2.   On relief the 138th Infantry Brigade will occupy the billets at present occupied by 139th Infantry Brigade.

3.   One section 178th Machine Gun Company of the two sections at present attached to 138th Infahtry Brigade will come under orders of 139th Infantry Brigade, the other section returning to its unit.

4.   ACKNOWLEDGE.

                                Sd/ G.THORPE Lieut - Col.
                                General Staff 46th Division

Issued at 8 p.m.

O.C.465th Field Co R.E.
O.C.466th Field Co R.E.
O.C.468th Field Co R.E.

            The above copy of 46th Divisional
Order 172, is forwarded for your information please.

                                Lieut & Adjutant R.E.
4/5/17.   for C.R.E. 46th Division

S E C R E T.   Copy No. 2.

46th DIVISION ORDER No. 173.

10th May, 1917.

Reference - LENS, 36c.S.W.1, 1/10,000.

1.   The 138th Infantry Brigade will relieve the 137th Infantry Brigade in the LIEVIN Sector on the 12th May.

       Relief to be completed by 4 a.m., 13th instant.

2.   The section of the 178th Machine Gun Coy. at present with the 137th Machine Gun Company will on relief return to their own Company and the section of the 137th Machine Gun Company attached to 178th Machine Gun Company to their Company.

3.   ACKNOWLEDGE.

Issued at 8 p.m.   sgd/ - - JOHNSON, Major.
                                       for Lt-Col. G.S., 46th Division.

2.

O.C. 465th Field Coy.R.E.
O.C. 466th Field Coy.R.E.
O.C. 468th Field Coy.R.E.

For information.

Lieut & Adjutant.R.E.
for C.R.E. 46th Division.

11:5:1917.

OO.169

46th Division.
C.R.E., 46th Division.
170th Tunnelling Coy., R.E.
3rd Australian Tunn.Coy., R.E.
Capt. Ball, R.E.

No. 211 (G.b.) 11th May, 1917.

Reference I Corps 1193/4 (G.b.) of 30/4/17:-

1.   4 Officers and 40 men of 170th Tunnelling Company, R.E., will be detailed for attachment to Right Brigade, 46th Division, instead of the party detailed from 173rd Coy., R.E.

2.   The senior Officer of this party will report as early as possible to C.R.E., 46th Division, for instructions.

Brigadier General,
General Staff, I Corps.

Copies to Controller of Mines,
          First Army.)
    C.E.) I Corps.   ) For information.
    "Q")   )

Secret

Copy No. 5

OPERATION ORDER No. 14.
by
Brig.-Genl. C.V.WINGFIELD STRATFORD. C.M.G.
C.R.E. 46th Division.

May 14th, 1917.

1.   Irrespective of Brigade reliefs, work by the Field Companies will be carried out as follows :-

465th Field Co.R.E., will work in the Left Sector.
466th Field Co.R.E., will work in the Right Sector.
468th Field Co.R.E. will work as detailed on the LIEVIN - ST PIERRE Line.

2.   O.C. Companies will arrange reliefs among the sections so that each section has 2 days rest in every 8 days.

3.   Any assistance required by Brigades will be given by the Field Company in whose sector it is required.   One section will be detailed for this work (this does not apply to the 468th Field Co.R.E).

Chas. C. Hinton
Lieut & Adjutant.R.E.
for C.R.E. 46th Division.

Copies to :-

O.C. 465th Field Co.R.E.   No.1
O.C. 466th Field Co.R.E.   2
O.C. 468th Field Co.R.E.   3
Headqrs, 46th Division "G".   4
War Diary   5
File.   6

O.C. 465th Field Co.R.E.
O.C. 466th Field Co.RE.
O.C. 468th Field Co.R.E.

      Reference Operation Order No.15. When the Monmouths are not available for work, O.C. Companies will ask for working parties from Brigades.

Chas. A. Hinton

Lieut & Adjutant.R.E.
for C.R.E. 46th Division.

14:5:1917.

Secret

Copy No. 6

OPERATION ORDER No.15.
by
Brig-Genl. C.V.WINGFIELD-STRATFORD. C.M.G.
C.R.E., 46th Division.

O.C. 1st Monmouths.   May 14th, 1917.

1.   Companies employed on night work will not be required
to work on Saturday nights.

2.   Companies employed on day work will not be required
to work on Sundays.

3.   This does not apply to any necessary work required
for the upkeep of the railways.

                                      Chas A. Hith
                                    Lieut & Adjutant.R.E.
                                    for C.R.E., 46th Division.

Copies to :-

O.C. 466th Field Co.R.E.   No.2
O.C. 467th Field Co.R.E.   3
O.C. 468th Field Co.R.E.   4
Headqrs, 46th Division "G".   5
War Diary   6
File   7

SECRET   Copy No 5

46th DIVISION ORDER No 175

Ref. Map - LENS 36.c. S.W.1
1/10,000   May 15th.1917

1. The 139th Infantry Brigade will on night 17th/18th.
May raid the German front line, NASH ALLEY-N,1.b.10.00 to
N.1.a.82,54.

2. On the same night a feint attack will be made against
HILL 65 as follows-

    At Zero-8 minutes, a barrage will be put on the
front of HILL 65, lifting off front line at Zero.-3 minutes.
A machine gun barrage will at Zero - 8 minutes be placed
by 138th Infantry Brigade on the approximate line M.30.d.9.5.to
M.24.d.75.42.
Futher details to assimilate attack or action of patrols will be
arranged by G.O.C.138th Infantry Brigade with Right Group Commander.

3. At Zero.:-

    (a)   Divisional Artillery will open barrage on the line
          N.1.d.16,45 to N.1.a.82,54. 6th Divisional Artillery
are arranging to continue this barrage to the old German front
          line at N.1.a.78,95.

    (b)   An enfilade barrage will be placed along the railway
          from N.1.c.98,42 to N.1.d.95,53.

    (c)   4.5" howitzers and trench mortars will deal with :-
          (i) The DYNAMITE MAGAZINE
          (ii) Trench junction just North of it N.1.d.17,80.
          (iii) Lines of houses running East and West on North
                side of CITE ST LAURENT.

    (d)   6th Divisional Artillery are arranging to fire on
          NETLEY Trench with 4.5" howitzers East of NASH
          ALLEY, also trench junction N.1.a.82,83.

    (e)   I Corps Heavy Artillery are engaging group of houses and
          dugouts about junction of LENS-LA BASSEE Road with railway
          in N.1.d. and trench junction on line of NUNS ALLEY.

    (f)   139th Infantry Brigade will arrange for a machine gun
          barrage on the East of CITE ST LAURENT and CITE ST EDOUARD
          138th Infantry Brigade barraging the Western exits of
          LENS.

4. At Zero, gas will be discharged from 750 projectors into
CITE ST LAURENT and CITE ST EDOUARD. O.C.'B'Special Company,
will arrange that no gas is liberated which would enter NASH
ALLEY north of DYNAMITE MAGAZINE N.1.d.30,68.

5. The Infantry will advance at Zero. The barrage will lift off
the front of attack at Zero plus 5, and form a box barrage,
4.5" howitzers on trenches NESTOR, NELSON and NETLEY in
addition to targets in para (3)-(c).

6. The Infantry will return at Zero plus 30 minutes. Artillery
fire will slacken down from Zero plus 40 minutes till the signal
'All clear' is given, when it will cease.
                                                  P.T.O.

7. The wire between N.1.a.85,45 and N,1.a.99.30.will be cut previously on the 16th and 17th. 2" Trench Mortars will cut a lane in the German wire about N,1.a.98.10

8. Zero will be communicated later.

9. Watches will be synchronized from Divisional Headquarters at 7 p.m. 17th May, and again two hours before Zero.

10. Acknowledge.

              Sd/ G.THORPE Lieut-Col.
              General Staff 46th Division

O.C.465th Field Co R.E.
O.C.466th Field Co R.E.
O.C.468th Field Co R.E.

       Forwarded for your information please.

May 16th 1917.   Lieut & Adjutant R.E.
              for C.R.E. 46th Division

SECRET   Copy No. 7

46th DIVISION ORDER No. 176

Reference Map -LENS 36.C.S.W.1   15th May.1917
    1/10,000

1. The 137th.Infantry Brigade will relieve the 139th.
   Infantry Brigade in the ST PIERRE Section on the 18th.
   May 1917.
      Relief to be completed by 4a.m.,19th.instant.

2.   All details of relief to be arranged by
   Brigade Commanders concerned.

3.   On relief, the section of 178th M.G.Co.will
   re-join their Company.

4.   The 178th.Machine Gun.Company will take over
   the defences of the RIDGE-VILLAGE and CRASSIER SWITCH
   line on the 18th instant.
      Two sections will form a permanent garrison
   of this line.   These guns being also used for
   Aint-Aircraft Defence.

5   ACKNOWLEDGE.

                                Sd/   Johnson Major.
                         for Lieut-Col.G.S. 46th Division.

C.O.465th Field Co R.E.
C.O.466th Field Co R.E.
C.O.468th Field Co R.E.

                         Forwarded for your information
please.

                                  Chas A Hinton
                                  ─────────────────
                                  Lieut & Adjutant R.E.
May 16th.1917   for C.R.E.46th Division.

S E C R E T.

ADDENDUM TO 46TH DIVISION ORDER No. 175.

Paragraph 4.

Add sub-para. (a). -

No. 4 Special Company (O Section) will fire 480 Bombs into NARWAL ALLEY, the same precautions being observed as in last part of para. 4.

ACKNOWLEDGE.

16th May /'17.
                                           sd/ - - Johnson. Major,
                                     for Lt-Col. G.S., 46th Division.

Issued to all recipients of Order No. 175.

2.

O.C. 465th Field Co.R.E.
O.C. 466th Field Co.R.E.
O.C. 468th Field Co.R.E.

For information.

May 17th 1917.
                                     Lieut & Adjutant.R.E.
                                     for C.R.E., 46th Division.

Secret.   G.190.

C.R.E.

          Reference Order No. 175 of the 15th.,
para. 8.

          Zero hour will be 2 a.m., 18th May.

17th May, /17.   Lieut-Colonel,
                              General Staff, 46th Division.

SECRET.  G 190

C.R.E.

Reference Order No.175 of the 15th para 8.

Zero hour will be 2 a.m. 18th.May.

                                      Sd/ R.G.Stone Captain
17th May /17.   for Lieut-Col.G.S.46th Division

O.C.465th Field Co R.E.
O.C.466th Field Co R.E.
O.C 468th Field Co R.E.

For your information please.

                                      Sd/ C.A.HINTON.
                                Lieut & Adjutant R.E.
17th May 1917.   for C.R.E.46th Division

46th Division wire begins.

" Reference Order No.177 to-day. Zero hour will be 2 a.m. 19th. AAA Acknowledge by wire" Ends.

O.C.465th Field Co R.E.
O.C.466th Field Co R.E.
O.C.468th Field Co R.E.

Reference Divisional Order 177,

Zero hour will be 2 a.m. 19th.

All working parties should be

withdrawn at 1 a.m.

ACKNOWLEDGE.

Lieut & Adjutant R.E.
for C.R.E.46th Division.

May 18th 1917.
9-50 p.m.

"A" Form.
MESSAGES AND SIGNALS.

Army Form C. 2121
(in pads of 100)

Secret

TO C.R.E.

Sender's Number: C.210
Day of Month: 18

Reference order 177 today ZERO hour will be 2 am 19th aaa Acknowledge by wire

All Coy
Ref ED Div Ord 177 Zero hour will be 2 am 19th. All working parties should be withdrawn at 1 am.
Acknowledge.   Chas A.H

From: Muriel
Place:
Time: 8.0 pm

SECRET.   Copy No. 6.

46th DIVISION ORDER No. 177.

18th May, 1917.

1. The 7th Sherwood Foresters will not be relieved to-night.

2. The raid arranged for night 17th/18th will be carried out to-night.

3. Further wire-cutting is being carried out to-day by I Corps H.A. and Trench Mortars.

4. G.O.C., 139th Infantry Brigade will arrange the fixing of Zero, and make any necessary amendments to the programme for night 17th/18th.

5. G.O.C., 139th Infantry Brigade will remain in command of PIERRE Sector for night 18th/19th. The necessary alteration in relief programme will be made between G.Os.C., 137th and 139th Infantry Brigades.

6. On no account must the relief be allowed to interfere with the keeping open of gaps in wire. Continuous machine gun fire and bursts of shrapnel must be kept up by night on this wire to prevent its repair, both before and after the raid, except for the time that patrols are out inspecting it.

7. ACKNOWLEDGE.

                                                 sd/ - - JOHNSON. Major.
                                 for Lt-Col. G.S., 46th Division.

2.

O.C. 465th Field Co.R.E.
O.C. 466th Field Co.R.E.
O.C. 468th Field Co.R.E.

For information.

                                               Lieut & Adjutant.R.E.
                                               for C.R.E. 46th Division.

May 18th, 1917.

SECRET.   Copy No.2

46TH DIVISION ORDER No.178.

Ref: Maps, LENS and LOOS,   22nd May, 1917.
     1/10,000.

1. The 137th Infantry Brigade will on Thursday, 24th May, attack and capture NASH ALLEY from N 1 a 98.40 to N 1 a 78.90 and NETLEY Trench between NASH and NOVEL ALLEYS.

2. Zero time will be communicated later to all concerned.

3. The artillery programme will include :-

   (a) <u>Wire-cutting</u> (to be completed by 6 pm, 23rd May). Wire in front of objective to be cut by I Corps H.A.
   Gaps will also be cut by I Corps H.A. on front of 8th Division north of H 31 c 9.0 during morning of 24th instant.

   (b) <u>Previous bombardment.</u>
       <u>By I Corps H.A.</u>
       (i)   T.M. emplacements H 31 d 28.52 and H 32 c 71.59 to be destroyed.
       (ii) FOSSE 14 to be shelled at intervals on 24th to prevent enemy observation, especially during period troops are forming in their assembly positions. (18-pdrs and Machine Guns will co-operate).
       (iii) DYNAMITE MAGAZINE.

       <u>By 9.45" Trench Mortars</u> - Old German front line and NETLEY Trench to be destroyed at a point about 100^X E. of NASH ALLEY.

       Except where stated otherwise stated, these bombardments are to be completed by the evening of 23rd May.

   (c) The artillery programme from Zero onwards is being issued separately.
       I Corps H.A are from Zero onwards dealing with :-
       (i)   DYNAMITE MAGAZINE
       (ii) Houses just South of railway in CITE ST LAURENT.
       (iii) Machine Gun positions as follows :-
             N 2 a 0.8, N 1 b 73.90, N 1 b 60.87,
             N 1 b 42.62, N 1 b 22.82, H 31 d 10.03,
             N 1 b 10.95.
       (iv) Strong Point about N 1 b 55.86.

4. On night 23rd/24th, gas will be discharged into CITE ST LAURENT and CITE ST EDOUARD by about 750 projectors, also by one section Stokes Mortars, under orders of O.C, 'B' Special Company, R.E. The hour for this operation will be fixed later.

5. At Zero, No.4 Special Company, R.E. will form a Smoke Cloud from about H 31 a 8.6 to H 31 b 8.8, and as far Eastwards as possible. To be fired in any wind except between N.N.W. and N.E.
   Ammunition allowed - 100 rounds - 50 heavy and 50 light.

6. 6th Division are co-operating as follows :-

   (a) From Zero onwards by Trench Mortars on enemy's front and support trenches at H 31 d 10.10, H 31 d 10.35 and Northwards.
   (b) By Stokes Mortar fire against breaches in enemy's front line.
   (c) By Lewis and Machine Gun fire to flank NASH ALLEY to stop counter attack over the top.
   (d) By rifle grenades fired from the HUMP, H 31 c 68.20.

7. Watches will be synchronized from Divisional Headquarters at 12 noon and again two hours before Zero.

8. 178th Machine Gun Company will attach one section to 137th Brigade Machine Gun Company for this operation. Section Commander will report at 137th Brigade Headquarters at 8 am, 23rd. Co-operation of 138th Brigade Machine Gun Company will be arranged between Brigades concerned.

9. ACKNOWLEDGE.

Issued at 8.20 pm.

sd/ G. THORPE. Lieut-Col.
General Staff, 46th Division.

2.

O.C. 465th Field Co.R.E.
O.C. 466th Field Co.R.E.
O.C. 468th Field Co.R.E.

For information.

Please ACKNOWLEDGE.

Lieut & Adjutant.R.E.
for C.R.E. 46th Division.

May 23rd, 1917.

S E C R E T.   Copy No. 2.

46TH DIVISION ORDER No. 179.

Ref: Trench Map, 1/10,000.   24th May, 1917.

1. The 139th Infantry Brigade will relieve the 138th Infantry Brigade in the LIEVIN Section on the night of 25th/26th May, 1917.
   Relief to be completed by 4 am, 26th instant.
   Details of relief will be arranged by Brigade Commanders concerned.

2. ACKNOWLEDGE.

Issued at 8 am.
sd/ - - - JOHNSON, Major.
for Lt-Col. G.S., 46th Division.

2.

O.C. 465th Field Co. R.E.
O.C. 466th Field Co. R.E.
O.C. 468th Field Co. R.E.

For information.

~~Please~~ ACKNOWLEDGE.

Lieut & Adjutant. R.E.
for C.R.E. 46th Division.

May 24th, 1917.

SECRET. 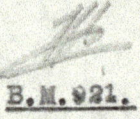 B.M.921.

Headquarters,
    139th Infantry Brigade.

      With reference to 46th Division Warning Order No.5.
I am making my Staff Captain responsible for the collection of stores, and the placing of these in position. The necessary carrying parties will be provided by the Reserve Battalion of this Brigade. It will therefore be unnecessary for you to bother about this. I quite understand you already have enough to do with organising the assembly trenches.

29th May, 1917.
                        Lieut-Colonel,
                Commanding 138th Inf. Brigade.

    Copy to :- 46th Division)
               C.R.E. 46th Div) For information.

WAR DIARY
or
INTELLIGENCE SUMMARY

Army Form C. 2118.

HQ R8462

Place	Date	Hour	Summary of Events and Information	Remarks and references to Appendices
SAINS en GOHELLE	June 1/1917		CRE visited. Adj't went to inspect work on 139th O.P. in ST PIERRE	See C. Buller Map reference sheet LENS 36c SW1 1/10000
	2nd		E.O. informed C.R.E. of R.E. work required from R.E.S. - went with Maj CRISSMAKER to ANCRES to see B.M. 139th Bde re working parties for night - Saw Brigadier & discussed R.E. work required - Saw O.E. 1st Monmouths re work for the night - Adj't making arrangements for laying out dummy figures to draw fire	
	3rd		Went with Adj't to see site selected for Dummies between CORKSCREW & COLLEGE TRENCH. Saw O.E. 1st Cup. & latticed with roads supply - & tramway schemes	
	4th		Went to see schemes of operations at MARKAPPEL farm carried out commenced & E.M. present - very successful. A quiet day - Saw O.E. C.P. & Cup with supply Off.	
	5th		Went to see B.G. 137 Bde at advanced H.Q. - Saw Lieut Annis & re shells here 466 Fd. RE.	
	6th		Went round front line trenches in night sector with O.E. 466 D.POR.E. from ASSIGN to ABSALOM. Work well in hand re approaching operations. Adj't laying out dummies on site at night.	
	7th		Went to see R. Wbs re troops reqd to assist in r LIEVIN to see O.E. 468 who had moved up preparing the operations - Saw O.E. 466 re re work for the night - Adj't out at night getting dummies into position.	

C.R.E. 46 Div

Army Form C. 2118.

WAR DIARY
or
INTELLIGENCE SUMMARY.
(Erase heading not required.)

Place	Date	Hour	Summary of Events and Information	Remarks and references to Appendices
SAINS en GOHELLE	June 8th		Saw E.O.R. at work required in future. v about preparation for operation twilight. Went out with G.S.I. horses B.G. 137th Bde – watched shelling of Hill 65 from COUGAR post. In alternoon saw Tramway officer at BULLY GRENAY & inspected work & line. In evening raid by 137th & 138th Bdns. – Sapper detailed for demolitions, salting troops & consolidation. Dummies put out by 137th infantry were very successful in throwing enemy trench fire – which was repeated on 3 occasions	2
	June 9th		Saw R.O.E. in morning. Then to LIEVIN saw O.C. 468 at work done of 79 in raid – an I mind & half lid killed & killed 5 N.C.Os & men & wounded 2 – Saw O.C. 465 at work done by them in raid – Lt Jones specially mentioned for good work – he succeeded in taking 4 prisoners – his task + assisted in making blocks & bombing dug outs	
	June 10th		Saw O.C. 465 at work – issued operation orders on same – Went to see strong pts 14 to 24 in LIEVIN. ST. PIERRE line with R.S.I. returned by 137th outlet H.Qrs & saw BGS. cmdg. – Saw R.O.E. in evening	
	" 11th		Went to BULLY GRENAY & saw O.C. 466 & 468 – went with O.C. 466 to make a reconnaissance of new line to connect ASSIGN trench with N.E. end of Bois de RIAUMONT. to defend right flank of line. Inspected 4 & 9 strong pts in LIEVIN – ST. PIERRE line – return to FOSSEU. – Saw R.O.E.	

CWE 46' div

WAR DIARY
or
INTELLIGENCE SUMMARY.
(Erase heading not required.)

Army Form C. 2118.

3

Place	Date	Hour	Summary of Events and Information	Remarks and references to Appendices
SAINS en GOHELLE	June 12th		R.E. mounted competition – went with G.S. 3 to see 13.B. 137th Bde and O.P. in Hirondelle Wood. Heavy shelling of RIAUMONT Wood – Saw O.C. 465, 466 & 27th R.E.	
	June 13th		Presentation of medals by Army Commander – Major MILLER 466 Tg Co received Military cross also Capt. Roberts 46 Sig'l. Coy. R.E. – went to BULLY GRENAY – saw O.C. Co. – Div mounted competition in afternoon.	
	14th		Went with O.C. 466 T'ng Co & inspected shaft to shafts 16 – 13 Saw O.C. 465 & 468	
	15th		Office work. Saw G.S.I. & afterwards had conference with O.C. Field Coys – operation orders got out & arrangements made for works to right – went to LIEVIN to see O.C. 468	
	16th		Went to see O.C. 468 at LIEVIN & D.G. 138 Bde – went with staff to see site for refilling station & went in respect – went to ANCRES & saw O.C. 253 Tunnelling Co. Capt. Hardman to 468 & 11th LOWBRIDGE to 465 arrived	
	17th		Went with G.S.2 round new trenches being dug & to see work done by 253 Tunnelling Co. in COWDEN trench & CROCUS trench Saw O.C. 468 at LIEVIN – 1	
	18th		Went to LIEVIN & saw O.C. 468 – Saw O.C. 253 Tunnelling Co & arranged work – went with G.S.I. & saw Br.G. 138.	

WAR DIARY or INTELLIGENCE SUMMARY

Army Form C. 2118.

C.R.E. 46th Div

Place	Date	Hour	Summary of Events and Information	Remarks and references to Appendices
SAINS en GOHELLE	June 19th		Went with G.O.C. to ANGRES and went round the new trenches dug in night. Went thro' CROCODILE to new trench CYCLIST to FOSSE 9, & thence to CORKSCREW. Went in afternoon to ANGRES & saw B.G. 138 & R.E. arrivals/reliefs for CORKSCREW adj. Went to see O.C. 468 at LIÉVIN. Saw O.C. 465 & 466 re work.	
	20th		Office work. Saw G.O.C. & G.I. — Went to LIÉVIN & saw O.C. 138 & O.C. 468. Made arrangements for digging new line — Capt. Hardman 468 (?) wounded.	
	21st		Went with G.S.I. etc & to reconnoitre railway cutting & inspect work done at night in new front line trenches — Went to 138 Hd & advanced H.Q. — to CHATEAU ABSALOM thro' to CYCLIST trench & then to CROCODILE & railway cutting & returned to LIÉVIN — Saw C.E. 1 Corps - B.G.E. & O.C. Cavalry - & O.C. 3rd AUSTRALIAN Tunnelling Co.	
	22nd		Saw G.O.C. & G.S. Went to BULLY GRENAY & saw O.C. Cavalry. to ANGRES & saw N.S.F. 137 at advanced H.Q. re work — then to 466 det. in CITÉ du RIAUMONT — Inspected dug outs in CHATEAU of ABSALOM trench & then to inspect work in front trench — Saw O.C. 468.	
	23rd		Saw G.O.C. & G.S. re work - & to ANGRES with O.C. Mammoths & arranged for work in A55IGN trench to new trenches to the Mosele - Saw O.C. 465 & 468. - Saw O.C. 468 re LIÉVIN	

C.R.E. 46th Div.

WAR DIARY
or
INTELLIGENCE SUMMARY.

Army Form C. 2118.

Place	Date	Hour	Summary of Events and Information	Remarks and references to Appendices
SAINS en GOHELLE	June 24th		Got instructions from to re work required. Saw O.C. Cavalry. O.C. 465 & O.C. 468. 73rd Companies & Explained requirements. Adjt. to dump to show offr 4 Canadian Div. the method we used for working dummy figures — went to inspect Bruch. & arranged to remove dumps. Saw O.C. 466 & Explained operation when a new sinking of 466 to Cr.	
	June 25th		Stayed in dugout of 137 for operation. Adjt went with G.S.2 to inspect work on new trenches — went to BULLY GRENAY & saw O.C. 465 & 468 & O.C. 2nd Cavalry Pioneers re work for night.	
	June 26th		to LIEVIN & saw O.C. 468 & Adjt Comdg 138 Fd Coy — inspected site of proposed dugout. Station instead in report respecting alterations — made KANGROS & saw O.C. 2nd Front thing to us. Adjt went with G.S.2 at 5.a.m. to see progress of work done in night — CRE & Adjt went up in evening & inspected all work necessary to be done at night. to	
	June 27th		Lt. MOUNTFORD. R.E. 468. P.W. — Adjt went round work in morning with G.S. 2 & inspected work — all of night work in K/12's & arranged work for night — Saw O.C. 2nd Cavalry Pioneers, O.C. 3rd Amalgam & O.C. Cavalry re work — went to LIEVIN & saw O.C. 468 & prior inst'ructions for night	
	June 28th		to LIEVIN & saw O.C. 466 & R.O. Comdg 137 Inf Bde — & took notes to explain to Adjt & had infor on casualties trenches sudden slightly burned were distributed to Adjt & which put up to keep hands during at operation places. Found trenches in good order 2 section of Rail field to allotted to Ampletilli as Western of cord to keep in Div. reserve. Operations was taken My card to kept in Div. reserve. Operations was taken at 7.10 p.m. on successful all objections taken	

C.R.E. 46 Div.

Army Form C. 2118.

WAR DIARY
or
INTELLIGENCE SUMMARY.
(Erase heading not required.)

Place	Date	Hour	Summary of Events and Information	Remarks and references to Appendices
SAINS en GOHELLE	June 29th		Conference at H.Q.R. — arrangements made for work tonight — recon: operation by 137 & 139 Bgds. — all objectives taken —	
	June 30th		Went with G.S.1. to LIEVIN & saw W.G. Cmdt 137 & 138 Bgds + made arrangements for night work — CRE 2nd Canadians came to see C.R.E. 46 div. re taking over line, etc. —	

C. Hughes Hallett W.G.
C.R.E. 46 Div.

Secret

<u>46th Division No. G.555/73.</u>

<u>REFERENCE 46th DIVISIONAL ORDER NO.182 AND AMENDMENT.</u>

The Raid on ALARM TRENCH by the 139th Infantry Brigade will now take place on the night of 9th/10th June 1917.

Artillery support will be arranged by the G.O.C., 139th Infantry Brigade with O.C., Right Group Artillery

Zero hour will be notified to all concerned by 139th Infantry Brigade.

acknowledge

Major.

7th June 1917.   General Staff, 46th Division.

Issued to recipients of Order No.182.

C O P Y.

SECRET.   Copy No.2.

46th DIVISION ORDER No. 189.

****

Ref: Sheet LENS,
1/10,000   June 12th, 1917.

1.   The 139th Infantry Brigade will relieve the 137th Infantry Brigade in the Left Section (ST PIERRE) on the night of the 15th/16th.
        Details of relief will be arranged by Brigade Commanders concerned.
        Relief to be completed by 4 am, 16th instant.

2.   Acknowledge,

                                       sd/ - - JOHNSON, Major.
                                 General Staff, 46th Division.

                           2.

O.C. 465th Field Co.R.E.

            The above is forwarded for your information.

                                         Lieut & Adjutant.R.E.
June 12th, 1917.   for C.R.E. 46th Division.

C O P Y

SECRET.   Copy No.2.

46TH DIVISION ORDER No. 190.

Ref: LENS Sheet, 1/10,000   June 12th, 1917.

The following operations will take place on the Divisional Front on the ~~13th~~, 14th and 15th June, 1917.

(i) On the 14th inst. The 137th Infantry Brigade will raid the enemy's trenches NARWAL and CONTRACT between N 7 . 97.50 and N 1 d 16.16.

(ii) Zero hour will be notified later.

(iii) The object of the raid is to establish identifications and destroy the enemy's defences and troops.

(iv) Details of artillery fire and barrages will be arranged by the C.R.A., 46th Division.

(v) The 138th Infantry Brigade will co-operate with a demonstration with Trench Mortars and M.G fire on FOSSE 3 for half-an-hour commencing at Zero hour.

(vi) Boiling Oil. At Zero hour, 'B' Special Company, R.E, will project Boiling Oil on to the DYNAMITE MAGAZINE defences.

Gas. At 2 am on the 15th instant (wind permitting), 'B' Special Company, R.E, will project gas on to NARWAL Trench, COWDRAY Trench, N 13 c 6.8 area and ALARM Trench.

The C.R.A. will arrange to shrapnel the gassed areas and approaches to these areas until daylight on 15th instant.

The object of this operation is to kill the enemy who may be endeavouring to repair their defences

Watches will be synchronised at 137th and 138th Infantry Brigade H.Q and Divisional H.Q at 12 noon on 14th instant.

sd/ - - - JOHNSON, Major.
General Staff, 46th Division.

2.

O.C. 465th Field Co. R.E.
O.C. 466th Field Co. R.E.
O.C. 468th Field Co. R.E.

For information.

June 13th, 1917.

Lieut & Adjutant.R.E.
for C.R.E., 46th Division.

ORDERS BY BRIGADIER-GENERAL C.V.WINGFIELD-STRATFORD.C.M.G.
C.R.E. 46th.DIVISION

O.C.465th Field Co R.E.
O.C.466th Field Co R.E.
O.C.468th Field Co R.E.
O.C.1st.Monmouths
3rd Australian Tunnelling Co.
253rd Tunnelling Co.
Headquarters "G" (for information)

1. O.C.465th Field Co.R.E. will arrange for the taping of a new line M.18.b.62.50 to M.7.c.00.41.on night of 16/17th. and will have a dump of stores collected at M.17.a.35.85. for the digging and wiring of trench on night of 17/18th.

2. O.C.466th Field Co R.E. will detail two Sections for making O.P's. at sites selected by C.R.A., an officer of 466th Field Co R.E. will be sent to C.R.A's office at 9 a.m.to-morrow to obtain instructions.
   Remainder of Company will be employed on S.P. as previously detailed.

3. (a) O.C.468th Field Co.R.E.will arrange for the taping out of a line of wire to protect the projected front assembly trench which will be wired on night of 17/18th. in addition to the taping out of the 2nd.line as directed in G/697/4 attached.

   (b) He will also have the trenches commenced tonight completed on night of 16/17th,and continued North from the "F" in FOSSE to CORKSCREW Trench at M.18.b.35.60.
   Troops available will be :-
   170 South Irish Horse) Rendezvous and arrangements for
   170 Corps Cyclists   ) tools to be made direct with O.Cs.
   400 136th Brigade ---- Details to be arranged with 136th.Bde.
   3 Companies 1st.Monmouthshire Regiment.

4. The O.C.Monmouthshire will have his Companies detailed as below.
   3 Companies for work as in 3 above,an officer to be sent to O.C.468th Field Co R.E.at POST OFFICE LIEVIN M.28.b.4.5. at 12 noon 16.6.17 to get instructions.
   Half Company for work on CHATEAU
   Half Company for work on Railways.

5. O.C.3rd Australian Tunnelling Co.will continue work on dugouts by CHATEAU and the deepening and clearing of CROCODILE and ABSALOM Trenches as previously directed.
   O.Cs will arrange for tools and assembly, work not to be commenced before 10-30 p.m.

6. O.C.253rd Tunnelling Co.will work on CROCUS and COWDEN Trenches and will make his own arrangements for tools and assembly , work not to be commenced before 10-30 p.m.

Chas. A Hutton

Lieut & Adjutant R.E.
for C.R.E.46th Division

June 15th 1917

G.697/4

C.R.E. 46th Division.
****

With reference to 46th Division Order No 191 15th June 1917.

Work will be carried out as follows :-

1. Night 15th/16th June

    (a) New trench to be dug M.24.c.85.75 to M 18.d.40.56
    Troops to be employed -
    South Irish Horse   (About 170 men)
    I Corps Cyclists   do
b   138th Inf.Bde.   (approximately 400 men)
    G.O.C.138th Infantry Brigade will arrange for a covering party of one complete company to be in position by 10-30 p.m. The work will be supervised by 468th Field Co R.E.

    (b) All available men of the 1st Monmouths will be employed on clearing existing assembly trenches in CITE DE RIAUMONT.

    (c) 3rd Australian Tunnelling Co. to complete dog-outs in CHATEAU. Remainder to clear ABSALOM and CROCODILE trenches (night work)
    253rd Tunnelling Co. to clear CROCUS and COWDEN trenches.

Night 16th/17th June

    As for night 15th/16th.June.
    In addition Trenches S.end of COPPER Trench to E. end of CORKSCREW Trench, and a second line about 75 Yds in front of this one to be taped by 465th Field Co R.E.

    468th Field Co R.E. to tape out second line on E.side of cutting parallel to one described in para 1 (a).

2. Work for succeeding days will be detailed later.

3. All men of the 3rd Australian Tunnelling Co will be billeted in LIEVIN, 253rd Tunnelling Co in ANGRES. 3rd Australian Tunnelling Co. will make their own arrangements for billets, 253rd Tunnelling Co being allotted theirs by 138th Infantry Brigade (Advanced H.Q. ANGRES M.27.c.6.0.)

Sd/ G. THORPE Lieut-Col.
General Staff 46th Division

15/6/17

S E C R E T. Copy No. 4

OPERATION ORDER No.22
BY
BRIG-GENL. C.V.WINGFIELD-STRATFORD. C.M.G.
C.R.E. 46TH DIVISION.

O.C. 466th Field Co.R.E. June 15th, 1917.

1. The 466th Field Co.R.E., will detail two Sections to work on O.Ps under instructions from the C.R.A.

2. An Officer will report to the C.R.A., at 9 am., on 16:6:17 to receive instructions.

                                               Lieut & Adjutant.R.E
                                        for C.R.E., 46th Division.

Copies to :-

C.R.A. 46th Div. No.2
Headqrs "G". 46th Div. No.3
War Diary. No.4
File. No.5

ORDERS
BY
BRIG-GENERAL C.V.WINGFIELD-STRATFORD C.M.G.
C.R.E. 46th DIVISION.

O.C.465th Field Co R.E.
O.C.466th Field Co R.E.
O.C.468th Field Co R.E.
O.C.1st Monmouths
O.C.3rd Australian Tunn.Co A.E.
O.C.253rd.Tunnelling Co R.E.
Headqtrs "G" 46th Division.

C.R.E. I Corps Troops.
138th Brigade.Headqtrs.
O.C.South Irish Horse
O.C.I Corps Cyclists.

Work on the night of 17th/18th.will be as follows :-

468th Field Co R.E.

1. Wiring of ~~~~~ trenches as taped out on night of 16/17th
2. Continuation of digging of trenches to N.of F in FOSSE to CORKSCREW TRENCH.
3. Troops available,
    - 3 Companies 1st Monmouths
    - 170 South Irish Horse
    - 170 I Corps Cyclists
4. O.C.468th Field Co R.E. to arrange direct with O.C.,parties as to time of assembly &c.,and to provide necessary guides and supervision as required.
5. Arrangements to be made with 138th Infantry Brigade for covering party.
6. Lieut MARSHALL to be detailed for taping out practice trenches,he should report to C.R.E.Headquarters at 1 p.m. on 17/6/17.

465th Field Co R.E.

Supervision of wiring and digging of trenches taped out on night of 16th/17th.

466th Field Co R.E.

Work on O.Ps and STRONG POSTS as arranged.

1st Monmouths.

Three Companies to be employed on wiring of new ~~~~~ trenches.
An Officer of each Company to get instructions from O.C., 468th Field Co R.E.at POST OFFICE,LIEVIN at noon on 17:6:17.

3rd Australian Tunnelling Co A.E.

Continuation of work on ABSALOM and CROCODILE Trenches,O.Ps., in BOIS de RIAUMONT and CHATEAU dug-outs.

253rd.Tunnelling Co R.E.

Continuation of work on CIRCUS and COWDEN Trenches.

All Os.C Companies will render daily to C.R.E.by 9 a.m. a short report on the work done the previous evening.

Chas. A. Hilton

Lieut & Adjutant R.E.
for C.R.E.46th Division.

June 16th.1917.

SECRET   Copy No 2

           46th DIVISION ORDER No. 195
           ****

                                          18th June 1917.

1.   On 19th June, 1917, the 138th Infantry Brigade will
   attack and consolidate the emeny trenches from M.30.d.20.80
   to M.30.b.15.50 from the junction of BALL and BATH to join
   with 4th Canadian Division in BRICK and BOOT Trenches.

2.   Artillery support will be arranged by G.O.C., 138th.
   Infantry Brigade. with O.C., Right Group.

3.   Two sections 178th Machine Gun Company are attached
   to 138th Machine Gun Company, for this operation.

4.   I Corps H.A. are arranging to fire from Zero+ 5
   minutes to Zero + 30 minutes on to :-
        N.25.a.61.09
        N.24.d.90.67
        N.19.c.00.95.

5.   G.O.C.138th, Infantry Brigade will arrange for
   inspection of wire tonight. Should further wire-
   cutting be required, he will arrange for 2" trench mortars
   to carry this out.

6.   Zero hour will be 2-30.p.m. 19th June.

7.   ACKNOWLEDGE.

                                   Sd/ G.THORPE Lieut-Col.
Issued at 8 p.m.   General Staff 46th.Division.

                    ****

O.C.465th Field Co R.E.
O.C.466th Field Co R.E.
O.C.468th Field Co R.E.

                    For your information please.

                                      Lieut & Adjutant R.E.
18th June 1917.   for C.R.E.46th Division.

SECRET.   Copy No 2

46th DIVISION ORDER No.196

Ref. LENS sheet 1/10,000   18th June 1917.

1. Wind permitting gas will be projected on to the emeny's front line to-night on the following areas- N.19.a., N.13.b., and c.,N.7.b.

    The 4th Canadian Division are also projecting gas on to FOSSE 3.

2. Zero hour will be 3 a.m. 19th instant.

3. ACKNOWLEDGE.

Issued at 6-30 p.m.   Sd/ R.G.STONE Capt.for
                                              Lieut -Colonel.
                                       General Staff 46th Division.

O.C.465th Field Co R.E.
O.C.466th Field Co R.E.
O.C.468th Field Co R.E.

For your information please.

                                       Lieut & Adjutant R.E.
June 18th 1917.   for C.R.E.46th Division.

S E C R E T.   46th Division. G.703.

138th Inf:Bde.   C. R. E.
139th   „   O.C. 1stv Monmouths.
O.C. South Irish Horse
O.C. Cyclist Bn.
O.C. Detachment 1st Cavalry Div.
3rd Aust:Tunnelling Co.
253rd Tunnelling Co.

※※※※※※※※※※※※※※※※※※※

During digging operations to-night the pass word will be "PLUM and APPLE".

                                sd/ V.JOHNSON, Major.
                                  for Lieut-Colonel.
18:6:17.   General Staff, 46th Division.

-2-

O.C. 465th Field Co.R.E.
O.C. 466th Field Co.R.E.
O.C. 468th Field Co.R.E.
C.R.E., I Corps Troops.

For information.

                                  Lieut & Adjutant.R.E.
June 18th, 1917.   for C.R.E. 46th Division.

SECRET. E 1081. 46th Division G.723.

C.R.E.
138th Inf:Bde
139th " "
1st Monmouths.
O.C. South Irish Horse.
OC, Cyclist Battn.
O.C. 2nd Cav: Bde Pioneer Bn.
3rd Aust: Tunnelling Co.R.E.
255rd Tunnelling Co.R.E.

During digging operations to-night the pass word will be the same as last night.

19:6:17.

sd/ G. THORPE, Lt-Col.
General Staff, 46th Division.

-2-

O.C. 465th Field Co.R.E.
O.C. 466th Field Co.R.E.
O.C. 468th Field Co.R.E.
C.R.E., I Corps Troops.

For information.

June 19th, 1917.

Lieut & Adjutant.R.E.
for C.R.E. 46th Division.

Secret   Copy No. _____

46th DIVISION   ORDER   No 198
****

Ref : Map, LENS 36.C. S.W.1. 1/10,000   22nd June 1917

1. The 137th Infantry Brigade will on 24th instant capture and consolidate the emeny's front and second lines AHEAD and ADMIRAL Trenches. Line to be consolidate to run along BOOT Trench, thence to M.30.b.5.4. thence along ADMIRAL Trench to M.30.b.35.98, thence to M.24.d.22.20.

2. I Corps H.A. are bombarding ADMIRAL and AHEAD trenches from ALICE Trench northwards from 10 a.m. to 7-45 p.m. 24th instant
   Divisional Artillery are co-operating as follows :-
   Enfilade fire on ALMANAC, ALICE and AGNES Trenches.
   Trench mortars will co-operate as follows :- 2" mortars by wire cutting in front of AHEAD Trench from ALICE Trench to M.24.d.22.20, 4.45" trench mortars bombarding on trench east of M.24.d.40.30

3. The infantry attack will take place from south to north Zero will be notified later.
                    Artillery
4. At Zero, Divisional will :-
   (a) Barrage AHEAD Trench from its junction with ALICE Trench to M.24.d.22.20 and ADMIRAL Trench from M.30.b.56.50. northwards, lifting as infantry advance is carried on.
   (b) 4.5" howitzers will bombard PIT in M.30.d. and embankments between PIT and River SOUCHEZ.
   (c) AGNES and ALMANAC Trenches will be kept under enfilade fire.
   (d) I Corps H.A. bombarding RESERVOIRS for 20 minutes with two 6" howitzers and blacking trench at M.24.d.75.42. with two more 6" howitzers for half-an-hour

5. Machine Gun barrages from Zero onwards will be arranged by Divisional Machine Gun Officer and will include an enfilade barrage on the approximate line N.25.a.3.1. to M.24.d.65.45 and an overhead barrage from the River SOUCHEZ to N.25.a.3.1. Arrangements will also be made for supporting the advance by direct machine gun fire at short range.

6. It is probable that 4th Canadian Division will at Zero attack the PIT in M.30.d. If this is arranged the necessary modifications will be made to the artillery programme.

7. Watches will be synchronised from Divisional Headquarters at hours to be notified later.

8. ACKNOWLEDGE.

                            Sd/ G. THORPE Lieut -Col.
                       General Staff 46th Division.

O.C.466th Field Co R.E.
3rd Australian Tunnelling Co A.E.
O.C.1st Monmouths.

            For your information please.
         ACKNOWLEDGE.

                              Lieut & Adjutant R.E.
                              for C.R.E. 46th Division.
June 23rd 1917.

Secret   Copy No 2

46th DIVISION ORDER No 200

Ref : Map LENS 36 C S.W.1
1/10,000

23rd June.1917

The following amendments and additions to Order No 198 will be made. :-

1. Bombardment by I Corps H.A. will commence at 11 45 am and continue till Zero.
   The bombardment by I Corps H.A. detailed in para 4 (d) of Order No 198 will commence at Zero.

2. Zero will be at 9-30 p.m.

3. The 4th Canadian Division are at Zero advancing their posts to the embankment at M.30.d.9.4 and the PIT at N.25.c.1.9.
   The howitzer fire detailed in Para 4 (b) of Order 198 will therefore not take place or the machine gun barrage from the river SOUCHEZ to N 25 a 3 1
   This advance by the 4th Canadian Division will be covered by a rolling barrage from the river SOUCHEZ northwards to M 30 b 8 2, carried out by Canadian Artillery.

4. The 46th Divisional Artillery barrage as detailed in para 4 (a) of Order 198 will remain stationary for five minutes, guns then being lifted off AHEAD and ADMIRAL Trenches 50 Yds at a time every 3 minutes from the southern limits of the barrage, re-opening fire on their new S.O.S. lines by batteries at a slow rate for 40 minutes.

5. Watches will be synchronised from Divisional H.Q. by telephone to I Corps H.A at 10 a.m. An Officer from Divisional H.Q. will bring the time to 137th. Infantry Brigade H.Q. at 2 p.m.
   Further synchronization of watches with I Corps H.A. will take place by telephone from Divisional H.Q. at 3 p.m.

ACKNOWLEDGE

                                   Sd/ G.THORPE Lieut-Col
O.C.466th Field Co R.E.General Staff 46th Division.
3rd Australian Tunn.Co.A.E.
O.C.1st.Bn.Monmouthshire Regt.

For your information please

ACKNOWLEDGE.

                                   Lieut & Adjutant R.E.
June 23rd 1917   for C.R.E.46th Division.

OPERATION ORDER   No.23.   Copy No. 4
By.
BRIG-GENL. C.V.WINGFIELD-STRATFORD C.M.G.
C.R.E. 46th DIVISION.

June 23rd 1917.

<u>466th Field Co R.E.</u>

1.   One Section of the 466th Field Co R.E. will be placed at the disposal of the 137th. Infantry Brigade for work to-morrow 24th./6/17 if required.

2.   The 466th Field Co.R.E. will keep in touch with 137th.Brigade to receive instructions.

3   ACKNOWLEDGE.

Chas. R. Keith
Lieut & Adjutant R.E.
for C.R.E.46th Division.

Copies to :-

137th Infantry Bde. No 2.
Headquarters "G" 46th.Divn. No.3.
War Diary   No.4.
O.O.File.   No.5.

"A" Form.
MESSAGES AND SIGNALS.

Army Form C.2121
(in pads of 100).
No. of Message ....

Prefix ..... Code ..... m.	Words	Charge	This message is on a/c of:	Recd. at .... m.
Office of Origin and Service Instructions.				Date ....
SECRET	Sent At ..... m. To By		.... Service. (Signature of "Franking Officer.")	From .... By ....

TO { CYLLENE

| Sender's Number. | Day of Month. | In reply to Number. | AAA |
| R.E.776 | 23rd | | |

Div^{al} Orders No.178 received please

From Bayard0
Place
Time 10.30 a.m.

The above may be forwarded as now corrected. (Z)

Censor.   Signature of Addressor or person authorised to telegraph in his name.

* This line should be erased if not required.
750,000. W 2186—M509. H. W. & V., Ld. 6/16.

"A" Form.
MESSAGES AND SIGNALS.

Army Form C.2121 (in pads of 100).

TO	CYLLENE

Sender's Number.	Day of Month.	In reply to Number.	AAA
*EB 349	23rd		

"Muriel" Order No 178 received

From: THROSTLE
Place:
Time:

No officer available
A. Huffer Sergt

"A" Form.
MESSAGES AND SIGNALS.

Army Form C.2121
(in pads of 100).

Prefix	Code	m.	Words	Charge	This message is on a/c of:	Recd. at	m.
Office of Origin and Service Instructions			Sent		Service.	Date	
			At	m.		From	
			To				
			By		(Signature of "Franking Officer.")	By	

TO: **CYLLENE**

Sender's Number.	Day of Month.	In reply to Number.	AAA
N 1537	23		

46th Division Order No 178 received and noted

From: **OSSIAN**

Time: 10.30 AM

SECRET.   Copy No.2.

46TH DIVISION ORDER No. 201.
****

Ref: Map, Sheet, 36.C, S.W.1.
  1/10,000   24th June, 1917.

1. A raid will be carried out by 139th Infantry Brigade on night 24th/25th June between the following points :- N 1 d 16.44 and N 1 d 11.20. A dummy raid will take place simultaneously on front N 7 a 95.65 to N 7 a 93.60. Zero time will be at 12.45 am, 25th instant.

2. The object of the raid will be to take prisoners, to destroy the enemy's personnel and trenches and to secure identifications.

3. The enemy's line will be entered at N 1 d 08.37 and N 1 d 10.27.

4. All ranks taking part in the raid will be searched before embarking on the raid to ascertain that no identifications are left on any men taking part in the raid.

5. I Corps H.A are co-operating by wire cutting at points of entry and by two false gaps, by destroying the concreted house at N 1 d 15.35 during raid by bombarding trench junction N 1 d 16.80, FOSSE 14, Trench junction N 1 d 83.50, Trench junction N 7 b 90.92 and houses around that point, trench junction N 7 b 95.46 and CONTROL Trench and houses from N 7 b 45.77 to N 7 b 75.88 and by counter battery work.

6. Divisional Artillery co-operation has been arranged by G.O.C., 139th Inf: Bde with O.C, Left Group.

7. Synchronization of watches will be arranged for by G.O.C., 139th Onf: Bde, who will receive time from Divisional Headquarters at 3 pm, I Corps H.A synchronizing with Divisional Headquarters as detailed in Order No. 200.

8. ACKNOWLEDGE.

                                    sd/ G.THORPE. Lieut-Col.
                                    General Staff, 46th Division.

-2-

O.C. 465th Field Co.R.E.

The above is forwarded for your information.

                                          C.B.Hutton
                                    Lieut & Adjutant.R.E.
                                    for C.R.E. 46th Division.

June 24th, 1917.

Copy No. 4

OPERATION ORDER No 24.
By
BRIG-GENL. C.V WINGFIELD-STRATFORD C.M.G.
C.R.E. 46th DIVISION.

O.C.465th Field Co R.E.
O.C.468th Field Co R.E.

June 24th 1917

1. The right boundary for work by 465th. Field Co.R.E. will be CROCODILE exclusive from 24th instant.

2. ACKNOWLEDGE

Copies to :-

Headquarters "G"
  46th Division.   No.3.
War Diary   No.4.
O.O.File.   No.5.

Lieut & Adjutant R.E.
for C.R.E. 46th Division.

Secret.   OPERATION   ORDER   No 25.
By
BRIG-GENL. C.V.WINGFIELD-STRATFORD C.M.G.
C.R.E.46th DIVISION.

Copy No 5

24th June 1917

O.C.465th Field Co R.E.
O.C.468th Field Co R.E.

1. The 465th Field Co R.E. will on the 26th instant take over from the 468th Field Co R.E. the work in front trenches CROCODILE inclusive to cross roads M.30.a.75.90.

2. ACKNOWLEDGE.

Chas A. Hutn
Lieut & Adjutant R.E.
for C.R.E.46th Division.

Copy to :-
    465th Field Co R.E.   No 3
    Headquarters "G"   No 4
    War Diary   No 5
    O.O.File   No 6.

"A" Form.
MESSAGES AND SIGNALS.

Army Form C. 2121.

TO CRE

Sender's Number.	Day of Month	In reply to Number	
G 882	26		AAA

Order 207 is cancelled AAA Operation will be carried out as ordered in Order 206 of 25th June 1917.

From GUNNER

Time 2.40 p.m.

(Sd) G Thorpe Lt Col

"A" Form.
MESSAGES AND SIGNALS.
Army Form C.2121
(in pads of 100)

Prefix ...... Code ...... m.	Words	Charge	This message is on a/c of:	Recd. at ...... m.
Office of Origin and Service Instructions.		Sent		Date ......
......		At ...... m.	...... Service.	From ......
......		To		By ......
		By	(Signature of "Franking Officer.")	

TO | 137 Bde.

Sender's Number. | Day of Month. | In reply to Number. | AAA
— | June 26th | — |

reference to Div. O.O. of today
directing "466 & 466 F.T. RE to be attached
to 137 Bde for operation".
I am sending Capt Davies down to
find out what is required. —
The Company has some important
work in hand at O.P.S, so if
with, I should like this to be
continued. Major Townsend is going
over a portion of the line with a view to
taking over some work from

From
Place 468 F.T.R which is the reason why
Time I am sending his 2d in command to see you

The above may be forwarded as now corrected.   (Z)
                                  Censor.   Signature of Addressee or person authorised to telegraph in his name.
* This line should be erased if not required.
750,000. W 2186—M509. H. W. & V., Ld. 6/16.

S E C R E T. 　　　　　　　　　　　46th Division.
　　　　　　　　　　　　　　　　　　G. 695.

137th Inf:Bde
138th   ,,
139th   ,,
C.R.A.
C.R.E.

On night 2nd/3rd July and night 3rd/4th the 2nd Canadian Division will relieve the 4th Canadian Division on our right, the 12th Canadian Infantry Brigade being relieved on our immediate right on the night of 3rd/4th July.

　　　　　　　　　　　　　sd/ G.THORPE, Lieut-Col.
June 28th, 1917.　　　　　General Staff, 46th Division.

-2-

O.C. 465th Field Co.R.E.
O.C. 466th Field Co.R.E.
O.C. 468th Field Co.R.E.

For your information.

　　　　　　　　　　　　　　Lieut & Adjutant.R.E.
June 28th, 1917.　　　　　for C.R.E., 46th Division.

SECRET   Copy No 2

46th DIVISION ORDER No.210

Ref: Map, LENS 36.c.S.W.1.1/10,000
and Special Map LENS (2) 1/10-000   29th June 1917

1. (a) The Division now holds the line along ADJACENT Trench
         from about N 25 central, thence AGUE TRENCH to N.19.ac
         7.8. thence ADROIT Trench to N 19.a.10.45.

    (b) 4th Canadian Division on our right occupy a line
         N.26.d.4.0 to N 26.d.0.0.to N.25.b.4.2.

    (c) The German Division opposite us is 11th. Reserve
         Division. an indifferent Division with low morals, who
         have already been badly punished this year on several
         occasions.

2.   On the 1st July, 46th Division will attack on a three
         Brigade front to secure the line from SOUCHEZ River at
         N,25.b.8.6. to N 20 c.0.2. ACONITE Trench and ALOOF Trench
         thence to N.13.a.95.65. This line will be joined up to
         our original front line by COLLEGE, CORNWALL and COMBAT
         Trenches.

3.   The 2nd Sherwood Foresters and the 9th Norfolks, 71st.
         Infantry Brigade, are under the 46th Division for this
         operation.

4.   Bombardment ny Heavy Artillery commenced to-day and will
         be continued throughout to-morrow. Detail of bombardments
         will be issued to all concerned.

5.   The infantry attack will take place at dawn on the 1st
         July: Zero hour will be notified later.

6.   Field Artillery and Machine Gun barrage maps are being
         prepared and will be issued to all concerned.

7.   Frontages are allotted as follows :-

         138th Infantry Brigade from river SOUCHEZ to road
         running E.N.E from M 24 d 7.4 exclusive.

         137th Infantry Brigade from above road inclusive to
         LIEVIN - LENS Road inclusive.

         139th Infantry Brigade and 2nd Sherwoods attached, from
         LIEVIN - LENS Road exclusive to our present left.

8.   2nd Cavalry Brigade Battalion, 9th Norfolks and 1st
         Monmouths will be in Divisional Reserve, located as follows:-

         2nd Cavalry Brigade Battalion   - CALONNE
         9th Norfolks.   - CITE ST PIERRE
         1st Monmouths   - LIEVIN
         To be in position by 2 am, 1st July.

9./

-2-

9. A preparatory operation will take place at 2.34 am to-morrow, 30th June, with a view to capturing the line N 19 c 7.8 - N 19 a 50.52 - N 13 c 35.02. This operation will be carried out by 137th and 139th Infantry Brigades under support of artillery barrage.
C.R.E will arrange that working parties in ABSALOM and CROCODILE Trenches are clear of these trenches by 2 am.

10. Orders will be issued as to times contact aeroplanes will call for flares. Flares will be carried by advanced troops.

11. If wind is favourable, O.C., 'B' Special Company.R.E. will project gas into CITE ST EDOUARD and N 13 at 11.30 pm, 30th June.

12. Correct time will be sent to Brigade Headquarters at 9 pm, 30th June.

13. 137th and 138th Infanrty Brigades Advanced Headquarters will be unchanged: 139th Infantry Brigade Advanced Headquarters will be at M 17 a 3.9. Divisional Headquarters will not move.

14. ACKNOWLEDGE.

Sd. G.THORPE, Lt-Col.
General Staff, 46th Division.

O.C. 465th Field Co.R.E.
O.C. 466th Field Co.R.E.
O.C. 468th Field Co.R.E.

The above is forwarded for your information.

Lieut & Adjutant.R.E.
for C.R.E. 46th Division.

June 30th, 1917.

OPERATION ORDER No 26.   Copy No 8
By
BRIG-GENL& C.V.WINGFIELD-STRATFORD C.M.G.

C.R.E. 46th DIVISION
****

O.C.465th Field Co R.E.
O.C.466th Field Co R.E.
O.C.468th Field Co R.E.   June 30th.1917

Reference Divisional Order No 210.

1.   For the operation detailed in the above order the following Sections will be attached for work under Brigades.:-

   465th Field Co. 2 Sections to work with 139th.Inf.Bde.
   466th Field Co 2   do   do   137th Inf.Bde.
   468th Field Co. 2   do   do   138th Inf.Bde.

   The remaining 2 Sections of each Field Co will be held in reserve for work under the C.R.E.

2.   Each Field Co will be prepared for demolition work and wire cutting.

3.   Forward dumps will be formed with such stores as are likely to be required,i.e. Sandbags,Picks,Shovels, Barbed wire,Screw Pickets,Tape,&c.
   Map reference of all forward dumps will be wired to the C.R.E. to-day by 6 p.m.

4.   Copies of Brigade Orders for the work of the two attached Sections will be forwarded to the C.R.E.for information.

5   ACKNOWLEDGE.

                                 Lieut & Adjutant R.E.
                                 for C.R.E.46th Division.
Copies to :-

   137th Infantry Brigade No 4
   138th   do   do   No 5
   139th   do   do   No 6
   Headquarters 46th"S"   No 7
   War Diary   No 8
   O.O.File   No 9

WAR DIARY
or
INTELLIGENCE SUMMARY.

C.R.E. 46th Div.

Vol 12

Army Form C. 2118.

Place	Date	Hour	Summary of Events and Information	Remarks and references to Appendices
SAINS en GOHELLE	July 1st 1917		C.R.E. went to LIEVIN with G.S.I. – Saw Brig.Genl. Comdg. 138 & 137 Bdes – arrangements made for carrying out of line.	
	2nd		Went to LIEVIN with G.S.2 & saw Inspection 138 & 137 – C.R.E. 2nd Canadian Came in and arranged about taking over line re – 466 & 468 1st/1st R.E. to hand over to R.E.s 2nd Canadian divs".	O.O. N° 28
	3rd		465 1st/1st relieved by 5th M.P.Coy 2nd Canadian div. – Sent in report on operations. – Adjt. went on leave.	
LA COMTÉ	4th		H'qrs. 46 div R.E. arrived at LA COMTE – went with R.E. round new area	
	5th		made R.E. arrangts. re divl. workshops & started on making targets for training purposes, baths & laundries, mr improvement to billets.	
	6th		making ranges, firing targets, in prove billets & training. C.R.E. finished?	
	7th		do	
	8th		do	
	9th		do	
	10th		do	
	11th		do	

HdQrs R.E. 46th Divn.

WAR DIARY
or
INTELLIGENCE SUMMARY.
(Erase heading not required.)

Army Form C. 2118.

Place	Date	Hour	Summary of Events and Information	Remarks and references to Appendices
LA COMTÉ	July 12th		Making new Range for Rifle meeting — R.E. Companies Training	
	13th		do —	
	14th		— do —	
	15th		Training	
	16th			
	18th			
	19th		Training & rifle meeting. CRE to see Corps CRE to make arrangements for relief of division & handing over	OO's 24.30
	20th		arrangements for new river shelters for repair at HESDIGNEUL made in MAZINGARBE	
	21st		466 left for SAILLY LABOURSE	
	22nd		466 — k— to SAILLY LABOURSE	
	23rd		465 & 4th GESTREVILLE en route to NOVELLES — ONE wood wind line unit	
	24th		CRE & 2nd Asst CRE visits 2nd Div K SAILLY & took over plans in Sullian sector. — Visited 466 Coys at LABOURSE & took round billets	
	25th		Moved to SAILLY. — Visited 466 Coys at LABOURSE & took round billets & instructed dumps	
SAILLY LABOURSE	26th		Went to see B O138 Area Roffe 468 & CRE 2 Canadian Divn to arrangements for tanks and dismounts for approaching operations	
	27th		Went to very new HQ Check at FOSSE 12 with CRE 1 Corps further arrangements with LGS O.K.E.	

HQ O/C RE 46 Div

Army Form C. 2118.

WAR DIARY
or
INTELLIGENCE SUMMARY.
(Erase heading not required.)

Place	Date	Hour	Summary of Events and Information	Remarks and references to Appendices
SAILLY LABOURSE	July 28th		Went to see work at FOSSE 12 - KNOYELLES & the 465th & round the OP/PU south of line with O.C. 466 & Lt MOUNTFORD - Laws work in progress - Friends my work & in bad state -	3
	29th		O.C. 170 Tunnelling Co - O.C. 466 line & to see last comms out of him. Went in wiring tree start of French with Flos & Subbies for VERMELLES front line - & works in O.P. in water tower VERMELLES	
	30th		Work round with sentries with O.C. 465 M.R.E. - afternoon saw O.E. 1 Coys & discussed trench policy with him. Lt S.H. Anf. read to select place as put line to france dammies	
	31st		Went with O.O.C. around head of trench N. Sector - a work being done by RE's & Pioneers - hung sitting in addit (Cpt. Stansfield RE) new version of armament of Block 5.1 & finally approval new version of armament of block strong.	

[signature]

SECRET   Copy No 9

OPERATION ORDER No 28
By
BRIG-GENL. C.V. WINGFIELD-STRATFORD C.M.G.
46th DIVISION.

O.C. 465th Field Co R.E.
O.C. 466th Field Co R.E.   2nd July 1917
O.C. 468th Field Co R.E.

1.   The dismounted portion of your Company will move
     from NOEUX LES MINES to GENTREVILLE area by bus
     to-morrow evening the 3rd instant, time to be
     notified later.

2.   Mounted portion and all transport will move
     to GENTREVILLE area tomorrow.

3.   Billeting parties consisting of 1 Officer and
     3 O.R. will be taken by lorry to the new area.
     They should be ready at their Headquarters
     at 8-30 a.m. and will be picked up by lorry.

4.   The 465th Field Co R.E. and the 468th Field Co R.E.
     will be billeted at GENTREVILLE and the 466th Field Co R.E.
     at HERLIN LE VERT.

5.   Details will be arranged in the new area with
     the Adjutant R.E.

6.   ACKNOWLEDGE.

                                    J.C. Marshall
                                       1 Lt RE
                                  Lieut & Adjutant R.E.
Copies to :-   for C.R.E. 46th Division.

     Headquarters 46th Divn.   No 4
     O.C. Signal Co R.E.   No 5
     A.D.M.S.   No 6
     D.A.D.V.S.   No 7
     O.C. Divnl. Train   No 8
     War Diary   No 9
     O.C. File   No 10

MARCH TABLE   JULY 2nd. & 3rd.

DATE	UNIT	DESTINATION	MOUNTED OR DISMOUNTED	REMARKS
July 2nd.	466th Field Co R.E.	MONTE LES MINES Huts.	Dismounted portion with necessary transport.	To move on completion of relief Billeting party to report to 2ND MAJOR MONTE LES MINES morning of 2nd.
	do. do	do	do	do
	467th Field Co R.E.	MOUDAIN	Mounted portion and remainder of transport.	To move on completion of relief Billeting party to report to 2ND MAJOR MOUDAIN on the morning of 2nd.JULY.
	468th.Field Co R.E.	do	do	do
3rd.	468th Field Co R.E.	MONTE LES MINES Huts.	Dismounted portion with necessary transport.	To move on completion of relief [illegible]
3rd.	466th Field Co R.E. } 466th Field Co R.E. } 466th Field Co R.E. }	GESTRUVILLE LOTIMAT CHILES.	Dismounted portion	by Busses [illegible]
	468th Field Co R.E. } 468th Field Co R.E. } 468th Field Co R.E. }	Do do	do	Details will be sent later.
			Mounted portion Transport.	

OPERATION ORDER No 29
BY
BRIG-GENERAL C.V. WINGFIELD-STRATFORD C.M.G.
C.R.E. 46th DIVISION
==

Copy No 7

JULY 20th 1917.

Reference E.1270 dated 19:7:16.

The following details of reliefs will be carried out by Field Companies

O.C. 465th Field Co R.E.
O.C. 466th Field Co R.E.
O.C. 468th Field Co R.E.

Unit of 46th.Dvn.	Relieved By	Date	To Relieve	Advanced party from 6th Dvn. Field Coy.	Date	Advanced party from 46th.Dvn. Field Coy.	Remarks.
468th.Fld. Co R.E.	12th.Fld.Co.	22nd.	509th.Fld. Co.R.E. at MAZINGARBE Headqtrs. L.25.b.30.	Will be sent to take over billets in GUESTREVILLE early on 22nd.	22nd.	2 Off.& 6 O.R. will take over from 509th.Fld. Co.on 21st.This party will be billeted by 509 Fld.Co.	O.C. 468th.Fld.Co.will arrange with O.C. 465th Fld.Co.to guard his billets after he leaves on 21st. instant, until advanced party of 509 Fld.Co.arrives. (No Lorry available to take advanced party.)
466th Fld. Coy.R.E.	509 Fld Co.R.E.	22nd.	12th.Fld.Co. R.E. at LABOURSE.H.Q. L.2.a.4.4.	Will be sent to take over billets in BAJUS on 21st. O.C.466th.Fld. Co.will arrange billets for this party.	22nd.	2 Off.& 6 O.R. will take over from 12th.Fld.Co. on 21st.This party will be billeted by the 12th.Fld.Co.	No Lorry is available to take advanced party
465th.Fld. Co R.E.	459th.Fld.Co.	24th.	459th Fld.Co. at NOYELLES (H.Q.L.11.d.4.6.	Will be sent to take over billets in GUESTREVILLE on 22nd.Billets will be found by 465th.Fld.Co for this party	24th.	2 Off.& 6 O.R. will take over from 459th.Fld.Co on 23rd.This party will be billeted by 459th.Fld.Co.	

Chas A Hulm
Lieut & Adjutant R.E.
for O.R.E.46th.Division.

SECRET.

Copy No. 15

OPERATION ORDER No 30
BY
BRIG-GENERAL C.V.WINGFIELD-STRATFORD C.M.G.
C.R.E. 46th Division.

July 29th 1917

O.C.465th Field Co R.E.
O.C.466th Field Co R.E.
O.C.468th Field Co R.E.

1. The undermentioned reliefs for August will take place

2. The 468th Field Co R.E.will be relieved by the 466th Field Co R.E.on 2nd August.
   The 465 Field Co R.E.will be relieved by the 468th Field Co R.E. on 14th August.
   The 466th Field Co R.E.will be relieved by the 465th Field Co R.E.on the 26th. August.

3. The Brigades relieve the day following in each case.

4. All arrangements for reliefs will be between O.C.Companies concerned and arranged to ensure continuity of work as far as possible.

5. O.C.Companies will be prepared to give their Brigade all information on engineering work in their Sector as soon as the incoming Brigade arrives

[signature]

Lieut & Adjutant R.E.
for C.R.E.46th Divn.

Copies to-
Headquarters "G"   No 4 to 7
C.E.I Corps.   No 8
O.C.Monmouths   No 9
O.C.253rd Tunn.Co.R.E. No 10
O.C.Signal Co R.E.   No 11
O.C.Divn.Train   Bo 12
A.D.M.S.   No 13
D.A.D.V.S.   No 14
War Diary   No 15
File   No 16

SECRET REF: C.R.E. OPERATION ORDER No 30.

O.C.465th Field Co R.E.
O.C.466th Field Co R.E.
O.C.468th Field Co R.E.

July 30th 1917.

1. The reliefs by Field Companies will be carried out one day earlier than is given in the above Operation Order.

2. ACKNOWLEDGE.

Chas. A Hunlin
Lieut & Adjutant R.E.
for C.R.E.46th Division.

Copies to :-
Headquarters G No 4 to 7
C.E.I Corps   No 8.
O.C.Monmouths   No 9
O.C.253rd Tunn.Co.R.E. No.10
O.C.Signal Co R.E.   No 11
O.C.Divnl.Train   No 12
A.D.M.S.   No 13
D.A.D.V.S.   No 14
War Diary   No 15
File   No 16.

E.R.E. 46 Div.

HQ RE 46
Vol 13

WAR DIARY
or
INTELLIGENCE SUMMARY
Army Form C. 2118.

Place	Date	Hour	Summary of Events and Information	Remarks and references to Appendices
SAILLY LA BOURSE	Aug 1st		Went to NOEUX with CRE 1 Corps troops and saw O.C. 465 T TRE & O.C. 508 A.T.C. — Went to FOSSE 12 — & saw O.C. 1st Monmouths — 466 T Tun. relieved 468 T Tun. in Hulluch sectr — saw K MARIONETTS to show how trench during picks	LENS 11 1/100,000 36c N.W. 3 1/10,000
	2.		— This work — & visited 468 T.C. — Very wet	
	3		— Saw O.C. 468 & visited FOSSE No 12 dump — saw O.C. 466 — & 1st Monmouths at MAZINGARBE — & O.C. 170 Tunnelly Co at NOEUX LES MINES — wet day	
	4th		Saw O.C. 465 T Tre & inspected work in line in ST ELIE sectr — Trenches in very bad state after wet weather. Went to Hulluch trenches to see about the visibility of new dug outs to increase accommodation required	
	5th		To MAZINGARBE home O.C. 466 T Tre — & saw O.E. 465 & 468 T Tre. Inspected transport & technical equipment of 465 & 468 T Tre. and from there visited work to advance VILS of 466 T Tre	
	6th		Went to see work in progress on LA ROUTOIRE Village line	
	7th		Went round work in line on Hulluch sectr — inspected work in Northern Redoubt — visited Curran & Bones huts — POSEN ALLEY & VENDIN C.Ts. — Went round with sectn	
	8th		Inspected work on RUTOIRE Farm dug outs — went round with sectn. WK of OC 465 (1st ELIE sectr) & visited work in progn	

C.R.E. 46 - Aus'n

WAR DIARY or **INTELLIGENCE SUMMARY**
Army Form C. 2118.

Place	Date	Hour	Summary of Events and Information	Remarks and references to Appendices
SAILLY LABOURSE	Aug 9th		Went round huts standing in areas. Saw O.C. 466 F.T. & C.E. I Corps at I Corps H.Qrs.	
		10h	Went round ST ELIE sect'n of line with O.C. 465 & inspected work in ST GEORGES tunnels & at RUTOIRE farm	
		11h	Went round HULLUCH sect'n with A/O.C. & O.C. 466 F.T.C. - visited LONE Works See O.O. N°31	O.O. N°31
			And HAY ALLEY subways - Saw O.C. 1st Monmouths	
		12h	Conference at H.Qrs. on points of work & scheme - Arrived extra sections 3rd Australians - 466 - 465 & 560 Coys.	O.O. N°32
			Saw O.C. 170 Tunnellin Coy - 3rd Australians round his sector	
		13th	Went Round O.C. 466 & went with him round his sector - inspected Lone Tree Redoubt - Went with G.S.I. to a Conference at Corps H.Qrs.	
		14th	Went round Mallock sect'n with O.C. Pioneers - & then inspected Curzon & Northern Saps Redoubt - Had a conference with O.C. 2.9.9. Pet Northern Saps Redoubt - Had a conference with O.C. 2.9.9.	
		15th	O.C. Pioneers saw work both in stores in Vermelles C.E. I Corps. & C.E. I Corps came & inspected Redoubts & all 3 Saps. & new standings	

10. R.E. 46th Divn.

Army Form C. 2118.

WAR DIARY
or
INTELLIGENCE SUMMARY.
(Erase heading not required.)

Place	Date	Hour	Summary of Events and Information	Remarks and references to Appendices
SAILLY LA BOURSE	Aug 16th		Went round St ELIE sector & inspected new advanced billets in Hulluch Alley & went round work in STANSFIELD — O.P. 1 tunnel & Orchard Alley — advanced billets & R.E. tunnel were too wet to be assembly for a raid.	
	17th		Went round Hulluch sector of line with Coy & inspected tunnels.	
	18th		Went with O.C. Pioneers round Hulluch sector - & discussed an additional dugout in Northern dug Redoubt — visited work at La Rutoire Farm. Letters re tunnelling work with O.C. 3rd Australians & G.S. & settled billeting arrangements & home stemming & loose soil tramway run.	O.S. No 33
	19th		Inspected work in St ELIE sector — visited billets Junction Keep & work to proper — visited La Rutoire & went with the 46th horse tank in Vermelles C.T.	
	20th		Went to see C.R.E. 2nd div re taking over a new piece of line to N. of St ELIE sector — Inspected various workshops —	V.O. No 34
	21st		Saw O.C. Pioneers & 466 Coy - inspected village line - & heard from them re Kings Way trench — Inspected work in 10th Avenue - Orchard Avenue & Rutoire	

C.R.E. 46th Div^n

Army Form C. 2118.

WAR DIARY
or
INTELLIGENCE SUMMARY.
(Erase heading not required.)

Place	Date	Hour	Summary of Events and Information	Remarks and references to Appendices
SAILLY LABOURSE	July 23rd 1917		Went round new CAMBRIN sector with V.C. 483 7th F.C. R.E. & O.C. 466 & 7th F.C. R.E. & made report on same to 46th Div. G.	4
	24		Inspected work in ST ELIE sector of line.	
	25		Inspected work in HULLUCH sector with O.C. 466 & 7th F.C. R.E. Inspected POSEN & 14 block to see if fit for troops engaged in raid.	
	26		Went to see trenches in CAMBRIN sector - Inspected Dump at POSEN 12 & saw O.C. 466 7th F.C.	
	27		Inspected work in St. ELIE sector with O.C. 468 F.C. - large explosion on tramline near PHILOSOPHE - German shell set light to trucks with ammunition.	
	28		Went to see CAMBRIN sector with O.C. 466 L.F.C. Aniseeds - & inspected proposed M.G. emplacements.	
	29		Inspected HULLUCH sector with O.C. 466 & returned by tramway - inspected M.G. in CHAPEL ALLEY.	a.m. — lost & lonely march M1
	30		Inspected work in ST ELIE sector & then returned by CAMBRIN sector. This work in progress.	
	31		Went with G.21 round St ELIE sector returning through HULLUCH sector. Sited 2 M.G. emplacements & saw work in progress of 3rd Ambulation tunnelling.	

31/7/17

E. Winfrith Martin Maj C.B.E.
C.R.E. 46 Div

SECRET   Copy No 5.

OPERATION ORDER No 31
BY
BRIG-GENERAL C.V.WINGFIELD- STRATFORD C.M.G.
C.R.E.46th DIVISION

O.C.465th Field Co R.E.   August 10th 1917.
O.C.1st.Bn.Monmouth Regt.

        The 465th Field Co R.E. will vacate the dugouts in JUNCTION KEEP to-morrow 11/8/17.

2.   O.C.Monmouths will arrange to move his men in on the same day.

3.   Moves must be arranged so that the KEEP is not without garrison at any time.

4.   Details will be arranged between O.C. concerned.

5.   ACKNOWLEDGE.

Chas A. Hinton

Captain & Adjt.R.E.
for C.R.E.46th Division.

Copy to :-
  Headquarters   No 3.
  File   No 4
  War Diary   No 5.

SECRET   Copy No 6

OPERATION ORDER   No. 32
By
BRIGADIER-GENERAL C.V.WINGFIELD-STRATFORD C.M.G.
C.R.E. 46th Division.

11th August 1917.

O.C.1st.Bn.Monmouthshire Regt.

1. Two Platoons of the 1st Bn.Monmouthshire Regt.will move from 10th AVENUE to billets in MAZINGARBE to-morrow 12/8/17.

2. Dugouts in 10th AVENUE to be vacated at a time to be arranged by O.C.Monmouths with 137th Brigade.

3. The above two Platoons will move to LE RUTOIRE FARM when the billets are available for occupation

Chas A Hutton
Captain & Adjutant R.E.
for C.R.E.46th Division.

Copy to :-
   137th Brigade No 2
   Headquarters G No 3
   466th Fld.Co. No 4
   File   No 5
   War Diary   No 6

War Diary

SECRET   OPERATION ORDER   No 33   Copy No. 15
BY
BRIG-GENERAL C.V.WINGFIELD-STRATFORD C.M.G.

================   August 19th 1917.

O.C. 465 Field Co R.E.
O.C. 466 Field Co R.E.
O.C. 468 Field Co R.E.
----

1. The following reliefs will take place.

2.   The 466 Field Co R.E. will be relieved by the 465 Field Co R.E. on 26th August.
                 The 468 Field Co R.E. will be relieved by the 466 Field Co R.E. on 7th September.
                 The 465 Field Co R.E. will be relieved by the 468 Field Co R.E. on 19th September.

3. The Brigades relieve two days following in each case.

4.   All arangements for reliefs will be between O.C.Companies concerned and arranged to ensure continuity of work as far as possible.

5.   O.C.Companies will be prepared to give their Brigade all information on engineering work in their Sector as soon as the incoming Brigade arrives.

                                       Capt & Adjt R.E.
                                     for C.R.E. 46th Division.

Copies to:-
Headquarters "G"   No 4 to 7
C.E.1.Corps   No 8
O.C.Monmouths   No 9
~~O.C. 253rd Tunn.Co.R.E. No 10.~~
O.C. Signal Co R.E.   No 11.
O.C. Divn Train   No 12.
A.D.M.S.   No 13.
D.A.D.V.S.   No 14.
War Diary.   No 15.
File.   No 16.

SECRET

War Diary

Copy No 7

OPERATION ORDER No 34
BY
BRIG-GENERAL C.V.WINGFIELD-STRATFORD C.M.G.

August 21st 1917.

O.C. 465 Field Co R.E.

The 139 Brigade will relieve the 99th Brigade (2nd Division) in the CAMBRIN sector, on the 26th August.

The 465 Field Co R.E. will relieve the 483 Field Co R.E. (3rd Division), (H.Q. BEUVRY) on the 25th August.

Arrangements will be made by O.C. 465 Field Co R.E. with O.C. 483 Field Co R.E. to take over the work, dumps &c, and reconoitre the line as early as possible.

Billets for the 465 Field Co R.E. will be settled later.

Acknowledge.

Chas. Atkin

Capt & Adjt R.E.
for C.R.E. 46th Division.

Copies to:-

C.R.E. 2nd Division   Nos 2 & 3
O.C. 466 Field Co R.E. No   4
O.C. 468 Field Co R.E. No   5
Headquarters 46th Division No 6
War Diary   No 7
File   No 8

WAR DIARY
or
INTELLIGENCE SUMMARY.
(Erase heading not required.)

Army Form C. 2118.

HQ R.E. 46 D.

SOS/14

Place	Date	Hour	Summary of Events and Information	Remarks and references to Appendices
SAILLY LABOURSE	Sept 1st		Inspected R.E. dump FOSSE 12 – Saw O.C.s 466 & 468 2/7 R.E. – 31 horses belonging to 466 2/7 R.E. hit by shrapnel in stampup – 14 killed – several drivers wounded	LENS II Trench Map LOOS 36c NW3 1/10,000 several 1/10,000
	" 2nd		Went round part of HULLUCH sector with O.C. 466 & inspected work St GEORGES & HULLUCH tunnels	
	" 3rd		O/S went round St ELIE sector with O.C. 468 – inspected gas doors being erected at entrances of tunnels – returned by Devon Lane & Chapel Alley	
	" 4th		Visited St ELIE sector with O.C. 468 2/7 R.E. – visited Junction Keep post – STANSFIELD got up to tunnel entrances, inspected work in BORDER & RAT CREEK tunnels – returned by Regent Lane – R.E.61 cmd situ new post for defence of Hulluch road	
	" 5th		C.E. came here & R.E. about new work in prospect. & went round afternoon HULLUCH sector with O.C. 466 2/7 R.E. – B.Mch gas shells at night – Mpse lines at SAILLY shelled in day time.	
	" 6th		went round St ELIE sector with G.O.C. 46 div. – In afternoon met with G.O.C. to see divisional school at VAUDRANGE	

WAR DIARY or INTELLIGENCE SUMMARY

Army Form C. 2118.

46th Div. R.E.

Place	Date	Hour	Summary of Events and Information	Remarks and references to Appendices
SAILLY LA BOURSE	Sept 7	7	Went with G.S.1 to see site for put suggested for post in HULLUCH road — then to inspect defences of RESERVE line — especially where it crosses Hulluch road — returning by VENDIN Alley.	
		8ʰ	Saw O.C. Australian Engt. Special C.R.E. & went with Webster. O.C. 465 to arrange for insertion of cylinders in line	
		9ʰ	Went to CAMARIN to see to shed for cylinders being put in — visited hence lines	
		10ʰ	CRE went on leave — Major Commander acting for CRE — went to see O.C. 466 & O.C. Pioneers — to arrange for gas cylinders	
		11ʰ	Went to MINNEQUIN to meet O.C. 465 — walked round line with him & G.S.1	
		12ʰ	Went round HULLUCH redts with G.S.2. Selected a site for a cement M.G. —	
		13ʰ	Went with O.C. & Capt. O.C. Special C.R.E. to inspect the cylinders put in line. Saw B.S. 139 Bde	

"HQrs. R.E. 46th Div"   3   Army Form C. 2118.

WAR DIARY
or
INTELLIGENCE SUMMARY.
(Erase heading not required.)

Place	Date	Hour	Summary of Events and Information	Remarks and references to Appendices
SAILLY LABOURSE	Sep. 14th		office work	
	15th		Saw OC 466 & inspected work on scheme in RUTOIRE Main & work in HULLUCH Sectr	
	16		had with Q.S. & wired front line & Hill 70 Sectr members from & previous dumps & light railway	
	17th		Col. Ian CE.1 Corps wfs I & had prepared communications for Hill 70 expls. Saw C.R.E. IInd Divn & arranged hurdling rev work on CAMBRIN Sectr.	
	18th		Saw O.S.1 about cork huras & hurdls. arranged for 2 Cos of Pioneers to assist on Hill 70 Sectn - POSEN ALLEY Willis on CAMBRIN Sectn for work on Hill 70 Sectn	
	19th		went standing to forward W.L. of 468 F.T.R.C. alterations with O.C. 466 around work in HULLUCH sectr & settled site for emplct M.G. emplct & work advanced tram lines for Hill 70 sectr	
	20th		went to 137, 138, 139 F.Coys & altn rounds with G.S.1. interviewed with OC 1/1 K PHILOSOPHE & discussed matters with OC 468 & 1/1 K Coys 139 Bn. - Reconnaissance work with & rear frontings of saturation 1/1st Coys 139 Bn. Reconnoitred road with Q & Q branch & settled work settled site of the road. Hill 70 sectn.	
	21		CRE's frontward & took over work for trial Commander. Saw CE.1 Corps & GS.1. after return in further schemes of dummy front line with Staff.	

WAR DIARY or INTELLIGENCE SUMMARY

Army Form C. 2118.

HQ R.E. 46th Div.

Place	Date	Hour	Summary of Events and Information	Remarks and references to Appendices
SAILLY LA BOURSE	Sept 22		Went with Adj. tree head of HILL 70 sector – inspected work in progress on gun emplacements in FOSSE 7. Inspected KINGSBRIDGE rail head & line inspected CRUCIFIX Dump LOOS – returned by GUNTRENCH & saw Pioneer dug out & POSEN ALLEY & LONE TREE trench.	
	23"		Conference with CE 1 Corps & Corps directors M.T. G.S.I. & A.Q.M.G. & settled rail & tram policy. Reconnaissance route from PHILOSOPHE to LOOS – saw O.C. 466 & inspected his horses.	
	24"		Inspected work in HILL 70 sector – saw B.G. 139 at Advanced HQ & went round work of 465 Fd Coy R.E. – & inspected trenches.	
	25"		Went round part of HULLUCH sector with OC 466 Fd R.E. inspected new B" HQ on 10th Avenue – Conference in afternoon at HQ 46" – went with G.O.C. round tram lines in SAILLY.	
	26"		Went round HILL 70 sector with OC 465 Fd R.E. & D.L. Pioneers – saw work in progress & new instructions re tram lines & trucks & distribution of Pioneers.	
	27"		Saw Corps Railway Officer i/c of Tram lines & discussed proposals with E.I. – C.E. 1 Corps came to see me about water & tram lines.	

WAR DIARY
or
INTELLIGENCE SUMMARY.

Army Form C. 2118.

HQ R.E. 46th Div.

Place	Date	Hour	Summary of Events and Information	Remarks and references to Appendices
SAILLY LA BOURSE	Sept 28th		Walk round ST ELIE sector with O.C. 468 FFVRE & inspected R.E. work. Saw B.G. 138th Bde & "B" Commander in line — heat n.k HULLUCH sector. Work all morning distributing details.	
	29th		Walk round Hill 70 Sector & inspected trenches & trek ways & HARRY road — Saw Brig Gen 139 Bde. Saw BGRE 49th.	
	30th		inspected horse standing. Saw O.C. 3rd Armoured train & O.C. 466 and 468 FFVRE — & O.C. 560 A.T.C.R.E. re work going on. Adj. made reconnaissance of routes in LOOS. — Saw O.C. 46th — who explained nature of dummies &c O.C. 467 & O.C. 468 & CRE.	

C. Humphreys Lieut Col R.E.
CRE 46

SECRET

46th DIVISIONAL WARNING ORDER No. 14

16th September 1917.

The following reliefs will take place :-

1. 20th September :- 139th Infantry Brigade to be relieved by 2nd. Division in CAMBRIN Section.

2. Night 20th/21st. September 137th Infantry Brigade to take over front from our Southern boundary to H.25.d.5.5. from 71st Infantry Brigade.

3. Night 22nd/23rd September 139th Infantry Brigade to take over front from H.25.d.5.8. to N.2.b.8.5.

4. Detailed orders will be issued later.

                                            Sd.G.R.SANDEMAN Captain for
                                       Lieut Col: G.S. 46th Division.

O.C.465th Field Co R.E,
O.C.466th Field Co R.E.
O.C.468th Field Co R.E.

For your information please.

                                       Captain & Adjutant R.E.
Sept 16th 1917.   for C.R.E. 46th Division.

OPERATION ORDER No 35
By.
MAJOR L.J.COUSSMAKER M.C.
COMMANDING ROYAL ENGINEERS
46th.DIVISION.

Copy No 21

O.C.465th Field Co R.E.
O.C.466th Field Co R.E.
O.C.468th Field Co R.E.

September 18th 1917

1. The 2nd.Division are relieving the 139th. Infantry Brigade in the CAMBRIN Sector.
Relief will be completed by 9 a.m.21st.Sept.

2. 46th Division will relieve the 6th Division as far South as NOGGIN TRENCH -N.2.b.5.8., Relief to be completed by 6 a.m.on 23rd September.1917.

3. 465th Field Co R.E.will take over the billets of the
509th.Field Co R.E. (rear H.Q. MAZINGARBE L.22.Central
(Forward H.Q.G,28.d.3.3.

and the work in the line from H.26.c.17.68.southwards on 22nd.September,O.C.465th Field Co R.E.to take charge at 6 p.m.22nd.September 1917.
465th Field Co R.E.will also take over the work in the line from the 12th Field Co R.E. from the right of the 509th Field Co R.E.Sector to N.2.b.5.8.,O.C.465th Field Company to take charge by 6 p.m. 22nd.September.1917.
465th Field Co R.E. will also take over the work from the 459th Field Co R.E. on the RESERVE LINE which comes in their new Sector.

4. The 466th Field Co R.E.will take over the work from the 509th Field Co R.E.from their(466) present right boundary to H.26.c.17.68.,O.C.466th Field Co R.E. to take charge by 4 a.m.21st.September.1917.

5. Reconnoitring of the work to be taken over will be carried out as follows :-

465 and 509 Field Coys. on 18th September
465 and 12th. do on 19th do) 10 a.m.Les Brebis
468 and 459 do on 19th. do) H.Q.12th.Fld.Co.
L.36.c.2.6.

466th and 509th.Field Cos.by arrangements between the Companies concerned.

6. The 465th Field Co R.E. will be relieved in the CAMBRIN SECTOR by 483thField.Co.R.E.and 226th.Fld.Co.R.E. on morning of 22nd.September, detailed arrangements to be made between O.C.Companies concerned.

7. On completion of all reliefs Boundaries will be as follows :-
(a) DIVISIONAL Southern Boundary :-
N,2.b.5.8.-NUNS ALLEY (excl)-H.31.c.7.4.-H.31.c.2.7.
SCOTS ALLEY (incl)-G.36.b.3.1.-ENGLISH ALLEY (excl:)-
G.29.d.7.1.-G.26.c.7.9.

(b) Between 139th and 137th Infantry Brigades :-
    H.25.d.3.8.-CHALK PIT ALLEY (to 139th Inf:Bde)-G.29.
    b.5.5.-G.29.a.2.8.

(c) Between 137th and 138th Infantry Bdes.- Unchanged.

(d) DIVISIONAL Northern Boundary :-
    CLIFFORD STREET-G.5.C.05.05 -HULLUCH ALLEY (incl) to
    G.8.a.80.40-North of VERMELLES-CHATEAU DES PRES(incl)

8.   ACKNOWLEDGE.

                                            Captain & Adjutant R.E.
                                            for C.R.E.46th Division

Copies to :-
    Headquarters " G" No 4
       do   Q No 5
    C.R.E.2nd.Division   6
    C.R.E.6th   do   7
    O.C.Signal Co R.E.   8
    O.C.1st.Monmouths.   9
    A.D.M.S.   10
    D.A.D.V.S.   11
    A.P.M.   12
    Divisional Train   13
    S.S.O.46th Din.   14
    O.C.3rd.Aust.Tunn.Co.15
    C.E. I Corps   16
    C.R.E.I Corps Troops 17
    File.   18
    War Diary   19.

OPERATION ORDER No 35   Copy No _____
By.
MAJOR L.J.COUSSMAKER M.C.
COMMANDING ROYAL ENGINEERS
46th.DIVISION.

O.C.465th Field Co R.E.
O.C.466th Field Co R.E.   September 18th 1917
O.C.468th Field Co R.E.

1. The 2nd.Division are relieving the 139th. Infantry Brigade in the CAMBRIN Sector.
   Relief will be completed by 9 a.m.21st.Sept.

2. 46th Division will relieve the 6th Division as far South as NOGGIN TRENCH -N.2.b.5.8., Relief to be completed by 6 a.m.on 23rd September.1917.

3. 465th Field Co R.E.will take over the billots of the 509th.Field Co R.E. (rear H.Q. MAZINGARBE L.22.Central (Forward H.Q.G,28.d.3.3.
   and the work in the line from H.26.c.17.68. southwards on 22nd.September,O.C.465th Field Co R.E.to take charge by 6 p.m.22nd.September 1917.
   465th Field Co R.E.will also take over the work in the line from the 12th Field Co R.E. from the right of the 509th Field Co R.E.Sector to N.2.b.5.8.,O.C.465th Field Company to take charge by 6 p.m. 22nd.September.1917.
   465th Field Co R.E. will also take over the work from the 459th Field Co R.E. on the RESERVE LINE which comes in their new Sector.

4. The 466th Field Co R.E.will take over the work from the 509th Field Co R.E.from their(466) present right boundary to H.26.c.17.68.,O.C.466th Field Co R.E. to take charge by 4 a.m.21st.September.1917.

5. Reconnoitring of the work to be taken over will be carried out as follows :-

   465 and 509 Field Coys. on 18th September
   465 and 12th.   do   on 19th   do) 10 a.m.Les Brebis
   466 and 459   do   on 19th. do) H.Q.12th.Fld.Co.
                                         L.36.c.2.6.

   466th and 509th.Field Cos.by arrangements between the Companies concerned.

6. The 465th Field Co R.E. will be relieved in the CAMBRIN SECTOR by 483thField.Co.R.E.and 226th.Fld.Co.R.E. on morning of 22nd.September, detailed arrangements to be made between O.C.Companies concerned.

7. On completion of all reliefs Boundaries will be as follows :-
   (a) DIVISIONAL Southern Boundary :-
   N,2.b.5.8.-NUNS ALLEY (excl)-H.31.c.7.4.-H.31.c.2.7. SCOTS ALLEY (incl)-G.36.b.3.1.-ENGLISH ALLEY (excl:)- G.29.d.7.1.-G.26.c.7.9.

(2)

(b) Between 139th and 137th Infantry Brigades :-
    H.25.d.3.8.-CHALK PIT ALLEY (to 139th Inf:Bde)-G.29.
    b.5.5.-G.29.a.2.8.

(c) Between 137th and 138th Infantry Bdes,- Unchanged.

(d) DIVISIONAL Northern Boundary :-
    CLIFFORD STREET-   -HULLUCH ALLEY (incl) to
    G.8.a.80.40-North of VERMELLES-CHATEAU DES PRES(incl)

8. ACKNOWLEDGE.

Chas. A. Hinton

Captain & Adjutant R.E.
for C.R.E.46th Division

Copies to :-
Headquarters " G" No 4
    do   Q No 5
C.R.E.2nd.Division 6
C.R.E.6th   do   7
O.C.Signal Co R.E. 8
O.C.1st.Monmouths. 9
A.D.M.S.   10
D.A.D.V.S.   11
A.P.M.   12
Divisional Train   13
S.S.O.46th Din.   14
O.C.3rd.Aust.Tunn.Co.15
C.E. I Corps   16
C.R.E.I Corps Troops 17
File.   18
War Diary   19.

C.R.E. 46th Div. AQ P₂ 46 D

Army Form C. 2118.

WAR DIARY
or
INTELLIGENCE SUMMARY.
(Erase heading not required.)

Oct 15

Place	Date	Hour	Summary of Events and Information	Remarks and references to Appendices
SAILLY LABOURSE	Oct 1st		Went with G.S.I. round Hill 70 sector and inspected tram lines & tracks - & site for T.M. emplacement —	Trench Map LOOS 36ᶜ NW 1/10,000
	2ⁿᵈ		Saw O.C. 465 & 466 F.T. R.E. & inspected work in MULWICH sector.	
	3ʳᵈ		Went round SOMME battlefield with H.Q. 46 Div.	
	4ᵗʰ		Visits 465 advanced H.Q. & saw O.C. 139 Bde.	
	5ᵗʰ		Inspected work in progress in ST ELIE sector	
	6ᵗʰ		Inspected work in MULWICH sector	
	7ᵗʰ		Saw O.C. 466 & O.C. and railway construction in his sector inspected 465 mine lines —	
	8ᵗʰ		Went round Hill 70 with G.O.C. & G.S.I. & inspected mine lines. Staffs & R.E. work in progress returns by Reserve line — 137 scale — A large party 500 men employed daily laying cable from POSEN ALLEY to O.G.1 at night	
	9ᵗʰ		Went round by the lines with 1 Corp Wireless officer to settle points for trench to terminate a scheme for extension of piped supply to ST ELIE sector	

WAR DIARY
or
INTELLIGENCE SUMMARY.
(Erase heading not required.)

Army Form C. 2118.

H.Qrs R.E. 46th Div.

Place	Date	Hour	Summary of Events and Information	Remarks and references to Appendices
SAILLY LA BOURSE	Oct 10th		Inspected village lines in order to put additional accommodation for Pioneers working in front trenches.	
"	11th		Inspected Hill 70 sector with O.C. 466 — also 800 men from Depot to be employed at night in clipping cable trenches – a funk of pioneers arrived at NOEUX LES MINES for work under CRE Ballasting tramways	
	12th		Inspected R.E. work. - for work on front line trenches in ST. ELIE sector with O.C. 466 T.T.R.E. 300 men from Depot Battalion continuing in clipping of cable trenches Ballasting tramways. 2 Coys of Pioneers from Depot at work.	
	13th		Saw O's C. 466 & 468 T.T: R.E. & inspected Adv. Dump of J.E. PHILOSOPHE with O.C. 466 — 9ml leading & warning arrangements required – Inspected village line Whited & work in dug outs & shelters for Pioneers, work on cable trench continued. My work & with Div."	
	14th		Inspected O.K. line trench & Von OP.	

A3834 Wt.W.4973/M687 750,000 8/16 D.D.& L.Ltd. Forms/C.2118/13.

WAR DIARY or INTELLIGENCE SUMMARY

Army Form C. 2118.

Place	Date	Hour	Summary of Events and Information	Remarks and references to Appendices
SAILLY LABOURSE	Aug 15th		Inspected HULLUCH section with 6-8.1 and HILL 70 section	3
	16th		Saw Bow'n Cunningham 139 Bde. Inspected RE work in HULLUCH section with O.C. 466 ? T RE	
	17th		Saw C.E. 1 Corps (Bg Gn'l G worth who had lectures on firm HQs Attornoon) Saw Lt Pierson & went round St ELIE sector. Transferred to 1st Army. Went in to HOHENZOLLERN & inspected with HE 218 & Q.S.1	
	18th		Saw Bn HQrs QM. Inspected HILL 70 sector & work in Reserve Trench. Saw B9 139 & 13th & R.E. 19 men & inspected plots in town & in a trench in Agnews in Village line.	
	19th		Inspected HILL 70 sector & Reserve line from LENS road by POTSDAM round to our sector. Inspected front line mineshafts, cellar strands & forward line. Saw C.E. 1 Corps	
	20th		Inspected RE work in St ELIE sector with Q.S.2	

HQ RE 46th Divn

Army Form C. 2118.

WAR DIARY
or
INTELLIGENCE SUMMARY.
(Erase heading not required.)

Place	Date	Hour	Summary of Events and Information	Remarks and references to Appendices
SAILLY LABOURSE	21		Inspected horse lines & office work	
	22		Inspected work Hill 70 sector & 3rd Brigade communication trench Reserve line & forward dumps	
	23		Saw OC 4 Bn — OC 3rd Australian Tunnelling Coy — & OCs 3rd A.T.s	
	24		O OC 466 A.T. Coy — Went round HULLUCH sector & inspected work done by Pioneers	
	25		Inspected RE work St ELIE sector & afterwards work at HULLUCH	
	26		Attended conference at Div HQn — discussed arrangements for laying out dummies in shell holes from line at old Hairpin road —	
	27		Inspected Kingsbridge dumps & saw RT1 & saw OC 4 Bn re ditmos [?] bullets — saw Bde Major 139	
	28		Inspected horse lines —	

A5834 Wt. W4973 M687 750,000 8/16 D.D. & L.Ltd. Forms/C.2118/13.

Army Form C. 2118.

H.Q. R.E. 46 Div

WAR DIARY
or
INTELLIGENCE SUMMARY.
(Erase heading not required.)

Instructions regarding War Diaries and Intelligence Summaries are contained in F. S. Regs., Part II. and the Staff Manual respectively. Title pages will be prepared in manuscript.

Place	Date	Hour	Summary of Events and Information	Remarks and references to Appendices
SAILLY LABOURSE	Oct 29th 1917		Inspected Hill 70 sectors & RE work in progress	
	30th	9.0	Inspected Hulluch sector	
	31st	3.0	CRE 38th Div enquiries & afternoon re his taking over Hulluch sector & back Hill 70 sector & returning by Hulluch sector to the 1st IAB Artly.	
			Army Commander's ideas to Divnl – Dummies attacks being use OK used attacks – Capture enemy's on attack with much stronger ideas in 70 deg MG & 2 FW explanations	

(signed) Henry Frend (Major) MG
CRE 46

C.R.E.
;------

2489/165/G

E2723/4.

Cancel my 2489/162/G dated 27th instant.

Moves of Depot Pioneer Battalion will be carried out as follows :-

1. 'C' and 'D' Companies at NOYELLES will relieve 'A' and 'B' Companies in TENTH AVENUE on 1st.November.

2. 'A'and'B' Companies on relief will move back to NOYELLES.

3. 'A' and 'B' Companies will move to rejoin Training Battalion at ALLOUAGNE on 2nd.November under arrangements to be issued by A.A.& Q.M.G.

4. Details of reliefs on 1st November will be arranged) by Major EVANS with 137th Infantry Brigade. Major EVANS will remain with 137th Infantry Bde in command of 'C' and 'D' Companies.

29/10/17   Sd/   G.R.SANDEMAN Captain
                                 for Lieut Col.G.S.46th Divn.

O.C.466th Field Co R.E.

Forwarded for your information please.

                                       Lieut & A/Adjutant R.E.
30/10/17.   for C.R.E.46th Division.

		Army Form C. 2118.
	WAR DIARY	
	or	
	INTELLIGENCE SUMMARY.	
	(Erase heading not required.)	

1 C.R.E. 46th Div.

Place	Date	Hour	Summary of Events and Information	Remarks and references to Appendices
SAILLY LABOURSE	Mar 1st		Saw O.C. 466, 77th R.E. and discussed R.E. arrangements for projected raid – Saw O.C. 465-977th R.E. and inspected R.E. work in Hill 70 sector – to finish work on tram line and water pipes – and Recon Trench	
	2nd		Inspected work in ST ELIE sector – went with G.S.I round the sector + Hus on party from Depot B about 400 men in dugout + Cab kitchen on Hill 70	
	3rd		Went round Hill 70 sector with G.S.I. inspected tram lines – heads supports + cable trench dug last night – In particular new trench tram line – 2 returned by POSEN ALLEY.	
	4th		Inspected Signal P/s & 4th Dyke hinge lines	
	5th		Inspected R.E. work in Hill 70 sector – also frozen work in this sector. Said Bye bye Emmet Scebt & 1/2 Pioneer	
	6th		Went with O.C. 461 77th 2nd ground HULLUCH sector & returned to Hill 70 sector – Saw work on main line. Saw O.C. 463 77th R.E.	

WAR DIARY
or
INTELLIGENCE SUMMARY

Army Form C. 2118.

14th yr R.E. 41st Divn

Place	Date	Hour	Summary of Events and Information	Remarks and references to Appendices
SAILLY LABOURSE	Nov 7th		Went to Hill 70 sector with G.S.O. 3 – visited new Divl. O.P. & fire instructions for improvement – Inspected R.E. & Pioneer work & saw the work done on earth hinds by Depot Battn. last night –	
	Nov 8th		Inspected R.E. work in St ELIE sector with O.C. 468 Pr. Fd. Co. R.E. Saw C.E. 1st Army & C.E. 1st Corps & A.N.E. – Cable trench (?) to forward O.P. & (?) for (?) Pt. 95 trenches a cable laid –	
	Nov 9th		Inspected work in FOSSE 7 refuges in dangerous – & arranged for clinometer examined hinds Hill 70 sector & R.E. & pioneer work Hill 70 sector – WINGLES watch tower & chimney (?) ring by both in thernville bright down by heavy artillery – Saw R.E. 4th Pr. Bn. & 139th Bde	
	Nov 10th		Inspected Hill 70 sector – & O.P. which had been hit by a shell – wet nasty day – examined tram lines –	
	Nov 11th		Office work & horse line inspection	

Army Form C. 2118.

WAR DIARY
or
INTELLIGENCE SUMMARY.
(Erase heading not required.)

A.G.R.E. 46th Div.

Instructions regarding War Diaries and Intelligence Summaries are contained in F. S. Regs., Part II. and the Staff Manual respectively. Title pages will be prepared in manuscript.

Place	Date	Hour	Summary of Events and Information	Remarks and references to Appendices
SAILLY LABOURSE	Nov 12th		Inspected R.E. work on Hill 70 sector & work by Pioneers also W.D. at HQ Armies. Hy. TK ALLEY & HUMBUG TRENCHES	
	Nov 13		had a walk with K. Lee D & Payne around - BOIS de NIEPPE & made arrangements for getting material to BETHUNE	
	Nov 14		Inspected R.E. work & PIONEER work at HILL 70 sector - x O.Ps trench at HULLUCH sector & R.E. work on CHALK PIT & POSEN ALLEYS - Inspected POSEN TRENCH →	
	Nov 15		Examined tram lines HILL 70 sector - saw OC 466 - & 455	
	Nov 16		Office work	
	Nov 17		Inspected 6 & 2.1 Coys me M.G. emplacements - visits [?] dumps	
	Nov 18		Made arrangements for parties returns called & when line strong enough [?] & sent in a report on working parties [?]	

Army Form C. 2118.

H.Q. " R.E. 46 Div

WAR DIARY
or
INTELLIGENCE SUMMARY.
(Erase heading not required.)

Place	Date	Hour	Summary of Events and Information	Remarks and references to Appendices
SAILLY LABOURSE	Nov 19th 1917		Went round Hill 70 with C.R.E. 1 — Saw V.C. of Battalions in line & Brig. Gen¹ 138	
	20th		Went round Hill 70 sector — orderly huts lines — O.P.s & Reserve line	
	21st		2 American R.E. Offrs came & were explained R.E. Organization — Sort R.E. Shops & Went with O.C. 466 to see Company organization — Composition of C.R.Es & C.E.'s Corps — Instructs present R.E. present when inspecting & training	
	22		Went round Hill 70 sector & inspected R.E. & Pioneers work. Also inspected Reserve line from CHALK PIT Dump forward	
	23		Inspected R.E. work HULUCH sector with O.C. 466 R.C.M. & parts out & new wire repairs in connection with the reserve line where it joins Hill 70 sector — Saw Lt. Pimeore future work — are dining Takes line in a new Cattle trough	
	24th		Went round Hill 70 sector with O.C. 468 — Saw O.C. Pioneers are now demolishing in before line — made arrangements to deepen cable trench with men from Depot Bn	

WAR DIARY
or
INTELLIGENCE SUMMARY.

(Erase heading not required.)

Army Form C. 2118.

HQrs. R.E. 46 Div.

Place	Date	Hour	Summary of Events and Information	Remarks and references to Appendices
SAILLY LABOURSE	Nov 25th		Prepared handing over report of Hill 70 sector — wished R.E. horse lines LABOURSE.	
	26th		Went round Hill 70 sector with C.R.E. 11th Division and G.S.I. 11th Div. Shewed them front line trenches, Reserve line O.B. trenches and water pipes etc. also Brigade & Batt Hd Qrs. Pioneers digging cable trench.	
	27th		Met C.R.E. 28th Division & took in CAMBRIN sector. Went in afternoon with staff to see front of sector.	
	28th		468 T.C.R.E. relieved in Hill 70 sector by 105 T.C.R.E. 11 Div. Went round CAMBRIN sector with C.R.E. 28 Div & O.C. 468 T.C.R.E. Afterwards went with Adj. to see work in St ELIE sector.	
	29th		Visited new Bn HdQrs & reported to G.S. 46 Div. Inspection of 466 & C.R.E. handed by G.O.C. went with Adj & Mr Hartwright Silt for dumps in STELIE sector for road.	
	30th		Went round HULLUCH sector with O.C. 466 T.C.R.E. Inspected work on turning water pipes —	C. Wingfield—Stratford Lt Col Cmdr. CRE 46 Div

SECRET

46th DIVISION ORDER No 260.

1. The 139 Infantry Brigade will give up from their present right to H.32.d.3.3. by 6 am, 8th November.

2. The southern boundary of the Divisional Sector will then run- H.32.d.3.3.- N.2.a.25.80., thence as at present.

3. Completion of relief to be wired to Divisional Headquarters.

4. Acknowledge.

7/11/17.
Sgd G.R.Sandeman, Captain,
for Lieut-Colonel,
General Staff, 46th Division.

2.

O.C.465 Field Co R.E.

The above copy for your information please.

7/11/17.
Lieut & A/Adjt R.E.
for C.R.E.46th Division.

S E C R E T

46th DIVISION WARNING ORDER No 267.

23rd November 1917.

1. The 11th Division will take over HILL 70 SECTION from 138th Infantry Brigade.
Relief to be completed by 6 am, 27th November.

2. 138th Infantry Brigade will take over the CAMBRIN SECTION from Right Brigade, 25th Division.
Relief to be completed by 6 am, 1st December.

3. Detailed orders will be issued later.

Sgd J.Dorling. Lieut-Colonel,
General Staff, 46th Division.

2.

O.C.468 Field Co R.E.

The above copy of 46th Division Order No 267 is sent for your information please.

23/11/17.

Captain & Adjutant R.E.
for C.R.E.46th Division.

O.C. 468th Field Co R.E.

A taking over party of the 67th Field Co R.E. 11th Division will be at your Advanced Headquarters LONE TREE REDOUBT at 10 a.m. to-morrow 25/11/17.

24/11/17.

Captain & Adjutant R.E.
for C.R.E. 46th Division.

Copy to C.R.E. 11th Division.

S E C R E T.   Copy No. 6.

ORDERS BY MAJOR R.K.A. MACAULAY D.S.O., R.E.,

A/C.R.E., 25th Division.

No. 161.

Map Reference,   25th November 1917.
BETHUNE 1/40,000.

1.   The 25th Division will be relieved in the GIVENCHY and CANAL Sectors by the 42nd Division on 27th and 28th inst. respectively.

2.   The 130th Fld. Coy. R.E. will be relieved by 429th Fld. Coy. R.E. on 27th inst. as from 6 p.m.

         The 106th Fld. Coy. R.E. will be relieved by 427th Fld. Coy. R.E. on 28th inst. as from 6 p.m.

3.   Taking over parties will meet Os.C. Fld. Coys. R.E. as under:-

429th Fld. Coy. R.E. at GORRE Brewery (F.3.c.4.3.) 130th Fld. Coy. R.E. morning of 26/11/17.

427th Fld. Coy. R.E. at LE PREOL (F.15.b.7.6.) 106th Fld. Coy. R.E. morning of 27/11/17.

4.   The 74th Brigade Group will come under the orders of the 46th Division at 6 a.m. on 29th November and will be relieved on the 3rd December rejoining the 25th Division on completion of relief. O.C. 105th Fld. Coy. R.E. will place himself in communication with C.R.E., 46th Division from whom he will receive his relief orders.

5.   Orders for moves of Fld. Coys. R.E. will be issued by Brigades.

6.   Completion of reliefs to be reported to this office.

7.   ACKNOWLEDGE.

                                                       R.K. Macaulay.
                                                                        Major R.E.,
                                                     A/C.R.E., 25th Division.

Copies to:-
No. 1. O.C. 105th Fld. Coy. R.E.
" 2. " 106th ditto.
" 3. " 130th ditto.
" 4. 25th Division "G".
" 5. C.R.E., 42nd Division.
" 6. C.R.E., 46th do.
" 7. File.
" 8. Diary.

Issued at 6 p.m.

SECRET.

C.R.E. ORDER NO. 34.

1. The 67th Field Coy R.E. (with attached Infantry) will relieve the 468th Field Coy R.E. in the Right Section of the 46th Division Front.

2. Relief will be completed by 6 p.m. 27th inst.

3. On completion of the relief the following will be the new Boundaries :-

    (a) Between Right Section and Centre Section
    N.8.b.87.87 to N.8.a.60.42 thence as at present.

    (b) Between Centre Section and Left Section
    H.32.d.40.10 to H.31.d.72.00 to H.31.c.00.60 to G.30.c.00.00.

    (c) Between 11th Division and 46th Division
    H.25.d.3.8. to H.25.c.5.2. and thence along CHALK PIT ALLEY (exclusive) to its junction with VILLAGE LINE at G.23.c.88.05 thence West to G.19.d.6.0 whence as at present

4. The 68th Field Coy R.E. will take over the forward billets vacated by the 67th Field Coy R.E. on the 27th inst.

5. ACKNOWLEDGE.

Copies sent to :-
  67th Field Coy R.E.
  68th Field Coy R.E.
  86th Field Coy R.E.
  32nd Brigade.
  33rd Brigade.
  11th Division.
  C.R.E. 46th Division.

Headquarters R.E.
26.11.17.

Lieut Colonel R.E.
C.R.E. 11th Division.

O.C.468th Field Co R.E,
O.C.1st.Monmouthshire Regt.

       Will you please have the Machine Gun Emplacements of the VILLAGE LINE in the HILL 70 SECTION cleaned out before the relief takes place.

25/11/17.

Chas A Austin
Captain & Adjutant R.E.
for C.R.E.46th Division.

O.C.468 Field Co R.E.

The attached copy of letter from C.R.E.11th Division is forwarded for your information please.

Captain & Adjt R.E.
for C.R.E.46th Division.

26/11/17.

G.S. 46th   Secret
Headquarters. 9.

C2995.

I have seen OC 1/ Monmouthshires &
report as follows:—

1/ OC Pioneers & OC Signals are
arranging details for filling in Cable
Trench in accordance with our
conversation of today.
  200 men will be supplied from
A. C. & D Coy Pioneers. — work on
tramlines having been suspended
for night 26/27th.
  B Coy will complete new
cut & work round towards Chalk
Pit in Reserve Line if time permits,
supplemented by any men that can
be spared after the working party
for Cable Trench is allowed for.

2/ Re billetting of Pioneers in view of
work to be done.

	Present Billets	Proposed Billets	Work
A Coy	Gun Trench.	Corons de Rutoire.	1 Digging in Pipe lines 2 Work on Village Line & 10th Avenue
B Coy	Northern Sap Redoubt & dugouts immediately to the South.	Remain as at present.	Work on Chalk Pit Alley.
C Coy	Village Line south of above.	Noyelles	Work as for A Coy.
D Coy	"	"	Work on tramline under RTO Kingsbridge. Vermelles & Cambrin.

As regards date of moving billets as

the men will be working in Hill 70 sector on night of 26/27th the move should be postponed if possible to 27/28th.

Can this be arranged please

3. In order to save the long walk on Routoire plain for 6 Cd it would be advisable to provide billets further up than Noyelles.

Will there be any to spare in 10th Avenue?

This presumes that they cannot remain for the present in their billets in the Village Line which is in 11th Division Area.

These billets were never used before by the 6th Division or Canadians & may not be wanted. If so could they remain where they are.

Sgd C. V. Wingfield-Stratford
C R E 46 Div.

25/11/17.

62995

SECRET

C.R.E. 46th Division.
****

1. The 67th Field Company R.E. (With attached Infantry) will relieve the 468th Field Co R.E. in the Right Section of the 46th Division Front.

2. The relief will be completed by 6 pm 27th inst.

3. On completion of the relief the following will be the new Boundaries :-

   (a) Between Right Section and Centre Section
   N.8.b.57.57. to N.8.a.60.42. thence as at present.

   (b) Between Centre Section and Left Section
   H.32.d.40.10. to H.31.d.72.00. to H.31.c.00.60. to G.30.c.00.00.

   (c) Between 11th Division and 46th Division
   H.25.d.3.8. to H.25.c.5.2. and thence along CHALK PIT ALLEY (exclusive) to its junction with VILLAGE LINE at G.23.c.68.05. thence West to G.19.d.6.0. whence as at present.

4. The 68th Field Coy R.E. will take over the forward billets vacated by the 67th Field Coy.R.E. on the 27th inst.

5. ACKNOWLEDGE.

25/11/17.

Sgd.
Lieut-Colonel, R.E.
C.R.E. 11th Division.

HANDING OVER STATEMENT
HILL 70 SECTION

Tramways (a) Supplies and R.E.Stores are brought to the front line by a 9 lb.track from KINGSBRIDGE - PHILOSOPHE to CURCIFIX LOOS and O.G.1 with branches from G.36.a.8.8. to H.31.d.5.5.

This line is available for mule traffic to TOSH ALLEY and from thence to NORTH and SOUTH Dumps O.G.1 by man haulage.

The tram line tracks to these dumps are partially ballasted with the exception of the forward portions) Pioneers are at present employed on this work, Slag is obtained from FOSSE 3 PHILOSOPHE and can be taken by lorry and dumped at FORT GLATZ and taken on from there by trucks, this saves the mules for this journey and provides a better supply than by ordinary trucks. There are no ballast trucks. The peice of line in G,35.a.needs particular attention.

(b) GREEN MOUND TRACK M.6.d.8.9. to H.31.b.1.3. == 16 lb. This line is laid and requires ballasting. Arrangements had been made to supply 40 men from the Pioneers to work under O.C.31st.A.T.Co.R.E. commencing Monday 26th instant for this work. C.R.E.11th Division will now provide the party

WATER LOOS SUPPLY This supply is from the pumping station at LOOS G.36.c.4.9. by a 4" main running on the East side of the LOOS HULLUCH ROAD to the tanks at Battalion Headquarters in TOSH ALLEY and tanks in CHALK PIT ALLEY. A forward 2" branch from G.36.a.7.5 supplying tanks in O.G.1 at G.31.b.2.2.

Protection is being provided for these tanks, the present arrangement being a temporary one. The pipe line is in working order.

Pumping hours are issued by Brigade.

HYTHE ALLEY Supplied by 2" branch from 4" main in NASH ALLEY& The water is pumped from FOSSE 12. The 2" pipe is not buried. This supply is not working at present owing to trouble at the pumping station. This is being attended to by C.R.E.1st.Corps Troops.

FOSSE 7 SUPPLY 2" branches from the main across the LA RUTOIRE Plain supply a 300 Gall.tank at G.28.c.9.1. (Advanced Field Co.H.Q.) to tanks at G.28.b.7.1.and to tanks in GUN TRENCH at G.30.a.1.5.

ROADS LENS BETHUNE ROAD. This is in good condition. Road should be patrolled as settlements frequently occur where trenches run under road.

CROSS ROADS at.G.34.d.7.7. to FORT GLATZ. This is in fair condition, from FORT GLATZ to the CRUCIFIX the road is bad.

HARRY ROAD From CRUICFIX through LOOS to O.G.1 is in fair condition and suitable for horse transport.

LOOS HULLUCH ROAD It is intended to use this road in the event of an advance, it is in a fair condition (See copy of report attached).

TRACKS /

TRACKS   The only track in this Section is shewn on accompanying map, the bridges are in good repair, but the mud track during wet weather is not fit for use.

VILLAGE LINE   Provides dugout accommoadation and Machine Gun defence for selected localities. The connecting trench has not been maintained, but is wired in front.

COMMUNICATION TRENCHES

RAILWAY ALLEY is in a good condition and the only one which has been worked on from the VILLAGE LINE to the front.

/11/17.

Brig-General
C.R.E. 48th Division.

CRE 46th Division
WO R6 462
Vol 17

Army Form C. 2118.

WAR DIARY
or
INTELLIGENCE SUMMARY.
(Erase heading not required.)

Place	Date	Hour	Summary of Events and Information	Remarks and references to Appendices
SAILLY LABOURSE	1.2nd		Went round Cambrin Sector with OC 105 Field Co R.E. (25th Division) & saw R.E. work in progress. 466th Field Co also accommodated this sector.	
	" 2nd		Went round Cambrin Sector with C.O.C. & R.C. of 8th Bde. (25th Division) 468th Field Co moved to Annequin taking over of the Cambrin sector from 105th Field Co.	
	" 3rd		G.O.C. inspected 465th Field Coys transport. Funeral of Col Tweeps OC 5th S Staffs. Went to Annequin with Adjutant to see 468th Field Co in new billets.	
	" 4th		Inspected St Elie Sector. Inspected Junction Keep & Lys Bns HQrs. Attended conference at Divisional H.Q.	
	" 5th		Inspected the billets of 1st Monmouths in Annequin & Cambrin. Arranged for more accommodation in Cambrin sector. Went with D.A.A.G. in afternoon to visit question of billeting areas.	
	" 6th		Saw OC 466th Field Co at Mazingarbe with reference of new second in command of the Company & water supply in Hulluch Sector. Met C.R.E. 42nd Division at Cambrin in the afternoon with reference to billeting area.	

Army Form C. 2118.

E.R. 46th Division

WAR DIARY
or
INTELLIGENCE SUMMARY.
(Erase heading not required.)

Instructions regarding War Diaries and Intelligence Summaries are contained in F.S. Regs., Part II. and the Staff Manual respectively. Title pages will be prepared in manuscript.

Place	Date	Hour	Summary of Events and Information	Remarks and references to Appendices
Sailly Labourse	Dec 6th		Adjutant inspected with Cambrin Scots	
		7th	Went to see demonstration for Mons Raid at Souchez: Went to relieve by G.S.O.I. First Army on Mortuary Station	
	" 8th		Visits Each Pit Alley & Trellis of 'A' Company 10th Monmouths, saw O.C. reserves having water pipes. Examined Pope Line & works in front. Went to lecture at First Corps School on the Battle of Cambrai.	
	" 9th		Office Work, saw O.C. 10th Monmouths & Machine Gun. Cmpds.	
	" 10th		Inspection of 468th Field Co. Transport by G.O.C. Inspected Cambrin sector with Adjt., saw Fountain Kepp Water supply tanks on railway cutting & advanced trellis of 468th Field Co. Inspected ballasting of tram line	
7th/11/14			Two successful dummy raids carried out, in conjunction with raid by 139th Inf Bde. owing to damage to frames on the Northern Dummy front. Only both covers 100 figures & displayed them in Drummond trench. Heavy shelling of working party.	
	" 19th		Went round Village Line in Cambrin Sector with G.O.C. & G.S.O.I. Visited O.C. Battalion who carried out raid. Saw O.C. 468 Field Co. & O.C. 465th Field Co.	

WAR DIARY
or
INTELLIGENCE SUMMARY

Army Form C. 2118.

C.R.E. 46th Division

Place	Date	Hour	Summary of Events and Information	Remarks and references to Appendices
Sally Labourd	Feb 13		SAVILE Tunnel blown in during night by T.M. fire. Inspected same with Adjt. in the morning & reported damage to C.R.E. Saw O.C. I Corps. C.R.E. & C.O. 138th Bde. with reference to repair works.	
	14th		Inspected pipe lines in 137th Bde. Sector & Chak Pit Alley to see site of new M.Gun Emplacements.	
	15th		Went with Adjt. to SAVILE Tunnel to make report for C.R.E. on works done during the night, on clearing tunnel & on new trench from Basin Alley to SAVILE Row. Went to Toulouse in afternoon at HOUDAIN on co-operation between R.E. & Infantry. O.C. Pioneers & Adjt. R.E. also attended. Tea with O.C. First Army.	
	16th		Adjt. went to SAVILE Tunnel to report progress of works during the night.	
	17th		Snow. Adjt. reconnoitred roads in Cambrin Sector with view of making dumps of wire & pickets, for wiring Village Line. Saw O.C. 1st Monmouths re works for 18th inst.	

WAR DIARY
or
INTELLIGENCE SUMMARY.
(Erase heading not required.)

Army Form C. 2118.

Instructions regarding War Diaries and Intelligence Summaries are contained in F. S. Regs., Part II. and the Staff Manual respectively. Title pages will be prepared in manuscript.

Place	Date	Hour	Summary of Events and Information	Remarks and references to Appendices
	18th		Went round Village Line with OC Monmouths. Saw OC 468 Field Co & works in Les Flectus	
	19th		Visited Tooo 7 Water Supply with Adjt. Saw new OC G Enples Clash Pri Alley. Inspected Tool Alley Water Supply. Reported latts to G.S.	
	20th		Adjt met Corps Water Supply Officer & OC 466 Field Co at Tooo 7 to advise what could be done to thaw Pipe Line. GSO I inspected RE workshops. Saw OC 170th Tunnelling Co. & discussed SOULE Tunnel dugout scheme.	
	21st		CRE went on tour with BG, 138th Bde & ADMS.	
	22nd		Adjt inspected Tool Alley Water Supply & MG Emple in Chalk Pri Alley. OC 468 Field Co visited Southern Part of Village Line in Les Flectus. Adjt saw GSOI. BETHUNE heavily bombed.	
	23rd		Saw GSOI. Office work in morning, went to DAC Hendykio to advise on new Trench in camp. Saw OC Monmouths with reference	

Army Form C. 2118.

WAR DIARY
or
INTELLIGENCE SUMMARY.
(Erase heading not required.)

Place	Date	Hour	Summary of Events and Information	Remarks and references to Appendices
Office Work.	Dec 24			
	25th		Snow Early. Started making snow plough. Christmas Dinner for Workshops Personnel.	
	26th		A.A. stopped in each and foot. Saw G.S.O.1 in the morning. Made arrangements for Glass Juice C.o. R.E. to see Norscism Regt at Villot Rinl in Cambrin Sector. Walks got through to Chain Pey Alley from LOOS.	
	27th		A.A. inspected Bath Lows at ANEQUIN. Saw Ad/C.R.E. went to rehard BETHUNE in afternoon to inspect stock of Forest timbers.	
	28th		Inspected work in Cambrin Sector, walked along new trench from Barts to Sasete & went in tunnel Inspected 4 Water mains returned via Cambrin. A.A. went with C.R.E. to Headquarters to explain organisation of R.E. to American General & Staff.	

WAR DIARY
or
INTELLIGENCE SUMMARY.

Army Form C. 2118.

CRE 4 Division

Place	Date	Hour	Summary of Events and Information	Remarks and references to Appendices
SAILLY	Dec 29	A.M.	Went with D.A.Q.M.G. to fix up new clothes store in SAILLY. Showed American Staff over workshops. Fosse 12, Kingsbridge Mine Yard & 109 Army Workshops BETHUNE. Explained how stores are got up to the line. Office work in afternoon.	
	" 30		A/y inspected Fosse 12. Office work.	
LABOURSE	" 31		Inspected 468th Field Co Transport Line & other Horse Lines in LABOURSE, Railhead & Ammunition Refilling Point. Saw O.C. 1 H Monmouths with reference to works in the Cambrin Sector. Capt wrote War Diary.	

C.R.E. Hand 9th 46th Div.

HQ RE 46D
9/1/18

WAR DIARY
or
INTELLIGENCE SUMMARY.
(Erase heading not required.)

Army Form C. 2118.

Place	Date	Hour	Summary of Events and Information	Remarks and references to Appendices
SAILLY LABOURSE	Jan 1st 1918		Fine. Snow & hoar frost on track. —	
		2"	Inspected ST ELIE sects. & CAMBRIN sects. & SAVILE tunnel & fine work. & to MAEUX - LES - MINES kit & put RE. work.	
		3"	and 1 Coy & walked with Officers at FOSSE 7. & walked up to 4th p'due line. Also saw O.C. 566. A.T. (CRE LOC, Minereo.	
		5"	Inspected MEDX. LES MINES camp. — Ammunition refilling point & railhead with B.A.G.M.G. — Saw B/OC re wiring of 4th line.	
		6"	Exped returns for leave. Saw B.G.C. 465 - 468. at Chalon	
		7"	Out & drove to visit French & others school de Genie. & refresh on new pond.	
		8"	Adutee. work normal — heavy fall of snow	
		9"	Adj. to Poiden & his hd. work in M.G. emplam. & Chalk Pit. Alley & village has being. — Heavy snow & very cold	
		10"	To BONEI with B.G.M. & to arrange for billets & Drill Gd.	

WAR DIARY
INTELLIGENCE SUMMARY

Army Form C. 2118.

C.R.E. 46th Divn.

Place	Date	Hour	Summary of Events and Information	Remarks and references to Appendices
SAILLY LABOURSE	Jan 11th		— nothing special —	
	19th		Went to BURNES with D.A.S.M.G. & Lts 465 & 466 — arranged billets	
	12th		CRE returned from CHALONS. Saw G.O.C. R.A.S.I. & reported re visit to French school	
	13th		Went to I Corps to discuss work on a 2nd Army line of defence	
	14th		reconnoitred Army line with G.O.C. & E.S.I from HOUCHIN to BEUVRY	
	15th		Very wet day	
	16th		Continued reconnaissance of Army line — heavy fall of broken during evening & thaws. Arranged for R.E.s & pioneers to clear same.	
	17th		Officers R.E. & D.M.G.O. 46th Divn visited portions of Maclean from Corps line. Saw B.G. 138 Bde & went to head of CAMBRIN sector	
	18th		Went with staff to fix sites for dumps of material to build new Army Line	
	19th		Preparing report on Army line — should receive subsidies in form	

C.R.E 46th div

Army Form C. 2118.

WAR DIARY
or
INTELLIGENCE SUMMARY.
(Erase heading not required.)

Place	Date	Hour	Summary of Events and Information	Remarks and references to Appendices
SAILLY LABOURSE	Jan 20" 1918	21-	C.R.E. 1st div came to see round yard and hutting area — went to see O.C. 468 Coy and hutting lines 466 37th Coy saw O.C. 465 & 466. Inspected site for new Hns H.Qrs. dug out. PHILOSOPHE.	
		22-	Went to see C.E. 1 Corps re Q.I. Corps on him line — went in afternoon with Bt. 465 & 7th Coy, D.M.G.O. 46 div & O.C. front M.G. position & made arrangements for tethring out.	
		23J	465 & 7th Coy moved to BETHUNE to work on line — moved to BUSNES.	
BUSNES		24h	Went with O.C. 465 & 7th Coy round head of Army line.	
		25d	Went to Army line — fixing details with O.C. 465 — Ali to GOMMECOURT re site for obs' corps.	
		26h	Went to H.Q.n 2° Canadian div: at Lem Pigare re fixing defence where boundary between Corps came — also heads went head of Army line.	

CRE 4th Div.

Army Form C. 2118.

WAR DIARY
or
INTELLIGENCE SUMMARY.

(Erase heading not required.)

Place	Date	Hour	Summary of Events and Information	Remarks and references to Appendices
BUSNES	Jan 27		Went to HOUCHIN to meet CRE 3 Canadian – he will sort out sitting on Canadian Corps Mining and permits. – Went on with OC 466 Field Coy & Div M.G.O. 4th and Army lines – went to see C.E. 1 Corps & his hutors work on Army line – Saw OC 466 & 466	
	28		him him of 466 FCoy at BUSNES	
	29		Inspected of work on Army line	
	30		du – & 1st Intrepids to make arrangements for parties in wires for Germans – arranged for this with Town Major VAUDRICOURT – 2 Officer & 20 R.E.s went to help 2 Bns of 139 Bde to work on parts in C.E. 1 Corps at VERMELLES.	
	31		Presentation of Summons or by 1st Army Commander at Div HQrs. – CB AdC to CRE & 2 a to Mil.Corps K 4th Army R.E. 4th divs – Went as alkokads to 1 Corps & walked round heads of then line with C.E. 1 Corps.	

© Major JS Matthews RE AD 466 Coy

S E C R E T

O.C. 46th Divisional Train.
S.S.O. 46th Division.

The following moves will take place :-

465 Field Co R.E. will move to BUSNES on January 17th.
466 Field Co R.E.   "   "   "   "   "   "   17th.
468 Field Co R.E.   "   "   " LABOURSE   "   17th.
Headquarters R.E.   "   "   " BUSNES   "   18th.

[signature]
Captain & Adjutant R.E.
for C.R.E. 46th Division.

15/1/18.
Copy to A.D.M.S.
        D.A.D.V.S.
        A.P.M.

S E C R E T.

46th DIVISION WARNING ORDER NO 274.
================================

6th January, 1918.

The 46th Division will be relieved in the line by the 11th Division: the relief will probably commence on 16th January. Further orders will be issued later to all concerned.

Sd. G.R.Sandeman, Captain.
General Staff 46th Division.

2.

O.C.465 Field Co R.E.
O.C.466 Field Co R.E.
O.C.468 Field Co R.E.

For information.

Captain & Adjutant R.E.
for C.R.E.46th Division.

6/1/18.

46th. Division. No. A2510/491

C.R.E.
O.C., 1st. Monmouth Regt.
'G'
****

    It has been arranged that the personnel employed with the Tramways shall be relieved on the 19th. instant by the 11th. Division.
    Officers and men of the 1st. Monmouth Regt. should rejoin their unit at NOEUX LES MINES on that date.

12th. Jany. 1918.

Lieutenant Colonel,
A.A. & Q.M.G., 46th. Division...

SECRET
O.C.465 Field Co R.E.
O.C.466 Field Co R.E.
O.C.468 Field Co R.E.

Reference Operation Order No 40

The reliefs of the Field Coys will be carried out as per attached table.

ACKNOWLEDGE.

Chas. A. Hurton
Captain & Adjutant R.E.
for C.R.E. 46th Division.

18/1/18.

Copy to Headquarters "G"
                       "Q"
       C.R.E. 11th Division.
       C.E. 1.Corps.
       46th Divisional Train.
       S.S.O.
       War Diary.
       File.

Name of Unit	To be relieved by	Date	Remarks
465 Field Co RE	86th Field Co RE.	22nd	465 Field Co R.E. with transport will be billeted in BETHUNE. (details later
466 Field Co RE	68th Field Co RE.	24th	466 Field Co R.E. with transport to march to BUSNES.
468 Field Co RE	67th Field Co RE.	24th	468 Field Co R.E. to move to LABOURSE - Horse Lines at VERQUIN (To be taken over from 68th Field Co R.E.) Relief to be completed by noon.
68th Field Co R.E.	468 Field Co RE	24th	

O.C.465 Field Co R.E.

   Please arrange for a billeting party to see the Town Major of BETHUNE at 10 am to-morrow 21st, to arrange for billets for your Company in detail.

20/1/18.

               Captain & Adjutant R.E.
               for C.R.E.48th Division.

Copy to Town Major, BETHUNE.

MARCHING IN STATE

Officers 5. O.R. 176

Animals   72

Vehicles   15

[Stamp: 485TH (N.M.) FIELD COY. No C/279 DATE 22/11/18 R.E.]

Major R.E.
O.C. 485TH (N.M.) FIELD COY R.E.

To
File/

C.R.E.
46th Div'n

> 466TH
> (N.M.) FIELD COY.
> R.E. (T.)
> No R.77
> Date 24-1-18

MARCHING IN STATE.

OFFICERS ----- 4.

O.R. ----- 167.

HORSES ----- 68.

MULES ----- 4.

VEHICLES ----- 14.

Major R.E.
O.C. 466TH (N. MIDLAND) F.D CO R.E.

C.R.E.
46th Div'n

> 466TH
> (N.M.) FIELD COY.,
> R.E. (T.)
> No. R 78
> Date 24-1-18

Reference. Operation Order No 40.

Move Completed.

For Map reference of billets, see
Location of Unit Return.
PLEASE.

O.C. 466TH (N. MIDLAND) F'D CO. R.E.

HQ RE 46 Div
Army Form C. 2118.

WAR DIARY
or
INTELLIGENCE SUMMARY.
(Erase heading not required.)

Places	Date	Hour	Summary of Events and Information	Remarks and references to Appendices
BUSNES	Feb 1/1918		Went to see work in HOUCHIN - LOCON line - saw O.C. 466Tox RETHUNE & O.C. 468 at LABOURSE - Conference in afternoon at Hofn on employment of what work required to know standings at LAPUGNOY - went to see 466 & O.C.E. Training in AIRE, BETHUNE canal.	
	2ⁿᵈ		Went to BETHUNE to see about work in HOUCHIN. LUCON line	
	3ʳᵈ		Went with D.A.D. to inspect new canal at BOMY - Saw R.E. dumps Wks	
	4ᵗʰ		" " " " " " " " to & to staff 55ᵗʰ Div"	
	5ᵗʰ		Went with D.V. Machine Gun Officer & O.C. 468 to S.E.T M.G. positions on Northern part of HOUCHIN - LOCON line - Saw work in progress	
	6ᵗʰ		Rode to HINGES to see O.C. Pioneers	
	7ᵗʰ		To BETHUNE to inspect work on Army line - O.C. 468 lecturing on works for O.C. 468s under orders to move to new area.	
	8ᵗʰ		466 & one left BUSNES with 138 Inf. Bde in order for BOMY area - Saw departure	
BOMY	9ᵗʰ		Hqrs. moved to BOMY - by march route via LILLERS - a host of a tactical march. Schiena - Hqrs found with 137 Inf. Bde. & Hqrs in order to BOMY area 468 continued its march to DENNE BROEUCK - roads very heavy & in falling wt.	

Army Form C. 2118.

409/m R.E. 40th Div

WAR DIARY
or
INTELLIGENCE SUMMARY.
(Erase heading not required.)

Place	Date	Hour	Summary of Events and Information	Remarks and references to Appendices
BOMY	10th July 1918		– inspected billets in	
	11th		inspected work on HOUCHIN. LOCON line – with O.L. 468	
	12th		Went to 1 Corps H.Qrs. & attd wards went with G.S. 1 Corps to site Tunnelers – Army Line	
	12th		– training in new area	
	14th		Went with G.S. 1 Corps to site more trenches – on Army Line – also wiring of ESSARS trenches – what work in progress	
	15th		training	
	16		do	
	17th		do – Went without progress of work in Army line & went round new extension of line round VERQUIN & MINX FOSSE with O.L. 468 & sited M.G. emplacements & wiring both done	
	18			
	19th		training – musketry, bridging &c	
	20th			

H.Q. 46 Div R.E.

Army Form C. 2118.

WAR DIARY
or
INTELLIGENCE SUMMARY
(Erase heading not required.)

3

Place	Date	Hour	Summary of Events and Information	Remarks and references to Appendices
BOMY	Feb 22" 1918	—	Went with CE.I Corps & G.I Corps round part of BEUVRY to site new army sited new defences on ARMY LINE by BEUVRY - went in bus to new army	
	23rd		ESSARS. HAMEL & R. LAWE - arranged for exercises with OC 429 & 1st Field	
			Coy	
	24th		do. inspected 466 F.T. Coy. at DENNEBRŒUCK	
	25th		D. Marshall to TOMMECOURT to make foundation for Div. Conf -	
			worning extra review for each move of div to take up part of Corps line	
	26th		Inspected 465 F.T. Coy at BUPAVAL	
	27th		went with 46 div staff - on counterattack scheme carried out with	
			our forces & RA.	
	28th		Gett's ready for move	

(signed) Philipps A.?.yu. B.G.
C.R.E 46 Div

SECRET.

O.C. 468th Field Co R.E.
O.C. 466th Field Co R.E.
O.C. 469th Field Co R.E.

The following extracts from 48th Divisional Order No 275 A are forwarded for your information please.

466th Field Co R.E. will cease work on wiring, after 7th Feby, and will hand over to 468th Field Co R.E.

468th Field Co R.E. will remain under O.R.I Corps at LaBOURSE, and will take over work on Army Line, after 7th instant, making arrangements **previously with** O.C. 466th Field Co R.E..

C.E. I Corps will issue further instructions regarding work by 1st Monmouths and 466th Field Co R.E. C.R.E. 48th Division will remain responsible for work on the NOEUX - LOOS Line, and a part of the 466th Field Co R.E. will be at his disposal for the purpose from C.E. I Corps.

Lieut R.E.
for C.R.E. 48th Division.

4/2/16.

p.a / / MOVES

C.E. 1st Monmouths

I should like to know ~~the~~ any arrangements that are made for relief of W? working under the C.E. 1 Corps

C Kingston Walpole
R.E.
46
P.T.O

CRE
46th Division

I saw the O.C. I Coy
a few days ago & he
asked me to allow
the Coys now working
to remain until
the end of the month
by which time, he
hoped to finish the
Bde H.Qrs at any
rate of "B" Company.

You will be interested
to know that K Coy
dug down 37 feet
in 12 hours. The
work was recently
visited by the Army
Commr who was very pleased.

[signatures]
13-2-18

S E C R E T

W A R N I N G O R D E R

24th February, 1918.

O.C.466 Field Co R.E.
O.C.468 Field Co R.E.

    The 468 Field Co R.E, will be relieved in the line on March 4th, by the 466 Field Co R.E, and will move to billets in the 42nd Division area (BUSNES district).
    The 466 Field Co R.E, will march to LABOURSE in two stages and will take over the work of 468 Field Co R.E..
    Two Officers of the 466 Field Coy R.E, should be sent in advance, to reach LABOURSE March 1st to take particulars of work in hand and make arrangements as to billets etc.
    Details of marches etc to follow.

Brig-General,
C.R.E.46th Division.

SECRET

O.C. 466 Field Co R.E.
O.C. 468 Field Co R.E.

Warning Order, sent in my E.3575 dated 24/2/18 is cancelled and fresh instructions as regards moves are being issued.

25/2/18.

Brig-General,
C.R.E. 46th Division.

SECRET

O.C. 465 Field Co R.E.
O.C. 466 Field Co R.E.
O.C. 468 Field Co R.E.

46th DIVISIONAL WARNING ORDER No 276.A.

1. Telephonic communication has been received from the 1.Corps that the 46th Division will start moving from the BOMY Area on 1st March, 1918, with a view to taking over a part of the Corps Line. Further orders will be issued on the subject later.

2. Acknowledge.

Christien Stratford
Brig-General,
C.R.E. 46th Division.

25/2/18.

SECRET.   Copy No. 2

46th DIVISION WARNING ORDER No. 276.A.

25th February, 1918.

1. Telephonic communication has been received from the I Corps that the 46th Division will start moving from the BOMY Area on 1st March, 1918, with a view to taking over a part of the Corps Line.
   Further orders will be issued on the subject later.

2. Acknowledge.

                                                Lieut-Colonel,
                                          General Staff, 46th Division.

Issued at 5.50 pm.

Copy No. 1. to C.R.A.
         2.   C.R.E.
         3.   Signals.
         4.   137th I.Bde:
         5.   138th :
         6.   139th :
         7.   1st Monmouths.
         8.   M.G. Battalion.
         9.   A.A. & Q.M.G.
        10.   Div'l: Train.
        11.   S.S.O.
        12.   A.D.M.S.
        13.   D.A.D.V.S.
        14.   A.P.M.
        15.   D.A.D.O.S.
        16.   Camp Commandant.

        17.   42nd Div:
     18/19.   I Corps.
     20/21.   File.
     22/23.   War Diary.

S E C R E T

O.C.465 Field Co R.E.
O.C.466 Field Co R.E.

    The enclosed March Table is forwarded for your information.

    R.E.Field Coys will move with the Brigade Groups in whose area they now billetted.

                                          Christopher Stafford

                                                  Brig-General,
25/2/18.   C.R.E.46th Division.

Copy to O.C.468 Field Co (for information)

Secret.   G.209/11.
---------   --------

C.R.A.
C.R.E.
O.C. Signals.
137th Infantry Brigade.
138th   -do-
139th   -do-
1st Monmouths.
A.A. & Q.M.G.
D.M.G.O.
O.C. Div'l Train.
S.S.O.
A.D.M.S.
D.A.D.V.S.
D.A.D.O.S.
A.P.M.
Camp Commandant.
I Corps.

      With reference to this office G.209/11 dated 21st. February, 1918, forwarding Orders for moves. Please substitute the enclosed March Table for the one already sent you, for the BUSNES Area. The old copy should be destroyed.

                                           Robert Evans Capt.
                             for   Lieut-Colonel,
25th Feb'y, /'18.   General Staff, 46th Division.

MARCH TABLE - Issued with 46th DIVISION ORDER No. G 207/11

1.	2.	3.	4.	5.	6.	7.	8.
Serial No.	Date.	Unit.	Starting Point.	Time.	From.	To.	Route.	Remarks.
1.	1st Day.	46th Div: Hqrs.	BOMY Chateau		BOMY	LABEUVRIERE.	ESTREE BLANCHE AUCHY-au-BOIS CAUCHY-à-la-TOUR AUCHEL MARLES-les-MINES.	
2.	do.	137th Bde Group.			EQUIRRE sub-area.	BURBURE LAPUGNOY Sub-Area	FONTAINE-lez-HERMANS - AMETTES HURIONVILLE - BURBURE-ALLOUAGNE.	All units of 137th Bde to be east of a N & S line through BOYAVAL by......m.
3.	do.	139th Bde Group.			ERNY ST JULIEN.	BUSNES Sub-Area	ESTREE BLANCHE or FERVIN PALFART AUCHY-au-BOIS ST.HILAIRE - LILLERS.	All units of 139th Bde group to be east of a N & S line through ENQUIN-les-MIMES by ......m.
4.	do.	138th Bde Group.	Under orders of E.G.C., 138th I.B.		WANDONNE Sub-Area.	ERNY ST JULIEN :: Sub-Area.	Shortest routes.	No units of 138th Bde Group to be east of a N & S line through BOMY before..... m.
5.	do.	46th D.A. Group.	Under orders of B.G.C., 46th D.A.		BOMY Art'y Sub-Area.	BUSNES Art'y Sub-Area.	Any roads between following boundaries:- Northern Boundary - PELLEFIN - FONTAINE-lez-HERMANS - AMETTES - AUCHEL - LOZINGHEM - LAPUGNOY - (all inclusive). Southern Boundary - HOUCHIN - PERNES - CALONNE-RICQUART - MARLES-lez-MINES (all inclusive).	No artillery units to be east of a N & S line through PELLEFIN before.......m.

- 2 -

1.	2.	3.	4.	5.	6.	7.	8.
Serial No.	Date.	Unit.	Starting Point. Time.	From.	To.	Route.	Remarks.
6.	2nd Day.	137th Bde Group.		BURBURE - LAPUGNOY Sub-Area.	FOUQUIERES Sub-Area.	LABEUVRIERE.	137th Bde Group to be clear of a N & S line through LAPUGNOY by..... m.
7.	do.	138th Bde Group.		ENNY ST JULIEN Sub-Area.	BURBURE - LAPUGNOY sub-area.	ESTREE BLANCHE or FEBVIN PALFART - BELLERY - BURBURE.	138th Bde Group not to cross a N & S line through HURIONVILLE before.... m.
8.	do.	46th Div. Art'y Group.		BUSNES Art'y Area.	(Probably) Line.		

MARCH TABLE - Issued with 46th Divisional Order No _____

1.	2	3	4	5	6	7	8
Serial No.	Date.	Unit	Starting Point.	Time	From	To	Route	Remarks

Serial No.	Date	Unit	Starting Point	Time	From	To	Route	Remarks
1.	1st Day.	46th Div Hqrs.	BOMY Chateau.		BOMY	LAMBUVRIERE	ESTREE BLANCHE-AUCHY-au-BOIS-CAUCHY-a-la-TOUR-AUCHEL MARLES-les-MINES.	
2.	do	137th Bde Group.			EQUIRRE Sub-area.	BURBURE LAPUGNOY Sub-Area.	FONTAINE-lez-HERLANS-AMETTES-HURIONVILLE-BURBURE-ALLOUAGNE.	All Units of 137th Bde to be east of a N & S line through BOYAVAL by _____ m
3.	do	138th Bde Group.			ERNY St JULIEN.	BURBURE Sub-Area.	ESTREE BLANCHE or PEDVIN PALFART AUCHY-au-BOIS-St HILAIRE-LILLERS.	All Units of 138th Bde Group to be east of a N & S line through AUCHIN-les-MINES by _____ m
4.	do	139th Bde Group.	Under orders of N.O.C., 139th I.B.		WANDONNE ERNY St JULIEN Sub-Area.	BURBURE Arty Sub-Area.	Shortest routes.	No Units of 139th Bde Group to be east of a N & S line through BOMY before _____ m
5.	do	46th D.A. Group.	Under orders of E.O.C., 46th D.A.		BOMY Arty Sub-Area.	Arty Sub-Area.	Any roads between following boundaries:- Northern Boundary. PRESSIN-FONTAIN-lez-HERLANS - AMETTES-AUCHEL - LOZINGHEM - LAPUGNOY - (all inclusive) Southern Boundary HOUCHIN - PERNES - CALONNE RICQUART - MARLES-lez-MINES (all inclusive).	No Artillery units to be east of a N & S line through PRESSIN before _____ m

2.

1.	2.	3.	4.	5.	6.	7.	8.
Serial No	Unit	Starting Point	Time	From	To	Route	Remarks
6. 2nd Day	137th Bde Group.			BUSSURU-LAPUGNOY Sub-Area.	FOUQUIERES Sub-Area.	LABEUVRIERE.	137th Bde Group to be clear of all N & S line through LAPUGNOY by _____ m
7. do	158th Bde Group.			SAINT ST JULIEN Sub-Area.	BUSNURE-LAPUGNOY Sub-Area.	LA TOMBE BLANCHE or FESTIN TALBART - BELLERY - BURBURE.	158th Bde Group not to cross a N & S line through AUCHICAVILLE before _____ m
8. do	28th Div Art'y Group.			BUSNES Art'y Area.	(Probably) line.		

S E C R E T

OPERATION ORDER No 41.
By Brig-General C.V.Wingfield-Stratford,C.B.,C.M.G.
C.R.E. 46th Division.

O.C.465 Field Co R.E.
O.C.466 Field Co R.E.
                                         February 28th 1918.

     The 465 and 466 Field Coys R.E. will move from the BOMY Area with the Brigade Group in whose area they are in at present,(Grouping Table attached)
     Details of relief of Field Coys of the 11th and 55th Divisions will be notified later.

ACKNOWLEDGE.

J Marshall
Lieut R.E.
for C.R.E.46th Division.

Copy to O.C.468 Field Co R.E.(for information)

S E C R E T

46th DIVISION ORDER NO 276.B.

Reference 1/100,000. HAZEBROUCK.5.A.& LENS 11 Sheets.

    The 46th Division is to move from the BOMY Area to take over part of the 1.Corps front from 11th and 55th Divisions.

    C.R.E.46th Division will arrange direct with C.R.Es of the 11th and 55th Divisions regarding the relief of the Field Companies.

    On completion of moves the 138th Infantry Brigade will hold the CAMBRIN Section and 137th Infantry Brigade will hold the CUINCHY Section, 139th Infantry Brigade will be in Divisional Reserve.
    Details regarding the Divisional and Brigade boundaries will be issued later.

    Preliminary March Tables for 1st and 2nd March in connection with above reliefs are issued herewith. Grouping tables for the march are shewn in Appendix A. Further March Tables will be issued later.

    Accomodation tables for the staging areas during the preliminary marches are issued herewith, Appendix 'B'.

                                      Sd/ F.H.DORLING. Lt Col,
28/2/18.   General Staff, 46th Division.

GROUPING TABLE   Appendix A

137th Infantry Brigade Group.

    137th Infantry Brigade.

    3rd N.Mid Field Ambulance.

    465th Field Co R.E.

138th Infantry Brigade Group.

    138th Infantry Brigade.

    2nd N.Mid Field Ambulance.

    466 Field Co R.E.

ACCOMODATION TABLE   Appendix B

LIGNY lez AIRE.......... LIGNY lez AIRE.............. 1200.
    Sub-Area   LA TIRMAND.................. 400.
                         FLECHIN..................... 820.
                         FLECHINELLE................. 350.
                         ESTREE BLANCHE.............. 300.
                         PIPPERONT................... 580.

AUCHY AU BOIS........... AUCHY AU BOIS............... 1000.
    Sub-Area.   WESTREHEM................... 800.
                         FONTAINE les HERMANS........ 2150.
                         NEDONCHELLE................. 800.
                         PEIFS....................... 600.
                         FEBVIN...................... 1270.

BUSNES.................. BUSNES......................
    Sub-Area.   BUSNETTES...................
                         L'ECLEME....................
                         CANTRAINNE..................
                         LE HAMEL.&
                         LENGLET.....................

HAM EN ARTOIS........... HAM EN ARTOIS...............
    Sub-Area.   ECQUEDECQUES................
                         & adjoining villages. (These villages will be
                                                notified later).

MARCH TABLE.

1	2	3	4	5	6	7
Serial Number.	Unit	Date	From	To	Route	Remarks.
1	138th I.Bde Group.	1st March.	BOMY Area. (WANDONNE)	LIGNY lez AIRE Area.	Any	
2.	137th I.Bde Group.	1st March.	BOMY Area. (EQUIRRE)	AUCHY au BOIS Area	Any	
3.	138th I.Bde Group.	2nd March.	LIGNY lez AIRE.	HAM en ARTOIS Area and ECQUEDECQUES.	Any	No Units of 138th I.Bde Group to be east of a N.&.S line through AUCHY au BOIS before 11-30 am. To be clear of a N.&.S line through WESTREHEM by 1 pm.
4.	137th I.Bde Group.	2nd March.	AUCHY au BOIS.	BUSNES Sub-Area.	Any	All Units of 137th I.Bde Group to be east of a N.&.S line through AUCHY au BOIS by 11 am.
5.	46th M.G.Bn.	2nd March.	BOMY Area.	AUCHY au BOIS. Area	Any	Not to cross a N.&.S.line through WESTREHEM before 1 pm.

MESSAGES AND SIGNALS.

TO: C.R.E. 46th DIVISION

Sender's Number.	Day of Month.	In reply to Number.	A A A
* EB115	26-2-18	E3575/1A	

Received.

From O.C. 466TH (N. MIDLAND) FD Co R.E.

From O.C 468th Field Coy R.E.
To CRE 46th Division

Your E.3575/1A received
please,

26-2/18

[signature]
Major R.E.

"A" Form
MESSAGES AND SIGNALS.

Army Form C. 2121
(in pads of 100).

TO C.R.E. 46th Division

Sender's Number: L.198
Day of Month: 26
AAA

Your E.33/5/1A received
& noted.

From
Place: 465th Field Coy. R.E.
Time:

Signature: E. Clarke Capt.

SECRET

C.R.E. 11th. Division
No. 4/58

C.R.E. 46th. Division

Reference your E.59 dated 28-2-18.

The 67th. Field Coy will be relieved in CAMBRIN Sector. The location of H.Q. is at ANNEQUIN (F.23.b.2.1.)

Arrangements will be made to billet the Officer of 465 Field Coy., from March 3rd.

Captain & Adjutant. R.E
for C.R.E. 11th. Division.

28-2-18

H.Q. R.E. 46 div

HQ RE 46 Div
Vol 20

WAR DIARY or INTELLIGENCE SUMMARY

(Erase heading not required.)

Army Form C. 2118

Place	Date	Hour	Summary of Events and Information	Remarks and references to Appendices
BOM?	1st March		Adj. to FOUQUIERES to see R.E. Dumps - & billets for H.Q. in the new area. - 465th Fd Coy marched with 137 Inf Bde Group and 466 Fd Coy with 138 Bde Group. - Snow is running - preparing to move to FOUQUIERES	HAZEBROUCK (Sta)
	2nd "		preparing to move to FOUQUIERES - Snow storm all day	
FOUQUIERES	3rd "	-	Left BOM? in snow for FOUQUIERES - went here 1st Wain be work on Army Line - Horse transport by march route. Stopping NEDONCHELLE en route for night.	
	4th "	-	Went to see C.R.E. 55th at LOCON to take over work - Saw O.C. Pioneers at LAPUGNOY - and C.R.E. 11th div at VERQUIN - also O.C. 468 at LABOURSE took over work on CAMBRIN & GUINCHY section from 11th + 55th respectively	
	5th "	-	Went to see work on Army Line - Horse lines of 465 & 466 Fd Coy RE at BEUVRY - Saw O.C. 466 Fd Coy RE & section of 468 workers at LE PREOL	
	6th "		Went round part of Army Line with Major ZEIGER in ESSARS locality and inspected sites for bridge head defences - In afternoon went with Adj round GUINCHY section & inspected part of village line	

HQ N.E. 46th Div.

WAR DIARY
or
INTELLIGENCE SUMMARY

Army Form C. 2118

2

Place	Date	Hour	Summary of Events and Information	Remarks and references to Appendices
FOUQUERES	7th	Morn	Conference at SAILLY LABOURSE - Called to 4.O.C. to explain situation and work to be carried out in new sector.	
"	8th	"	Reconnaissance of village line by CRE with Adj. & Arrow Officer - Send in what R.O.C. & arranged for carrying out work.	
"	9th	"	Reconnaissance of LE PRÉOL locality defence with O.C. 468 T.Tus & Adj. & Sent return to R.O.C.	
"	10th	"	Inspected KANTARA Dumps with Adj. - also work on S.A.A Dump & LE QUESNOY & was being made - also hose lines 465-Y-Tys being made. Conference at 139 Bde HQrs called by 4.O.C. - A.D.M.S. came to see no front making a new advanced dressing station at FOSSE 9. - arranged to inspect a site with him tomorrow.	
"	11th	"	Inspected site at FOSSE 9. ANNEQUIN - also Bde HQrs in FOSSE - Afterwoon went to see CRE 42nd Div at LABEUVRIERE & later on AIRE Bridge in CANAL in Army line defence -	
"	12th	-	Inspected work at LE PRÉOL locality with P.S. 2 & CAMBRIN to see work of PIONEERS in village line - Saw advanced Wkshops 465-Y-Tys	

Army Form C. 2118

H.Q. R.E. 46 Div

WAR DIARY
or
INTELLIGENCE SUMMARY
(Erase heading not required.)

3

Place	Date	Hour	Summary of Events and Information	Remarks and references to Appendices
BEUVRIERES	March	13h	Instructed work LE PREOL heavily - instructed horse lines of 2/5 at BEUVRY - only went to VERMELLES to select site for new dumps.	
		14h	Instructed work in Village line - a good deal of shelling going on	
		15h	Saw OC Pioneers & OC 466 at SALLY - AOC 466 at ANNEQUIN - Saw BG 137 Bde & went with him to select a new site for Bde HQrs. Saw BG 139 Bde & his new adv' HQ (not in ANNEQUIN FOSSE) - went to DWL RE Dumps at KANTARA - 4 men wounded therein by shelling - Lt GAMMAGE reported unfit & evacuated by ADMS.	
		16h	Went to see OC 466 re plans for new Bde HQrs - Instructed work in VILLAGE line - also instructed wire reputed damaged by shelling inspected side for another BdeHQrs - reported result to BGE	
		17h	Major MILLER OC 465 returned from leave then to see BG 137 Bde - afterwards saw OC 466 & OC 468 - Instructed him lines of billets 466 Bty at BEUVRY. Instructed horse lines 465 & 466 Bty at VERBRIGNEUL	

1875 Wt. W593/826 1,000,000 4/15 J.B.C. & A. A.D.S.S./Forms/C. 2118.

H.Q. R.E. 46th Div.

WAR DIARY
or
INTELLIGENCE SUMMARY

Army Form C. 2118

4.

Place	Date	Hour	Summary of Events and Information	Remarks and references to Appendices

FOUQUIERES

March 18th — Round with Gen. I. to 137 Bde H.Qrs. & from thence to see work on new M.G. emplact in RESERVE line and O.P. at MUNSTER tunnel. RESERVE trench & round O.P. being heavily shelled — returned by Sussex VALLEY & inspected M.G. emplacements Sussex TRENCH — Risk (m new position near FOUNTAIN KEEP — returned to ROUTE 2 at 6 switchalets ROUTE 3 — and new work (m.s) in at ANNEQUIN TRENCH — Sec. O.C. 468 and 468 Tr. R.E.

19th — Major MILLER reported in fit for his work ready to round is his leave. Saw O.C. M.G. Btn. & arranged 5(?) new CAMBRIN trench work with him. Very wet day.

20th — Road with O.C. M.G. Btn. & inspected M.G. emplact CAMBRIN & arranged new work with Lt 4 H 7 7TH. Inspected work on ANNEQUIN TRENCH & Sec N.E. 139 Rd. Ordered work in LE PREOL trench in afternoon.

21st — Road with Staff to recomnoitre site for Dummy road at GUINCHY. by brick stacks.

HQ R.E. 46th Div.

Army Form C. 2118

WAR DIARY
or
INTELLIGENCE SUMMARY
(Erase heading not required.)

Instructions regarding War Diaries and Intelligence Summaries are contained in F. S. Regs., Part II. and the Staff Manual respectively. Title Pages will be prepared in manuscript.

Place	Date	Hour	Summary of Events and Information	Remarks and references to Appendices
FOUQUIERES	March 1916	22	Saw C.E. 1st meen at SAILLY & afterward went with one of his officers to lay out new HQrs at ANNEQUIN JESSE – inspected work at LE PREOL recently & mine at LA BASSEE canal damaged by shell fire – Rode	
		23	Major Miller etc. 466 left for Base. inspected work on LE PREOL bridgehead	
		24	Saw C.E. 466 1st OR E at ANNEQUIN – ordered work in case of attack German offensive began South	
		25	Inspected head of line CAMRIN sector – Willage line & damaged rifle line	
		26	warning orders to be in readiness to move 26/27 received 8 a.m. – arrangements made accordingly – later in day orders to take over Hill 70 Lens & from the Southern River to the Canadian & to hand in present line to 55th & 11th divisions – made rd handing over reports	
		27	Went to see C.R.E. 4th Canadian at BRAQUEMONT - CRE 11th Div	
		27	Came over CRE 46 in interim – Pioneers moved to VIEUX-LES-MINES	
		28	466 & 468 move to LE BREBIS & ABLAIN ST NAZAIRE	
			Went with Adj to see church at LE BREBIS –	
			Went to BRAQUEMONT to see CRE 4th Canadian – Col. Pimera	

WAR DIARY
or
INTELLIGENCE SUMMARY

Army Form C. 2118

Place	Date	Hour	Summary of Events and Information	Remarks and references to Appendices
BRAQUEMONT	March 29th 1918		moved to BRAQUEMONT & both on at 12 noon - went to see LENS ROAD dump & DR 46b at AIX-NOULETTE	
		30th	Went round villages here with Lt. 46b & visited advanced HdQr 46r & LENS REDOUBT	
		31st	Inspected work on back beds & working up approaches with trenches & roads (Organs)	

C. Major R.A.M.C.
A.D.S. 46th

S E C R E T

O.C.465 Field Co R.E.
O.C.466 Field Co R.E.
O.C.468 Field Co R.E.(for information)

CO MOVES.

    Herewith Copy of 46th Divisional Order No 276.C
in continuation of 46th Divn Order No 276.B, for your information
and necessary action.

Acknowledge

1/3/18.

Lieut R.E.
for C.R.E.46th Division.

SECRET

46th DIVISION ORDER No 276.C

Reference- 1/100,000 HAZEBROUCK 5.A and LENS 11 Sheets.
1/20,000 36.C.N.W. and 36.B N.E.   1st March 18.

1. The moves given in March Table attached will take place in continuation of those ordered in 46th Divisional Order No 267.B.
   Distances between units on the march will be maintained in accordance with First Army Instructions.(Traffic)

2. Preliminary reconnaissances will be made and all details of Brigade reliefs in the line will be arranged by Brigadiers of 138 and 137 Infantry Brigades with Brigadiers of 32nd and 164th Infantry Brigades in the CAMBRIN and CUINCHY Sections, respectively.

3. Moves of the Divisional Artillery are shewn on the attached March Table. Necessary arrangements regarding any reliefs of Artillery in the front line will be made by the C.R.A.46th Division.

4. The Divisional and Brigade boundaries, Brigade Headquarters, and billeting areas for Reserve Brigade will be as follows:-

   Right Division Boundary. G.3.c.0.1.- G.9.b.3.5.- G.7.b.2.9.-
                             F.28.c.0.7.- E.30.a.0.5.

   Left Division Boundary.   BETHUNE- LA BASSE CANAL (exclusive)

   Inter Brigade Boundary.   Between 138th and 137th Brigades -
   LEWIS ALLEY- LEWIS KEEP = LEWIS ALLEY - CHURCH WEST KEEP- (A.25.b.32.58.) (all inclusive to 137th Infantry Brigade) A.19.d.0.0.- F.24.c.9.2.- F.24.c.6.2.- F.29.a.3.0.

   Right Brigade Headquarters.- CHATEAU-des-PRES.
   Left Brigade Headquarters.- Will be notified later.
   Reserve Brigade Headquarters.- BEUVRY.

   The western limits for the billeting areas of the Battalions of the Brigades in the line will be a N.&.S.line through F.29.a.3.9.
   139th Infantry Brigade in Divisional Reserve will have two Battalions in BEUVRY and one Battalion in LE PREOL

4. Moves of units not mentioned in March Table attached will be arranged by A.A.& Q.M.G.

5. Arrangements will be made by O.C.46th Bn M.G.Corps to take over Armour Piercing S.A.A.in Machine Gun Positions on relief.

6. 46th Divisional Headquarters will close at 12 noon on 3rd March and open at PRIEURE ST PRY Chateau (FOUQUIERES) at the same hour.

7. The command of the CAMBRIN Section will pass from G.O.C.11th Divn to G.O.C.46th Division at 12 noon on 5th March.
   The command of the CUINCHY Section as far north as the LA BASSE Canal (exclusive) will pass from G.O.C.55th Divn to G.O.C.46th Divn at 12 noon on 6th March.

8. Completion of Brigade reliefs in the line will be notified by wire to 46th Divisional Headquarters.

9. ACKNOWLEDGE.

                              Sd/ F.P.DORLING. Lt Col,
                              General Staff, 46th Division.

MARCH TABLE Issued with 46th Division Order No 276.Q.

1	2	3	4	5	6	7
Serial No	Unit	Date	From	To	Route	Remarks
1.	138th I.Bde Group (less 1.Btn)	3rd March	HAN EN ARTOIS.	NOEUX & VERQUIGNEUL.	Any	1.Btn 138th I.Bde remains at ECQUEDECQUES. 2nd N.Mid Field Amb to BETHUNE. 138th I.Bde less 1 Btn comes under orders G.O.C.11th Divn on arrival at NOEUX & VERQUIGNEUL.
2.	466 Field Co RE.	"	-do-	BUSNES Sub-Area.	Any	To Join 137th I.Bde Group- 137th I.B to notify 138th I.B village 466 Field Co is to proceed to.
3.	46th Bn M.G. Corps.	"	AUCHY-au-BOIS Area.	FOUQUIERES.	PERFAY - AUCHELL - MARLES.	
4.	1.Bde R.F.A. 46th Divn	"	BOMY.	St HILAIRE. Art'y Area.	Any	
5.	465 Field Co RE.	"	BUSNES Sub-Area.	NOEUX & VERQUIGNEUL.	Any	To rejoin 138th I.B.Group, 138th I.B.to notify to 137th I.B. village 465 Field Co is to proceed to.
6.	46th Divn H.Q. less R.A.H.Q.	"	BOMY.	FOUQUIERES.	-	Dismounted portion parade BOMY Chateau 10 am on 3rd March, Stage night 3/4th NEDONCHELLE to be arranged by "Q".
7.	138th I.B.Group. (less 1.Btn)	4th Mar.	NOEUX & VERQUIGNEUL	Line (CAMBRIN Section)	Any	
8.	137th I.B.Group. (less 1.Btn).	"	BUSNES Sub-Area.	BEUVRY.	BUSNETTES-CHOCQUES.	137th I.B. less 1 Btn comes under orders of G.O.C.55th Divn on arrival at BEUVRY. Not to enter BEUVRY before 2 pm. BUSNES Sub-Area should be clear by noon. 3rd N.Mid F.Amb to BETHUNE.
9.	1.Bde R.F.A.46thDiv."	"	ST HILAIRE.	BEUVRY Area.	Any	Details regarding BEUVRY Area will be no later.
10.	46th D.A.Group. (less 1.Bde R.F.A.)	"	BOMY Area. Art'y	ST HILAIRE. Art'y Area.	Any	
11.	137th I.Bde Group. (less 1.Btn)	5th Mar.	BEUVRY.	Line (GUINCHY Section)	Any	

1	2	3	4	5	6	7
12.	1 Btn 137th I.B.	5th March.	BUSNES Sub-Area.	BEUVRY.	Any	To move under orders of GOC 137th I.B and to come under command of G.O.C.55th Divn on arrival at BEUVRY until completion of relief. Btn to be in BEUVRY at 2-30 pm.
13.	1.Batt 138th I.B.	"	ECQUEDECQUES.	BEUVRY.	Any	To move under orders of GOC 138th I.B Not to enter BEUVRY before 3 pm.
14.	1.Bde R.F.A. 46th Div.	"	BEUVRY.	Line		
15.	46th Bn M.G.Corps.	"	FOUQUIERES.	46th Divn Area.	Any	FOUQUIERES to be clear by noon. Accomodation 2 Coys and H.Q. at BEUVRY 2 Coys at BETHUNE. to be arranged by Q.
16.	139th I.B.Group.	"	ERNY ST JULIEN Area	AUCHY AU BOIS Sub-Area.		
	1st N.M.F.A.				Any	To be billeted as far east as possible.
17.	139th I.B.Group.	6th"March.	AUCHY AU BOIS Sub Area.	BEUVRY & LE PREOL.		2.Btns BEUVRY, 1 Btn LE PREOL. Dismounted personnel by bus or lorry. Arrangements for busses will be notified later.
	1st N.M.F.A.					1st N.M.F.S. to BETHUNE.
18.	1st Monmouths.	"	LAPUGNOY.	SAILLY LABOURSE.	Any	
19.	1.Btn 137th Bde	"	BEUVRY.	ANNEQUIN & TOURBIERES.	Any	To move under orders of GOC 137th Bde
20.	1.Btn 138th Bde.	"	BEUVRY.	ANNEQUIN.	Any	To move under orders of GOC 138th Bde

N.B. Distribution of Field Ambulances after arrival at BETHUNE will be arranged by A.D.M.S.

O.O. Moves

SECRET.   S.G./105/G.S.

419 Field Co.R.E.	164 Infantry Bde.
422 Field Co.R.E.	165 Infantry Bde.
423 Field Co.R.E.	166 Infantry Bde.
427 Field Co.R.E.	Divisional Train.
1/4th.N.Lanc.R.E.	G.H.Q. 46th. Division.

1. The 46th. Division will take over portion of the 1st.Corps Front between 55th. Division and 11th.Division.

2. On completion of the relief the Southern Boundary of the 55th. Division will be the LA BASSEE CANAL (inclusive).

3. The relief of infantry will be completed by 8 A.M. March 8th. 1918.

4. On completion of relief the Divisional Front will be held by 2 Brigades in the Line, and one Brigade in Divisional Reserve. 165 Infantry Bde. will be on the Right,(H.Q. CANAL HOUSE) and 166 Infantry Bde. will be on the Left. (H.Q. LOISNE). 164 Infantry Bde. will be in Divisional Reserve (H.Q. VERDIN-les-BETHUNE).

5. The Field Company Relief will be as follows :-

    (a) On 4th.March, 419 Field Co.R.E. will take over all the Forward Work of 422 Field Co.R.E. North of the CANAL, and hand over all Back Area Work North and South of CANAL to 422 Field Co.R.E.

    (b) On the same day 419 Field Co.R.E. will take over all Forward Work in New Right Brigade Sector, from 422 Field Co.R.E.

    (c) On March 8th, 422 Field Co.R.E. will hand over all work South of CANAL to 466 Field Co.R.E., 46th. Division.

6. The Boundary between Brigades will be as follows :-

    A.9.d.75.75.(PRIMROSE ISLAND to LEFT BRIGADE).
    A.8.central(GORBACHEV ROAD to RIGHT BRIGADE.LE PLANTIN South
                                            to LEFT BRIGADE).

7. The moves of Field Companies will take place in accordance with attached Table.

8. Defence Schemes, Trench Maps, Aeroplane Photographs, Programmes of work, etc; will be handed over.

9. Command of the New Right Section will pass to Brigadier-General Commanding 165 Infantry Bde. on completion of relief on March 4th. Command of the remainder of the Front held by 164 Infantry Bde.will pass to Brigadier-General Commanding 167 Infantry Bde. on completion of relief on March 8th.
Command of that portion of the 55th. Divisional Sector South of LA BASSEE CANAL will pass to G.O.C. 46th. Division at 12 noon March 4th.

10. Completion of reliefs to be reported to this office by wire.
11. A copy of 422 Field Coy's. Handing Over Notes to reach this office by 9.0 P.M. 5th.March.
12. Acknowledge.

R.Carr

Issued at 11.0 A.M.   Captain & Adjt.R.E., for,
2nd.March 1918.   C.R.E., 55th. Division.

MOVEMENT - TABLE.

Serial No.	Date.	Formation of Unit.	From.	To.	Relieved by.	Remarks.
1.	Mar.4th.	423 Field Co.R.E.	LE PREOL.	MEURCHIN (E.5.c)	4th Field Co.R.E.	4th Field Co.R.E.will/take over work until the 5th.Mar. Location of billets will be notified later.
2.	Mar.4th.	4th Field Co.R.E.	LE PREOL.	LE QUESNOY.		Location of billets will be notified later.

MESSAGES AND SIGNALS.

TO: CRE HH Div

Sender's Number: N 20H
Day of Month: 2
AAA

| 46th | Divl | order | 180 |
| received | and | noted | |

From: 465 Field Coy R.E.

C Claridge Capt

To/ C.R.E. 46th DIVISION.
138th Inf Bde

466TH
(N.M.) FIELD COY.,
R.E. (T.)
No. R 180
Date 1-3-1918

Marching in State

Officers	5
O.R	172
Horses	69
Mules	4
Vehicles	15

O.C. 466TH (N. MIDLAND) FD Co R.E

From O.C

To O R.E.
46th Division

No. C.439
Date 1.3.1918

MARCHING IN STATE

OFF	O.R.	ANIMALS	Remarks
4	184	1/3	5 O.R. incl. Ambler 2 sick & unable to march

R. Partridge Capt
FOR O.C. 465TH (W.M.) FIELD COY. R.E.

From A.C.

C.143
2.3.1918

MARCHING IN STATE

OFFICERS	O.R.	ANIMALS	REMARKS
4	182	1/3	5. O.R. conveyed by Fd Amb 28th inst unable to march. 2. O.R. proceeded to ALLOUAGNE 2nd Lt

Ashley
Capt.

MESSAGES AND SIGNALS.

Army Form C. 2121.
(In pads of 100.)

TO: C.R.E. 46th DIVN
137 I.B. 138 I.B.

Sender's Number: FB 125
Day of Month: 3-3-18

AAA

MARCHING IN STATE

OFFICERS	5
O.R.	170 } Includes
HORSES	71 } attached
MULES	4
VEHICLES	15

From / Place: O.C. 466 Field Coy. R.E.

MESSAGES AND SIGNALS.

Army Form C. 2121.
(In pads of 100.)

TO: CRE 46th Divn
~~187 F A~~
~~DAC F B~~

Sender's Number: SB 126
Day of Month: 3/3/18
AAA

Move completed HQ Coy 46
N: 54 Billet Busnes
(Map reference Bethune Obtained
Sheets) F.26.c.2.5.

From: O.C. 466 Fd Coy R.E.

"C" Form.
MESSAGES AND SIGNALS.

Army Form C. 2123.
(In books of 100.)

Prefix.... Code.... Words. 10

Charges to Collect

Service Instructions.

Received From .....
By N.W

Sent, or sent out.
At.........m
To.........m
By

No. of Message.........
Office Stamp

Handed in at....... Office 9.55 m. Received 9.15 m.

TO CRE 46 Div

Sender's Number	Day of Month	In reply to Number	AAA
S 64	3	41	
Received			

FROM 137 S.B.

TIME & PLACE

*This line should be erased if not required

"A" Form.
MESSAGES AND SIGNALS.

Army Form C. 2121.
(In pads of 100.)

Prefix... Code........ m	Words. Charge.	This message is on a/c of:	Recd. at ...... m.
Office of Origin and Service Instructions.	Sent At........m.	..................Service.	Date................
	To.............		From ....
	By.............	(Signature of "Franking Officer.")	By ....

TO { CRE. 46th DIVN
137th Inf Bde

Sender's Number.	Day of Month.	In reply to Number.	AAA
EB.132.	4/3/18		

MARCHING IN STATE

OFFICERS	5	
O.R.	172	} Includes
HORSES	71	} attached
MULES	4	
VEHICLES	15	

From O.C. 466TH (N. MIDLAND) FD CO R.E.

Place
Time

The above may be forwarded as now corrected. (Z)

Censor. Signature of Addresser or person authorised to telegraph in his name

Major

"A" Form.
MESSAGES AND SIGNALS.

TO: C.R.E. 46th DIVISION

Sender's Number: EB 124
In reply to Number: E 3614
AAA

Received.

Amendments to
OO #1

From / Place: O.C 466 Field Coy R.E.

To
C.R.E.
46th DIVN

B/F 310
27-3-18

SECRET

The 466 Field Coy will move, leaving ANNEQUIN at 7.30 am. 28th inst.

Transport rendez-vous near CHURCH LABOURSE at 8.30 am.

ROUTE

NOEUX LES MINES.

Pᴇ SAINS

BOYEFFLES

Pᴛ SERVINS.

GOUY SERVINS

ABLAIN St NAZAIRE

This Unit does not possess any Maps of the new area. Can you supply PLEASE

To CRE
46th Division

> 466th
> (N.M.) FIELD COY.,
> R.E. (T.)
> No. R 6
> Date 28/3/18

Marching in State

Officers.	6
O.R.	168
Horses.	66
Mules.	5
Vehicles.	14

[signature]
Maj. R.E.

O.C. 466th (N. Midland) Fd Co. R.E.

"C" Form
MESSAGES AND SIGNALS.

Army Form C. 2123.
(In books of 100.)

No. of Message

Prefix	Code	Words	Received. From... By...	Sent, or sent out. At ___ m. To... By...	Office Stamp
Charges to Collect					
Service Instructions: by phone					

Handed in at _____ Office ___ m. Received ___ m.

TO

*Sender's Number	Day of Month.	In reply to Number	A A A
N730	24		

Ref your order no 43 2 sections for Lime March 8.30 AM AAA 2 sections for Ammo transport March 10.30 AM

FROM
PLACE & TIME

* This line should be erased if not required.

"A" Form.
MESSAGES AND SIGNALS.

Army Form C. 2121.
(In pads of 100.)

TO: GAPE

Sender's Number: M732 Day of Month: 28 AAA

Marching in state

1. Off   162 O.R.

71 Animals

15 Vehicles

From: GIN

Cartridge Capt

46th (North Midland) Divisional Engineers

C. R. E.

46th DIVISION

APRIL 1918.

HQᵈ R.E. 46ᵗʰ divⁿ

HQ R.E. 46 D

Vol 21

WAR DIARY
or
INTELLIGENCE SUMMARY
Army Form C. 2118

Place	Date	Hour	Summary of Events and Information	Remarks and references to Appendices
BRAQUEMONT	April 1ˢᵗ 1918		Inspected R.E. work going on in front line - and work being done by Pioneers in LENS Rd SWITCH and VILLAGE LINE.	
	April 2ⁿᵈ		Inspected work on LENS Rd Switch and VILLAGE line - & ST. PIERRE SWITCH. Reconnoitred CRASSIER SWITCH.	
	3ʳᵈ	-	Saw O.C. 466 ? Coy at his new billet in BULLY GRENAY - in afternoon accompanied R.O.E. & G.S.I. and examined ST PIERRE switch & decide on future action.	
	4ᵗʰ		Inspected work in JOSTRA between POSTS 11 and 16 & work on LENS Rd Switch & village line accompanied by Adjᵗ. Saw O.C. Pioneers. R.O.E gave me instructions for future work.	
	5ᵗʰ	-	Inspected works on JOSTRA & work done on new line - went by CROCODILE & CAVALRY trenches - and by new trench to CORKSCREW - gave an amended programme of work to Pioneers. Saw O.E. & explained same - Same works made.	
	6ᵗʰ		Rode to la BRETIS & saw O.C. 466 & made enquiries re complaint against Major B. of taking their work whilst on march - explanation quite satisfactory & referred same. Saw Pioneers & major line.	
	7ᵗʰ		Walked to walk - only two French to Gun trench to inspect sites for M.G. emplacements to reinforce Rest Line - which head to be put in order for defence - went to Pioneers selected ?	

1875 Wᵗ. W593/826 1,000,000 4/15 J.B.C. & A. A.D.S.S./Forms/C. 2118.

HQ. RE 46th Divn.

Army Form C. 2118

WAR DIARY
or
INTELLIGENCE SUMMARY

(Erase heading not required.)

Instructions regarding War Diaries and Intelligence Summaries are contained in F.S. Regs., Part II. and the Staff Manual respectively. Title Pages will be prepared in manuscript.

Place	Date	Hour	Summary of Events and Information	Remarks and references to Appendices
BRAQUEMONT	8th April 1918	-	Work in LENS Rd Switch – VILLAGE Line (??) on – + work on RED LINE + M.G. emplacements commenced –	
	9th	-	R.E. work and work by Pioneers on Pioneer Keys – Germans attacks No 9 La BASSÉE canal to FLEURBAIX –	
	10th	-	when reserve brigade on 46th divs line to 3rd Canadian. Adj. 3rd Canadian divs came to make arrangements for relief.	
	11th	-	9 p.m. handing over to H.Q. C.R.E. 3rd Canadians – Adj. took over 46th div: Mess & mess –	
	12th	-	Went over 465 & 466 F. Co R.E. who were aroused at their vans. Head Quarters in LE BREBIS & BILLY GRENAY after heavy bound on to 3rd Canadians – Instructed CO BRUAY to arrange for HQ. Wells there – German restricted ROBECQ –	
BRUAY	13th	-	H.Q. R.E. moves to BRUAY – 465 & 468 F.Co to BARLIN & 466 to HOUDAIN approved R.E. 1 Corps –	
	14th	-	Visited R.E. Canteens and instructed billets –	

H.Q. R.E. 46th Div —

WAR DIARY
or
INTELLIGENCE SUMMARY

Army Form C. 2118

Place	Date	Hour	Summary of Events and Information	Remarks and references to Appendices
BRUAY	15th April 1918	—	Companies cleaning up — baths — etc —	
	16th	—	Went to AVEHY au BOIS with Adjt. to arrange to take over from equipment & reserve the amt of early move — made arrangements unloading 466th F.R.E. moved to BARLIN	
	17th	—	Saw all companies — went with Adjt. to select fresh fm to practice an attack — arrangements made to use 1 rifle range by Co.	
	18th	—	Warning order received 3.40. a.m. the units to move at 1 hour notice after 6 a.m. — Div. notice accordingly & everything kept ready to move — visited all 3 companies. Major Hardman O.C. 466 admitted to Hospital — also Lt Broadhead — Genl —	
	19th	—	Visited Coy at BARLIN — saw practicing attack formations & div. musketry — order of 1 hour notice extended to 4 hours	
	20th	—	Visited Coys at BARLIN — & remained training ground with Adjt.	
	21st	—	Church Parade of all 3 Companies at BARLIN — a good show. Fielding to 15" & 9" H.V. guns at BRUAY	

HQ. R.E. 40th div.

WAR DIARY
or
INTELLIGENCE SUMMARY

Army Form C. 2118
4

Place	Date	Hour	Summary of Events and Information	Remarks and references to Appendices
BRUAY	April 22nd 1918		Sapper & R.E. pltn in marching order with Transport at BARLIN – a mg got turned out – Shelling of BRUAY continued & 4 casualties to HdQrs R.E. 1 killed 3 wounded – warning was to this to move & later overhead of line from rijn Re 3rd division & 53rd div. Bde. left of 1st division –	
	23rd		warning orders confirmed – went with Adjt to see CRE, 1st div. at GOSNAY & CRE 3rd div. at LABOUVRIERE – In return saw O.P. at BARLIN	
GOSNAY	24th		moved from BRUAY to GOSNAY – Wrote in same place as CRE Was in our 1915 before HOHENZOLLERN attack by 48 div, saw C.E.. Cpl(?) & made arrangement for transfer etc. – 2" D'AINSCOUTH reported in putting by 465 – CRE. – 466 moved to Tobacco putting. LA BASSÉE canal – 465 moved to BETHUNE – Adjt went beforehand to BETHUNE & found billets for 465. – 468 moved to BRUAY	
	25th		visited ↑ CREs in billets & Pioneers also billeted in BETHUNE Saw S.O.C. & arranged in formation for printing for pionk works – Received instructions	

HApr. 46th dut RE.

Army Form C. 2118

WAR DIARY
or
INTELLIGENCE SUMMARY
(Erase heading not required.)

Place	Date	Hour	Summary of Events and Information	Remarks and references to Appendices
GOSNAY	April 26 1918		Saw M. Pimeiro at BETHUNE & discussed programme of work – hunt from Lt. 466 Field Coy in billets at Labourse – afterwards discussed with Capt. Waite to be him a friends – a good deal of shelling of certain number of casualties to 465 people in billets.	5
	27th		C.R.E. came over Cell – Adj tree Campaign –	
	28		Adj. made reconnaissance of roads in forward area receiving enemy Lieut Thompson 466 Field Coy Wounded	
	29		Officers went Capt to Ram Caus RE dump.	
	30		468 Field Coy relieved 465 Tuesday. General Heath & Gen Atkinson visited CRE 46th Division with Brandon of Light Sun 98 with ref to new line from LE QUESNOY to CEARS	

Army Form C. 2118
Sheet 1.

WAR DIARY
or
INTELLIGENCE SUMMARY

(Erase heading not required.)

Hd. Qrs. R.E. 46th Div.
May 1918
Refer to ref. map. France 1/20,000
sheet 36A S.E. & 44B N.E.

Place	Date	Hour	Summary of Events and Information	Remarks and references to Appendices
GOSNAY	1.5.18		Major E.J. WALTHEW M.C. R.E. joined at Hdqrs. on appointment as C.R.E.	
	2.		Brig. General C.V. WINGFIELD-STRATFORD C.B. CMG. R.E. left the division for England on relief by Lt.Col. E.J. WALTHEW R.E.	
	3.		C.R.E. and Adjt. visited Field coys. at BRUAY, BETHUNE, & LE QUESNOY.	
	8.		466th Fd. Coy. relieved 468th Fd Coy. in ESSARS sector on 7/8th May	App. I
	9) 10)		468th Fd. Coy. moved to FOUQUIÈRES on receipt of orders for move of Div'l Reserve into assembly position. The Coy. stood down and returned to rest billets at 7 a.m. on 10th.	App. II
	12.		468th Fd Coy. relieved 465th Fd. Coy. in GORRE sector on 11/12th May	App. III
	16.		465th Fd Coy. relieved 466th Fd Coy. in ESSARS sector on 15/16th May	App. IV
	20.		466th Fd. Coy. relieved 468th Fd Coy. in GORRE sector on 19/20th May	App. V
	22.		468th Fd Coy. relieved 466th Fd. Coy. in ESSARS sector on 21/22nd May (Adjt. R.E.)	App. VI
	22.		Lt.Col. WALTHEW M.C. and Capt.F. HINTON M.C. & look stock by a shell and both killed instantaneously whilst on the N. bank of the LA BASSEE canal (about 1000 yds N.E. of BETHUNE) whilst reconnoitring the BUZARD area. Bmaps W.D. ZELLER M.C. and Capt. H.J.C. MARSHALL (bott. from 468th Fd Coy.) assumed the duties of R.E. and Adjutant respectively.	App. V
	23.		468th Fd. Coy. relieved 465th Fd. Coy. in GORRE sector on 22/23rd May	
			Lt.Col. WALTHEW and Capt. HINTON were buried at FOUQUIÈRES cemetery at 3 p.m. both impressive honours.	
	25.		465th Fd.Coy. relieved 468th Fd. Coy. in ESSARS sector.	App. VI
	31.		466th Fd. Coy. relieved 465th Fd. Coy. in GORRE sector	App. VII
			The work executed during the month consisted of the following principal items:-	

Army Form C. 2118.

Sheet 2

WAR DIARY
or
INTELLIGENCE SUMMARY.
(Erase heading not required.)

Place	Date	Hour	Summary of Events and Information	Remarks and references to Appendices
Adv. Hqrs. R.E. 46th Div.	May 1918		Refs. No. France ½,000, and Sheet 36A S.E. & 44 N.E.	

Works carried out during the month:—

(1) Extension of Deccauville Track from F.8 cent. for a distance of 2500 yds. to ESSARS (X.25 cent.). This job was carried out by No. 10 Foreways Coy. assisted by working parties from 1st Monmouth Regt. (Pion?). O.P. on the extension of this line for horse traffic is now in hand. The fast track from GORRE to LOISNE was also put in order, and a siding laid to KANTARA DUMP (F.5 c.9).

(2) 1200 yds. of new Pte French track dug and boxed by 1st Monm. Regt. (Pion?) from F.4 b.4.2 to F.5 b.6.6. This Trench formed an extension to the main line of resistance on the R.d. 4th Div. sector. 150 yds. of breastwork constructed in rear of wood in F.4 d.

(3) Inter Brigade Ledger for ESSARS Sector was put in hand at E.18 d.64, and improvements carried out to existing bde. Hdqtrs. at E.4 b.70. Improvements were also carried out at batt. Ldgrs. at X.15 a.73, X.20 a.16, X.20 d.63, F.3 b.55. Inc. battn. Ldgrs. erected at F.10 a.4.6.

(4) Two new Regt. Aid Posts constructed at W.3 b.6.91 and F.3 b.4.6, and improvement to existing R.A.P. at X.20 d.38.

(5) New R.A. Group Hdqrs. constructed at E.18 b.42, and F.13 a.91.

(6) Four Sections R.E. (i.e. the four Bde. Sector) been continuously employed as guards and demolition parties on the canals & railway bridges on the divisional front.

J. T. Pennefeather
Lt. Col.
C.R.E. 46th Div.
3.4.18

SECRET

OPERATION ORDER No 50
By Lieut Col L.J.Walthew.M.C. C.R.E.46th Division

O.C.466 Field Co R.E.
O.C.466 Field Co R.E.
O.C.468 Field Co R.E.

The 466th Field Co R.E. will relieve the 468th Field Co R.E. on the night 7/8th May, and day of the 8th May, 1918, to be completed by noon 8th May.

Completion of relief will be wired to this office.

ACKNOWLEDGE.

(signed)

Captain & Adjutant R.E.
for C.R.E.46th Division.

May 4th 1918.

Copy to Headquarters "C"
"D"
O.C.Signal Co R.E.
O.C.Div Train.
D.A.D.V.S.
War Diary.
File.

SECRET

App. II

OPERATION ORDER No 81
By Lieut Colonel E.J.WALTHEW, M.C. C.R.E.46th Division.

O.C.468 Field Co R.E.
O.C.466 Field Co R.E.
O.C.468 Field Co R.E.

The 468 Field Co R.E. will relieve the 466 Field Co R.E. on night 11/12th and day of 12th May 1918, to be completed by noon 12th.

Completion of relief will be wired to this office.

ACKNOWLEDGE.

[signature]
Captain & Adjutant R.E.
for C.R.E.46th Division.

May 9th 1918.

Copy to Headquarters "G"
            "   "Q"
    O.C.Signal Co R.E.
    O.C.Div Train.
    D.A.D.V.S.
    War Diary.
    File.

S E C R E T

App. III

OPERATION ORDER No 52
By Lieut Col E.J.Walthew.M.C. C.R.E.46th Division.

O.C.465 Field Co R.E.
O.C.466 Field Co R.E.

    The 465 Field Co R.E. will relieve the 466 Field Co R.E. on night 15/16th May 1918, and day of 16th, to be completed by noon May 16th.

    Completion of relief to be wired to this office.

    ACKNOWLEDGE.

Captain & Adjt R.E.
for C.R.E.46th Division.

12-5-18.

Copy to Headquarters "G"
           "   "Q"
    O.C.Signal Co R.E.
    O.C.468 Field Co R.E.
    O.C.Div Train.
    D.A.D.V.S.
    War Diary.
    File.

SECRET

App IV

OPERATION ORDER No 53
By Lieut Col E.J.Walthew.M.C. C.R.E.46th Division.

O.C.466 Field Co R.E.
O.C.468 Field Co R.E.

The 466 Field Co R.E. will relieve the 468 Field Co R.E. on night 19/20th May 1918 and day of 20th May, to be completed by noon 20th May 1918.

Completion of relief to be wired to this office.

ACKNOWLEDGE.

Chas. A Hutn

Captain & Adjt R.E.
for C.R.E.46th Division.

17-5-18.

Copy to Headquarters "G"
" "Q"
O.C.465 Field Co R.E.
O.C.Signal Co R.E.
O.C.Div Train
D.A.D.V.S

App V

SECRET

OPERATION ORDER No 54
By Lieut Col E.J.Walthew.M.C.C.R.E.46th Division.

O.C.465 Field Co R.E.
O.C.468 Field Co R.E.

The 468 Field Co R.E. will relieve the 465 Field Co R.E. on night 23/24th May, and day of 24th, to be completed by noon May 24th, 1918.

Completion of relief to be wired to this office.

ACKNOWLEDGE.

Captain & Adjt R.E.
for C.R.E.46th Division.

21/5/18.

Copy to Headquarters "G"
" "Q"
O.C.466 Field Co R.E.
O.C.Signal Co R.E.
O.C.Div Train.
D.A.D.V.S.

This order was cancelled, owing to gas casualties in Rf. Bde., the Bde. & Fd. Coy. in Rt. (Gorse) sector being relieved on 23/25 d. May).

SECRET   W.D   App VI

OPERATION ORDER No 55
By Major W.D.ZELLER.M.C. A/C.R.E.46th Division.

O.C.465 Field Co R.E.
O.C.466 Field Co R.E.

1. The 466 Field Co R.E. will relieve the 465 Field Co R.E., *in the ESSARS Sector* on night 25/26th May, and morning of the 26th, to be completed by 11 am, May 26th 1918.

2. Completion of relief to be wired to this office.

3. O.Cs concerned will make their own arrangements re handing over parties.

4. From this time onwards Field Coys will relieve at the same time as their Brigades.

5. ACKNOWLEDGE.

24th May 1918.

Captain R.E.
for A/C.R.E.46th Division.

APP VII

SECRET

OPERATION ORDER No 56
By Major W.D.Zeller.H.C. A/C.R.E.46th Division.

O.C.465 Field Co R.E.
O.C.468 Field Co R.E.

1. The 465 Field Co R.E. will relieve the 468 Field Co R.E. in the GOREE Sector on night 30/31st May, and day of 31st May,1918.

2. O.Cs concerned will make their own arrangements as regards handing over.

3. Relief to be completed by 11 am 31-5-18.

4. Completion of relief to be wired to this office.

5. ACKNOWLEDGE.

May 28th 1918.

Captain R.E.
For A/C.R.E.46th Division.

Copy to Headquarters "O" & "Q"
O.C.466 Field Co R.E.
O.C.Signal Co R.E.
O.C.Div Train.
D.A.D.V.S.

Army Form C. 2118.

WAR DIARY
of
INTELLIGENCE SUMMARY
(Erase heading not required.)

Hdqrs. R.E. 46th Div.

June 1918.

Reference Maps - France 1/20,000
1/40,000 Sheet 36A S.E. 46B
44.3 N.E.

Place	Date	Hour	Summary of Events and Information	Remarks and references to Appendices
GOSNAY	1st June 1918		Major (act/Lt.Colonel) H.T. MORSHEAD joined R.E. hdqrs. (from 11th Div.?) and assumed the duties of C.R.E.	
"	4th		Capt. H.J.C. MARSHALL appointed adjutant 46th Div. from 1st June.	Apx. I
"	8th		Major W.D. ZELLER left R.E. hdqrs. on appointment to E.S. Army School of Instruction at YALEON s/SOMME. 466th Fd. Coy. relieved 466th Fd. Coy. in ESSARS sector.	Apx. II
"	9th		466th Fd. Coy. relieved 466th Fd. Coy. in GORRE sector. Reserve Fd. Coy. billeted in FOUQUIÈRES (E 20 b cent.) instead of GONNEHEM. 466th Fd. Coy. billets at CHICORY FACTORY (F 7 a 4.9) received a severe gas-bombardment during night 8/9. The gas poisoning occurred owing to men inadvisedly re-entering the building when blankets, food, etc. had still saturated with gas. The following morning however, many cases of discipline was good & no casualties occurred during the bombardment. The remainder of the company Major DAVIES, 2 officers, 4 GS O.R. (including attached infantry) being evacuated to F. Amb. and one section of 466th Fd. Coy. from L. sector were were withdrawn into rest billets at FOUQUIÈRES on morning of 9th (bridge portals re) in R. sector.	Apx. III
"	15th		detailed in order to carry on the essential R.E. duties (bridge portals re) in R. sector. 466th Fd. Coy. returned to CHICORY FACTORY (clearing one section 466th Fd. Coy.)	Apx. IV
"	20th		Capt. (act/Major) H.M. FORDHAM arrived from 36th Div., on appointment as OC 466th Fd. Coy. vice Major H.T. DAVIES.	

Army Form C. 2118.
Sheet 2

WAR DIARY
or
INTELLIGENCE SUMMARY.
(Erase heading not required.)

Hdqrs. R.E. 46th Div.   June 1918   Refer map, France 1/40,000 Sheet 36A S.E. & 44 B. N.E.

Place	Date	Hour	Summary of Events and Information	Remarks and references to Appendices

The most important works carried out during the month are:-

(1) Playing of 9'6" trestles Decauville track from ESSARS to GLATIGNIE'S FARM (X20 b09) with a branch to LE HAMEL (X27 a 28). This was carried out by No. 10 Railway Coy., with working parties from 41st Div.

(2) An elaborate programme of revetment & repairs to Trenches was put in hand. The main reserve line (LIVERPOOL LINE) being undertaken throughout by the infantry in the line, and the NEWCASTLE LINE (with extension on R.F. over GORRE +STAFFORD Bridges over LA BASSÉE CANAL) by 2 coys 1/Monmouth Regt. (Pioneers)

(3) New Brigade Hdqrs. were completed & occupied for ESSARS sector - also numerous company & Batt. Hdqr. shelters erected in Bn. sectors.

(4) Guards & demolition parties were continued on all important bridges in the divisional sector. A slight economy was effected by substituting infantry guards for a proportion of the R.E. personnel employed. Pontoon bridges are in course of replacement by cork & barrel pier bridges.

(5) A considerable amount of work was done by the reserve Field coy. in providing hutting accommodation at BEUVRY & HESDIGNEUL aerodromes for Divl. Reception Camp & D.I. hwg respectively, provision of inviolable rifle ranges, tubed water supply &c. Also strengthening cellars of BETHUNE prison to form battle Hdqrs. for 2 inf. Bdes. if required.

During the month, a change was made in the policy of relieving Field coys. in the line simultaneously with their all R.P. instead 1st Brigades. The Field Coys. will normally remain 8 weeks in a sector before relief. Sanction from the G.O.C. D.O. OI.P.Y. was also received for the permanent attachment of 1 officer + 60 o.R. from each inf Bde. to a Field coy.

H.T. Morshead Lt-Col.
C. R. E. 46th Division.

SECRET

OPERATION ORDER No 57
By Lieut Colonel R.T.Morshead.D.S.O.C.R.E.46th Division.

O.C.466 Field Co R.E.
O.C.468 Field Co R.E.

The 468 Field Co R.E. will relieve the 466 Field Co R.E on night 3/4th June, and day of 4th June, relief to be completed by noon 4th June, 1918.

Completion of relief to be wired to this office.

ACKNOWLEDGE.

Captain & Adjt R.E.
2nd June 1918.   for C.R.E.46th Division.

Copy to Headquarters "G" & "Q"
    O.C.466 Field Co R.E.
    O.C.Signal Co R.E.
    O.C.Div Train.
    D.A.D.V.S.

SECRET   Copy No _____

46th DIVISIONAL R.E. ORDER No.59.
by Lieut-Col.H.T.MORSHEAD.D.S.O.,R.E.
Commanding Royal Engineers.

O.C.466th Field Co R.E.   6th June 1918.
O.C.465th Field Co R.E.

1. The 466th Field Co R.E. will relieve the 465th Field Co.R.E. in the GORRE Sector on the night 7th/8th June and day of 8th June, relief to be completed by Noon 8th June.

2. The 465th Field Co R.E. on relief will move to billets in FOUQUIERES (E.20.b.central) instead of to BRUAY.

3. Completion of relief to be wired this office.

ACKNOWLEDGE.

Copies to :-
    Headquarters "G"
        "   "Q"
    O.C.Signal Co R.E.
    O.C.469th Field Co R.E.
    O.C.Divnl.Train.
    War Diary
    File.

                                          Captain
                          Adjutant R.E.46th Division.

SECRET

46th Divisional R.E. Order No 60
By Lieut Colonel T.H.Morshead.D.S.O. C.R.E.46th Division

O.C.466 Field Co R.E.
O.C.468 Field Co R.E.

    One Section of the 468th Field Co R.E. will relieve the 466th Field Co R.E., guarding Bridges &c on the morning of the 11th inst.

    On relief the 466th Field Co R.E. will move to billets in FOUQUIERES.

    Details of relief to be arranged between O.Cs concerned.

    The Pioneers attached to 466th Field Co R.E. will not be relieved.

    ACKNOWLEDGE.

Marshall
Capt RE
for Lieut Colonel,
C.R.E. 46th Division.

June 10th 1918.

Copy to H.Q. "G"
       137 Brigade
       138 "
       War Diary.
       File.

SECRET   46th Divisional R.E. Order No 61
By Lieut Col.H.T.MORSHEAD. D.S.O. R.E.
Commanding Royal Engineers 46th Division

O.C.466th Field Co R.E.
O.C.468th Field Co R.E.

1. The 466th Field Co R.E. will relieve one Section of the 468th Field Co R.E. in the GORRE Sector on 16th June, relief to be completed by midnight 16/17 June.1918.

2. Details of relief will be arranged between the O.Cs. concerned.

3. On relief the Section of the 468th Field Co R.E. will revert to the ESSARS Sector.

ACKNOWLEDGE.

Copy to Headquarters "G"
            "   "Q"
          137th Inf.Bde
          138th Inf.Bde
          War Diary
          File.

                                                  Captain R.E.
                                    Adjutant R.E.46th Division

Secret.   G.45/3.

E4564

137th Infantry Brigade.
138th   :   :
139th   :   :

The Divisional Commander has decided that a party from each infantry brigade is to be permanently attached to the Field Companies, R.E, for work under the C.R.E.

2. Each brigade will therefore furnish 1 officer and 60 O.R's (including 6 N.C.O's) for duty as under -

    137th Inf:Bde - 466th Field Company, R.E.
    138th :   :   - 468th   :   :   :
    139th :   :   - 465th   :   :   :

The men detailed need not necessarily be skilled tradesmen.

3. It must be understood that these infantry will work permanently with the Field Companies, R.E, to which they are affiliated, irrespective of the location of the infantry brigade from which they are detailed.

                                        [signature]
                                        Lieut-Colonel,
                                        General Staff, 46th Division.

18th June, 1918.

Copy to C.R.E. ✓

Copy to Coys

WAR DIARY or INTELLIGENCE SUMMARY

Army Form C. 2118.

Instructions regarding War Diaries and Intelligence Summaries are contained in F. S. Regs., Part II. and the Staff Manual respectively. Title pages will be prepared in manuscript.

(Erase heading not required.)

Headquarters R.E. 46th Division
July 1918.
Refce Map. France 1/29,000
Sheet 36A. S.E.
" 44B. N.E.

Place	Date	Hour	Summary of Events and Information	Remarks and references to Appendices
Gosnay	5		Work on Defences of Canal Bridges East & Newcastle Line continued. Two parties of 250 men each provided by the Divisional Reception Camp.	#
	6th		Lieut (A/Major) H.T.Davis returned to 466th Field Co. from Hospital. Reverts to his substantive rank.	#
	7		465th Field Co R.E returned 468th Field Co R.E in Goosnay Sector	APR I #
	10		Lieut Col T. Davies 466th Field Co reports to 18th Corps School	#
			New Line of Retention erected on Assignments in Land for removal of Bn.H.Q. to P.1.d.40.70.	#
	21		Wiring of New Line of Retention commenced from existing wire at P.2.6.7.1. to Sunny Corner at F.7.d.6.central.	#
	25		Lt.Col. H.T. Mossload to Paris on 10 Days leave. Major H.N.Fordham assumed duties of Acting C.R.E.	#
	30		Culverts removed from LOISNE STREAM. X.21.a.2.u to facilitate float of works.	#
	30		G.O.C. reviewed this and concrete Emplacements at Coy. on Sector. H.Q. all to 60	#
			Prepared for refuse & loopholed.	
			The most important works carried out during the month are:-	
			1. Construction of double D.P. at LOISNE CHATEAU Lught no. X.28.a.74. Dye plates & concrete works carried out by 466 Field Co RE. 330 Tons Cement used.	
			2. The erection of a concrete Block Shelter at by 468 Field Co RE	
			3. The erection of Mois Pit Boxes at X.20.c.25.20, X.26.a.50.35, C.5.C.45.50 E.6.a.25.00.	
	8th 10. 12		4. E.C.t.S. FORGE Bridge (F.8.C.45.45) demolished by enemy shell fire. Re-erected by 466 Field Co RE. C.C. congratulated 466 Field Co on rapidity with which work was executed.	
			5. Protected cookers in PRISON BETHUNE continued by 465 & 468 Field Coys R.E	

Std 9.2

Army Form C. 2118.

Headquarters R.E. Maps Ref. France 1/20,000
46th Division. Nieppe
WAR DIARY 36A. S.E.
or 144 B. N.E.
INTELLIGENCE SUMMARY.

(Erase heading not required.)

Instructions regarding War Diaries and Intelligence Summaries are contained in F.S. Regs., Part II. and the Staff Manual respectively. Title pages will be prepared in manuscript.

July 1918.

Place	Date	Hour	Summary of Events and Information	Remarks and references to Appendices
	(6)		General Work in erecting Company & Battalion H.Q. Shelters in both sectors continued. Two new Bn. H.Q. started in Left Sector seeing to line of Retention covering tracks.	
	(7)		General & demolition traces were continued on all important bridges in the Divisional sector. Pontoon Bridge replaced by corks & barrel faux bridge.	
	(8)		Work continued on revetment of LIVERPOOL LINE & NEWCASTLE LINE	
	(9)		Bridges & gaps in wire provided for fire guns of GORRE & ESSARS GROUPS.	
	(10)		Gaps 5' wide, at 300 yards intervals, formed in wire of LIVERPOOL, MANCHESTER, DURHAM, NEWCASTLE & BETHUNE LINES. Concertina coils & gap signs being provided.	
	(11)		Fumigator erected in VAUDRICOURT WOOD (E.28.C.4.6) and TOUPIÈRES BATHS (E.20.6.50.55) Improvements of Toilets, Cooking & sanitary arrangements in VAUDRICOURT CAMP proceeding.	
	(12)		Improvements of Divisional Reception Camp in American Wood. J.E.Q. proceeding. Water supply run to this Camp.	
	(13)		North Midland Dump formed at E.16.a.31. consequent on change of Corps & abandonment of New Minx Dump.	

July 1918.
Trouhaut.

J. R. Forham
Major
Lt Col.
C.R.E. 46th Division.

APP. I

S E C R E T

46th Division R.E. Order No 82
By Lieut Col H.T.Morshead.D.S.O. R.E.
Commanding Royal Engineers 46th Division.

O.C.465 Field Co R.E.
O.C.468 Field Co R.E.

1. The 465 Field Co R.E. will relieve the 468 Field Co R.E. in the ESSARS Sector on July 7th 1918, relief to be completed by midnight 7/8th July 1918.

2. Completion of relief to be wired to this office.

3. Details of relief, and handing over of forward and back area work will be arranged between O.Cs concerned.

4. ACKNOWLEDGE.

J Marshall

Captain & Adjt R.E.
for C.R.E. 46th Division.

July 4th 1918.

Copy to H.Q. "G" & "Q"
Inf Brigades.
O.C.466 Field Co R.E.
O.C.Signal Co R.E.
O.C.Div Train.

WAR DIARY of INTELLIGENCE SUMMARY

Army Form C. 2118.

HdQrs. R.E. 46th Div.

August 1918

Refs to:- France 1/40,000 Bethune Combined Sheet
WB R & 46 D

Place	Date August	Hour	Summary of Events and Information	Remarks and references to Appendices
GOSNAY E 25 a 7.4	1st		A new divisional line of relation from LAMOTTE FMS (X 26 d) to LIVERPOOL LINE (X 28 c) was decided on and taped out on the ground. Laying of the line commenced - to D.A.C. Dragons employed carrying lining materials to site.	
	2nd			
	3rd		46th Div. Horse Show. Toolcart of 1st Jersn Dragon entered from all 3 field coys.	I
	6th		Capt. O'Sullivan (2nd i/c 466th Fd Coy) transferred to 4th Div. on appointment as O.C. 529 Field Coy.	
	7th		468th Fd. Coy. relieved 466th Field Coy. in right (GOSNAY) sector.	
	9th		Lt Col. Boustead returned from 10 days Paris leave.	
	12th 23rd		Chief Engr. 5th Army inspected new line of relation with C.R.E.	
			2nd Portuguese Field Coy. and 2nd Portuguese Field Coy. attached to Division for instruction. These troops were advised to look on the line of relation, thus releasing 1st Moor. Regt. (Div) he look on roads & drains.	
	31st		XIII Corps Horse Show. First prizes won as follows by Div. R.E.:- Poison Dragons, 465th Fd. Coy. Toolcart, 466th Fd. Coy.	II
			The principal work executed during the week was the alignment, tracing, & partial completion of breastwork of a new divisional line of relation (half rear & support lines) in accordance with XIII Corps Defence Scheme. Towards the end of the week, the enemy commenced a retirement on the Whole front, and work on the structure was accordingly suspended on 31st. It was decided the Div. Engr. ie Division as well as the Portuguese troops be lent on repairs to roads, bridges, and light railways as the line advanced. Other work completed erection of 8 More pill-boxes for Machine Guns, and 4 concrete shell shelters for M.G. teams.	

3/9/18

J T Boustead
Lt Col.
C.R.E. 46th Div.

SECRET

46th Division R.E. Order No 62/A
~~OPERATION ORDER~~
By Major H.M.FORDHAM.M.C. A/C.R.E.
46th Division.

O.C.466 Field Co R.E.
O.C.468 Field Co R.E.

The 468 Field Co R.E. will relieve the 466 Field Co R.E. on Monday August 6th 1918, relief to be completed by midnight, 6th.

Details of relief to be arranged between O.Cs concerned.

Completion of relief to be wired to this office.

ACKNOWLEDGE.

Marshall
Captain & Adjt R.E.
46th Division.

5/8/18.

Copy to Headquarters "G"   137 Brigade.
              "   "Q"   138   "
       O.C.465 Field Co R.E.   139   "
       O.C.Signal Co R.E.
       A.D.M.S.
       O.C.Div. Train.
       War Diary
       File.

S E C R E T 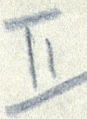 Copy No 9

46th DIVISION R.E. ORDER No 64.
By Lieut Colonel, H.T. Morshead. D.S.O.
C.R.E. 46th Division.

Ref Map - France 1/20,000 Sheets 36.A.S.E. & 44.B.NE.

1. 24th Battalion Portuguese Infantry and 2nd Field Co Portuguese Engineers on attachment to 46th Division, will work as follows :-

    1 Section Field Co and 1 Company Infantry - on Grouse Butts of NEWCASTLE SUPPORT LINE, F.8.a. and c - remainder of Field Co and Infantry on new Line of Retention (NEWCASTLE Front Line) X.28.c., and X.27.d. and c.

    Details of work have been pointed out on the ground to Officers of the 2nd Portuguese Field Co.

2. Working Parties will proceed daily by train, leaving LA PIERRETTE Siding (E.27.b.1.6) at 3-15 am, and will draw tools on arrival at KANTARA Dump.

    Train will return from EMPIRE SIDING F.8.b.central, at 10-30 am.

3. Sunday will be observed as a day of rest.

4. O.C. Portuguese Field Co will be technically responsible for the conduct of the work, and for the transport of the stores forward from KANTARA Dump, as required. He will also arrange with the O.C. 24th Portuguese Infantry Battalion regarding the distribution of the latter on the works.

5. A minimum of 75% of the ration strength of units will be expected to be available for work daily.

6. 2nd Portuguese Field Co will send a Daily Work Report to C.R.E. 46th Division by cycle orderly each evening.

H.T. Morshead
Lieut Colonel,
C.R.E. 46th Division.

25th August 1918.

Copy No 1 to British Mission with 2nd Portuguese Bde.
    2   "   "   Officer with 24th Portuguese Inf Battn.
    3   "   "   "   "   2nd Portuguese Field Co.
    4. "   Headquarters "G" 46th Division.
    5. "   "   "Q"   "
    6. "   137th Infantry Brigade.
    7. "   138th   "   "
    8. "   139th   "   "
    9. "   O.C. 1st Batt Monmouthshire Regt.
    10 "   War Diary.
    11 "   File.

Handwritten notes page — content largely illegible tabular pencil notes rotated on the page.

	Plus week	Queens	Vol.		Dec		Total		"A" shaded		"B"	
	0	0R	0	0R	0	0R	0	0R	0	0R	0	0R
5 June	42	774	—	147	42	921	2	41	40	880	10	198	23	68
4 Leic.	30	687	2	41	32	728	1	21	32	707	+16	193	16	514
6 Leic.	40	688	—	82	40	760	3	37	37	693	9	172	28	56
										735				

112 2149   2   290   114   2439   6   99   109   2280   42   563   67   137

Lt. R.G.Brown   W 6/11
Capt. W.R.Bull   W 7/11

4 | Pte | J.C. Nichols | joined
Leic | 2/Lt | A.R. Roe | "

5 | 2/Lt | Buttles K. 7/11
Leic | Lt | H.B. Byles W | do
     | Lt | J. Coleman W 7/11

68
5·19
1·53
———
14·6

AORS 462
Ref. Maps, France 1/40,000:-
Béthune Combined Sheet, & sheets 62c & 62D

Army Form C. 2118.

WAR DIARY
of
INTELLIGENCE SUMMARY.
(Erase heading not required.)

H.Q. R.E. 46th Division.
September 1918.

Instructions regarding War Diaries and Intelligence Summaries are contained in F. S. Regs., Part II. and the Staff Manual respectively. Title pages will be prepared in manuscript.

Place	Date Sep	Hour	Summary of Events and Information	Remarks and references to Appendices
GOSNAY (near HESDIGNEUL)	1st		Major F.D. POWELL DSO. MC. proceeded Choissy (Wood killing) and Lieut BAKER wounded, whilst reconnoitring forward Routemaps during the Germans retirement. Capt. LOWBRIDGE appointed OC. 466th Fd. Coy. Lt. JONES, late 466th Fd. Coy. Capt. LOWBRIDGE	
(BETHUNE SHEET) E 25. a. 74	1st to 8th		From 1st to 8th the whole strength of Div R.E. and Pioneers together with attached Portuguese troops, was concentrated on repairs to roads, bridges, installation &c in the area left by the Germans in their retirement from LE TOURET, LACOUTURE, RICHEBOURG, and on the establishment of dumps restored R.E. Dumps in the cleared and g.s. trash tracks in the recovered area	I
-do-	8th		Consequent on the shortening of our front, the 46th Div. British the 19th Div. extended their right flank so as to relieve the whole 46th Div front on night 8/9th and during the two following days, the field coys. moved out to the training areas at BUSNES, FOUQUERES, and LOZINGHEM. (D.R.E.O. b/s) respective brigade-groups into training areas at the div. commd's HQ. Reserve. Div. HdQrs. remained at GOSNAY, and the Div. commd's HQ. Reserve.	
BEAUCOURT EN L'HALLUE (Par D'AMIENS)	12th 13th		During 12th & 13th the 46th Div. moved by strategic trains to 4th Army back area – detraining at CORBIE, HEILLY, ARISEMONT. Div. remained in G.H.Q. Reserve, being placed under III Corps for administrative purposes. Div. Hdqrs. Established at BEAUCOURT sur L'HALLUE. Field coys. remained with their respective brigade-groups at BONNAY, RIBEMONT, & LA HOUSSOYE, and both employed daily until 18th in drill and lime-training practice.	
BOUVINCOURT & TERTRY	18th 19th		Personnel of Div. moved by 'bus into IX Corps area. Transport by road in two marches. Div. Hdqrs. established at CAURIGNY FARM near TERTRY	
VRAIGNES	20th		On 20th and 21st the 46th Div. relieved respectively the 1st Brigade 1st Div. and the whole 4th Australian Div. in the line. Div. Hdqrs. moved to VRAIGNES.	II

Sec 52 D.D & L. BELLENGUISE
(A7011) Wt. W.1377/M2931 750000 5/17 Sch 52 Forms C2118/14

Page 2
Army Form C. 2118.

WAR DIARY

H.Q. R.E. 46th Div.   Ref. Maps, France 1/10,000

INTELLIGENCE SUMMARY

September 1918   Sheet 62 C. old & D

Place	Date	Hour	Summary of Events and Information	Remarks and references to Appendices
VIRAIGNES	22nd		Secret warning orders received for the Division to be prepared to storm ST QUENTIN CANAL, as part of the troops of an operation to take place probably on Sep 29th. Reconnaissances & forward area & roads for in hand, & arrangements for bridging forces &c. made with C.E. IX Corps.	
	23rd		Lieut. E.T. MORGAN M.C. and 2nd Lt. I. BLACKLOCK re-joined 466th Fd Coy from Base & rediq Vice Capt. LOWBRIDGE (appointed O.C. 466th Fd Coy) and Lt. BOWEN (to England, sick)	
	24th		2nd Lt. R.D.T. COLLIER joined 466th Fd Coy from Base for duty vice Lt. BOXER (wounded 1-9-18)	
	25th		Lt. Col. H.T. MORSHEAD (wounded while reconnoitring forward roads for pontoon bridges) evacuated to No. 48 C.C.S. Major W.H. HARDMAN assumed temporary command of Div. R.E.	
	27th		Lt Col MORSHEAD returned temporarily to Div Hrs for duty during operations on 29th inst.	
	28th		Lt Col. W. GARFORTH D.S.O. M.C. R.E. arrived on appointment as C.R.E. 46th Div.	
	29th		Advanced R.E. Headquarters established near VENDELLES. See Appendix	III
	30th		Engaged in operations (in conjunction with Division) in the attack Detailed congratulations from G.O.C. & Engineer in Chief as appendix.	IV

Marshall Capt & Adjt

W Garforth Colonel
C.R.E. 46 Division

O.C. 465th Field Co R.E.
O.C. 466th Field Co R.E.
O.C. 468th Field Co R.E.
O.C. 1/1st. Monmouthshire Regt.

WARNING ORDER

The 46th Division is being relieved by a portion of the 19th Division commencing on the night 5/6th September 1918.

2. Representatives from 465th Field Co R.E. and 468th Field Co R.E. on bicycles will meet representatives of a Field Co R.E. of the 19th Division at ESSARS Church at 9-30 a.m. to-morrow morning, and will show them work in hand.

3. Work to-morrow will be as usual except that as many men may be kept behind as are required to load Pontoons Etc.

Lieut-Col.
C.R.E. 46th Division

4/9/18.

SECRET

46th Divisional Royal Engineer Order No 65
By Lieut-Col. H.T. MORSHEAD D.S.O.
C.R.E. 46th Division.

September 5th 1918.

Ref.Map. France 1/40,000 BETHUNE Combined sheets

1. The 19th Division are taking over the 46th Divisional front to-night.

2. Infantry Brigade Groups are moving as follows :-
On Sept.5th. 137th Inf.Bde Group to ALLOUAGNE, LOZINGHAM BURBURE (probable billets for 466th.Field Co R.E.)

On Sept.6th. 138th Inf.Bde Group to VERQUIN, VAUDRICOURT FOUQUIERES (Billets for 468th Field Co R.E.)

On Sept 7th. 139th Inf.Bde Group to MARLES-Les-MINES, LAPUGNOY, AUCHEL.

3. Divisional R.E. Order No 65 is cancelled. Field Companies will move and billet under orders of the G.O.C. of their respective affiliated Brigades.

4. Portuguese troops attached to 46th Division will come under orders of the C.R.E.19th Division from 6 a.m. Sept.6th.

5. 1/1st. Monmouthshire Regt (Pioneers) will not move. Divisional Headquarters are remaining at GOSNAY.

6 ACKNOWLEDGE.

Marshall
Captain & Adjutant R.E.
46th Division.

Copies to :-
465th Field Co R.E.	No.1.	H.Q.137th Inf.Bde	No 9
466th Field Co R.E.	No 2.	H.Q.138th do	No 10
468th Field Co R.E.	No 3.	H.Q.139th do	No 11
War Diary & File	No 4.5.	C.R.E.19th Divn.	No 12
1/1st.Monmouthshire	No 6	C.R.E.55th Divn.	No 13
Headquarters "G"	No 7	C.E.XIII Corps.	No 14
" "Q"	No 8	British Officer att.2nd.Fld.Co.C.E.P.	1
		Divisional Train.	16.

SECRET

Copy No 14

46th DIVISIONAL R.E. ORDER No 66
By Lieut Colonel H.T. MORSHEAD. D.S.O.
C.R.E. 46th Division.

Ref Maps -:
1/40,000, Sheets 62.B. and 62.C.   September 20th 1918.

1. The 46th Division is taking over a portion of the 1st Division, and 4th Australian Divisional fronts, as under :-

   (a) On night 20/21st, 139th Infantry Brigade relieves the Left Brigade (2nd Infantry Brigade,) 1st Division.

   (b) On night 21/22nd the 138th Infantry Brigade relieves the 4th Australian Division.

2. (a) Reliefs of Field Coys and Pioneers will take place as detailed overleaf. Details will be arranged direct between units concerned.

   (b) Work in each case will commence on morning of the 21st.

   (c) Map locations of unit's headquarters will be reported to this office immediately on arrival.

3. Divisional Headquarters closes at CAUVIGNY FARM tomorrow evening, and opens at VRAIGNES.

4. Boundaries after completion of relief are shown on the enclosed tracing (issued with copies No 1,2,3, and 4 of these orders).

5. ACKNOWLEDGE.

                                        Lieut Colonel,
                                        C.R.E. 46th Division.

Issued at 9-45 pm

    Copies No 1,2,and 3 to 465, 466, and 468 Field Coys R.E.
           No 4 to 1st Monmouthshire Regt (Pioneers).
           No 5 and 6 to 46th Division "G" & "Q".
           No 7,8, and 9 to 137, 138, and 139 Infantry Brigades.
           No 10 and 11 to C.R.E. 1st Div; and C.R.E. 4th Aust Div } for information
           No 12 to C.E. IX Corps.
           No 13 and 14 to War Diary and File.

46th Div Unit	Unit relieved	Nature of Work	Remarks
465 Field Coy R.E.	1 Section of 409th Field Co. R.E.	Work on dugouts – MAISSEMY and VADENCOURT	Representatives to take over bivouacs from the 409th Field Co. R.E., and from 26th Field Co R.E., as already arranged verbally.
	3 Sections of 26th Field Co R.E.	Roads and bridges – VERMAND.	
466 Field Coy R.E.	12th Australian Field Co R.E.	Trestle Bridge at R.8.a.5.8.	Representatives to be at railway Bridge – R.8.a.5.8. at 7 am on the 21st inst to take over work and bivouacs.
468 Field Co R.E.	13th Australian Field Co R.E.	Water Supply – Roads – and accomodation in Left Brigade area.	
1st Monmouths & 6th Welch Regt. Pioneers.	1 Company of	Road improvements – VERMAND – V.D.COULZ – to R.G.a.	
	2 Companies of 4th Australian Pioneer Batn.	Road improvements – V.D.COULZ – JEANCOURT – LE-VERGUIER.	

VERY SECRET   Copy No 13

46th DIVISIONAL R.E. ORDER No 67
By Major W.H.HARDMAN.M.C. A/C.R.E.46th Divn.

Ref Maps.
1/20,000, Sheets 62.B. and 62.C.   September 27th 1918.

1. On "Z" Day the 46th Division, as part of a major operation will cross the ST QUENTIN Canal between G.34.d.0.3., and G.22.b.6.0. and advance to the GREEN LINE.

2. The 30th American Division is operating on the left.

3. The 137th Infantry Brigade will capture 1st and 2nd objectives BROWN LINE.

4. The 138 and 139th Brigades will cross on footbridges erected by 465 and 466 Field Coys.

5. Horse Transport Bridges will be erected by 32nd Division.

6. The Field Coys and 1/1st Monmouths will be employed as detailed on attached "Outline of Work".

7. HEADQUARTERS. Divisional H.Q. will be at R.8.b.6.0.,
S.E.of VENDELLES.

Brigade H.Q. - 137 - G.21.c.15.65.

138 - G.21.d.7.8.

139 - G.25.d.4.5.

8. ACKNOWLEDGE.

Captain & Adjt R.E.
46th Division.

Copy No 1 & 2 to H.Q. "G" & "Q"
3.4.& 5 to Field Coys.
6 to 1/1st Monmouths.
7.8.& 9 to 137.138.& 139 Infantry Bdes.
10 to C.R.E.32nd Division.
11 to C.E.IX Corps.
12 & 13. War Diary & File.

VERY SECRET.

WORK FOR FIELD COMPANIES & PIONEER BATTALION ON "Z" DAY & FOLLOWING.

466 Field Co R.E.

3 Sections to be placed at the disposal of 157th Infantry Brigade for assistance in the use of expedients for crossing Canal. These Sections will be available for assistance in examining dugouts etc, if so required.

1 Section - Reconnaissance of captured area up to Blue Line.

for
(Water Supply.
(Roads.
(Dumps.
(Booby Traps.

465 Field Co R.E.

2 Sections - Cork Pier Bridges, and repair of any existing footbridges, - Maintainance of means of crossing.

2 Sections - Reconnaissance in 139th Brigade captured area beyond Blue Line,

for
((Water Supply.
(Roads.
(Dumps.
(Booby Traps.

468 Field Co R.E.

2 Sections - Cork Pier Bridges and repair of any existing footbridges, - Maintainance of means of crossing.

2 Sections - Reconnaissance in 138th Brigade captured area beyond Blue Line,

for
(Water Supply.
(Roads.
(Dumps.
(Booby Traps.

1/1st Monmouth Pioneers.

1. Carrying parties for Cork Pier Bridges - 200 men.

2. Tracks for transport from Ridge to sites of Horse Transport Bridges (to be erected by 32nd Divisional Engineers).

On completion of the above work the Pioneers will move forward on roads beyond the Canal (the division of labour on roads East of the Canal between 32nd and 46th Divisions has not yet been mutually arranged between C.R.Es).

The R.E. Sections with 137th Infantry Brigade will form up and move as arranged between 466 Field Co and 137th Brigade.

The parties of Sappers and Pioneers dealing with the Cork Pier Bridges will form up in front of 138 and 139 Infantry Brigades and will follow close behind the 137th Infantry Brigade, constructing the Bridges at the earliest possible moment.

The party of Pioneers working on the Horse Transport Tracks will form up in front of the 138 and 139 Infantry Brigades, and will commence work as soon as the Canal is crossed by the 137th Infantry Brigade.

Sections for reconnaissance of captured areas will form up behind the Brigade with which they are working, and move forward with them.

Field Company Headquarters, and Pioneer Bn Headquarters will be established in neighbourhood of present front line as soon as Infantry pass through.

-2-

Transport.

Tool Carts and technical wagons will be ready to move at half an hours notice after Zero plus eight hours.

Pontoon and Trestle Wagons, with teams and brakesmen will move on Y/Z night (to rendezvous) appointed by C.R.E., 32nd Division, and will come under his orders.

App^n III

46th DIVISION

Report on Work of Field Companies R.E. & Pioneers during Operations of 29th September 1918.

ATTACK ON BELLENGLISE.

465 Field Co R.E. Company was divided into 3 Sections for the attack at 5-50 am. 2 Sections followed 137th Infantry Brigade, as guides to carrying parties which were furnished by 1st Monmouthshire Battn.

2/Lieut BLACKLOCK was in charge of party on Left of Brigade front, and 2/Lieut AINSCOUGH of that on the Right.

On reaching the St QUENTIN Canal these Sections repaired 6 Footbridges across the Canal. At 12-30 pm 20 men of these Sections were handed over to 466 Field Co R.E., and a Horse Transport Bridge was built by them over damaged dam at G.34.d.6.5., under Lieut JAMES of the 466 Field Co R.E.

The Third Section under Lieut ROME examined dugouts and part of the Tunnel to North of Main Road through BELLENGLISE, and after rendering them safe proceeded to work on road repair.

466 Field Co R.E. Nos 1.2.&.4 Sections took up positions with the 6th North, 5th and 6th South Staffords respectively, on the night of September 28th. No 3 Section in Reserve for clearing dugouts.

Jumping off lines were taped out by 4-30 am on Sept 29th. The 3 first mentioned Sections went over with the Battalions at "Zero" (5-50 am).

On reaching the Canal Sections effected rough repairs to standing bridges, and assisted Infantry in crossing by means of ropes etc.

Before reaching the Bridge Cpl OPENSHAW accounted personally for a Machine Gun Nest. He subsequently led the Infantry across PONT RIQUEVAL Bridge under Machine Gun fire and bayoneted two of the Pioneers in charge of the demolition of the Bridge, before they could effect the demolition, and received the surrender of a third who was able to point out the positions of the demolition charges.

Sapper GILLHAM swam the Canal with a rope and pulled many men over, also under Machine Gun fire.

All Bridges across the Canal were found to be charged for demolition, and charges were withdrawn, and the Bridges rendered safe by 9-0 am.

On the orders of C.R.A. 32nd Division men of 465 and 466 Field Coys worked on repairs of damaged bridge across Canal, completing it for Field Guns by 3-15 pm.

Lieut FOX with No 3 Section did good work in clearing dugouts, and removing charges for demolition of same. This Section while carrying out this work took over 100 prisoners.

468 Field Co R.E. Two Sections were detailed for the erection of Cork Pier Bridges across the Canal, but it was found that the existing Bridges could be repaired more expeditiously. One Stone Bridge (WATLING STREET) and four wooden bridges were repaired very rapidly and demolition charges withdrawn.

The remaining two Sections were divided in three parties and attached as follows :-
```
        No 1   attached to 4th Lincolns    ) 138th
        No 2      "      "  5th    "       ) Brigade.
        No 3      "      "  5th Leicesters.)
```

These three parties were detailed to examine Roads, Water Supplies, Booby Traps etc, and carried out their work effectively.

O.C. 465 Field Co R.E.
O.C. 466 Field Co R.E.
O.C. 468 Field Co R.E.

App. IV

Office copy

1. The Engineer in Chief G.H.Q. has written to ask me to convey to your Companies his very best congratulations for the work done on September 29th.
   He wishes to let you know how very proud he is of you all.

2. I am forwarding his letter to your C.R.E, Lieut Colonel MORSHEAD, and attach a copy of my reply to the E-in-C.

3. I may add that congratulations from the Engineer in Chief direct to Divisional Engineers are very rarely given, and that you may regard General HEATH's appreciation as a great compliment, which in my opinion you richly deserve.

2/10/18.

Lieut Colonel,
A/C.R.E. 46th Division.

INSTRUCTIONS FOR FIELD COMPANIES & PIONEERS in amplification of

"OUTLINE OF WORK"

FOOTBRIDGES   Three Footbridges per Brigade (i.e.,138 and 139) must be got across the Canal at the earliest possible moment, and will be fit for use by the time the BROWN LINE is captured.   Arrangements will be made to inform the Brigades and C.R.E of the progress of the work, and every assistance must be given to Brigade guides.

Cork Pier material will be dumped as far forward as possible, and two carrying parties, each of 120, 1/1st Monmouths will carry the material forward.   Arrangements will be made between Field Coys and 1/1st Monmouths.

On completion of the carrying, the 1/1st Monmouths will rendezvous in the neighbourhood of the present front line.

On completion of the Cork Pier Bridges the R.Es will repair existing footbridges, and will maintain all footbridges and means of crossing.

HORSE TRANSPORT BRIDGES.   These will be made by 32nd Division. The Pontoons and Trestles of the 46th Division will be allotted as follows :-

     465 Field Co R.E.)
     466 Field Co R.E.)   - 206th Field Co R.E.

     468 Field Co R.E.   - 219th Field Co R.E.

These will be handed over (at a rendezvous to be notified later) on Y/Z night.

HORSE TRANSPORT TRACKS. 1/1st Monmouths, less parties detailed for carrying cork piers will prepare Horse Transport Tracks forward to the Canal, as on attached tracing.   These will be pushed on with all speed to enable 32nd Division Pontoon Wagons to approach the Canal.

ROADS.   The roads beyond the Canal will be worked on by Pioneers of 32nd Division, and 46th Division, in accordance with attached tracing, (to be sent later).

FORMING UP POSITIONS.   These will be as notified on "Outline of Work". A tracing is attached showing Infantry positions, and arrangements will be made with the units concerned with regard to routes etc to forming up positions.

R.E.RECONNAISSANCE PARTIES   These will push forward as soon as possible.   It must be impressed upon these parties that they are quite useless unless full and frequent reports are sent back.   NIL reports must not be disregarded.   The parties must not degenerate into souvenir hunters.

FIELD COMPANY H.Q. & 1/1st MONMOUTHS Bn H.Q.   These will be established in present front line.   Units will make arrangements as to report centres, so that advanced parties can send back their reports without delay.

TRANSPORT.   Technical vehicles will be held in readiness to move as detailed in "Outline of Work".   Horse Lines must be prepared to move forward, a storekeeper being left in charge of any stores left on present Horse Lines.

EXPEDIENTS.   The R.E.Sections with the 137th Infantry Brigade will move as arranged between Field Co and 137th Inf Brigade.

Army Form C. 2118.

Headquarters R.E.
46 Division

WAR DIARY
or
INTELLIGENCE SUMMARY.

(Erase heading not required.)

October 1918

Vol 27

Place	Date	Hour	Summary of Events and Information	Remarks and references to Appendices
BECCELISE	1/11/18	—	Report on R.E. work during operation of Sept 29th.	APR I
	2/10/18		Headquarters R.E. moved to LA BARAQUE on rd BELLENGLISE established Advanced H.Q.	APR II
	3/10/18	6:5 AM	46th Division attacked & captured the line SEQUEHART (exclusive) - MONTBREHAIN (see appendix III attached) (R.E. did not take part in this operation)	APR III
			including RAMICOURT.	
	9/10/18		Headquarters R.E. moved to MAGNY-LA-FOSSE	
			465 Field Coy left BELLENGLISE moved to LEVERGIES also 466 Field Co also moved to LEVERGIES. 468 Field Co moved to H.21.d.20.10. (Sheet 62.B)	
	10/10/18		Headquarters R.E. 465 Field Co & 468th Field Co R.E. moved to FRESNOY-LA-GRAND	
			466 Field Co R.E. moved to J.2.d.8.7. on rd BOHAIN	
	10-16/10/17		Companies employed on repairing forwards, improving billeting accommodation, Water supplies, destroying German "Booby Traps" etc. Marking tracks for guidance on 17/10/18 roads	APP IV
FRESNOY-LA-GRAND	17/10/18		46th Division attacked enemy trenches ANDIGNY-LES-FERMES. Field Corps. employed on construction of roads, & assisting Demoray Engineers & Pioneers in consolidating positions gained	APP V
	18/10/18		46th Division relieved in the Line by 6th Division. 46th Division brought in Corps Reserve.	

Army Form C. 2118.

WAR DIARY
or
INTELLIGENCE SUMMARY.
(Erase heading not required.)

Instructions regarding War Diaries and Intelligence Summaries are contained in F. S. Regs., Part II. and the Staff Manual respectively. Title pages will be prepared in manuscript.

Place	Date	Hour	Summary of Events and Information	Remarks and references to Appendices
FRESNOY-LA GRAND	19-26/10/18		Field Coys General training. Lieut. A. BOWEN struck off the strength. 465 Field Co.	
	26/10/18		466 Field Co R.E. moved from J.2.d.8.7. to BOHAIN to FRESNOY-LE GRAND	
"	20/25/10/18		Companies undertook General training, Musketry, Dress etc. also improvements to roads & general improvements to billeting accommodation.	
"	26/10/18.		Divisional "Guard of Honour Parade" & Presentation of medals by G.O.C. 126 French Division, Sergt. AN MASKERY 466 Field Co. R.E. & Sapper DEIGHTON Signal Co R.E awarded the "Croix de Guerre"	
	27/10/18		Field Coys continued training	
	28/10/18		Field Coys & Signal Co R.E. with transport were inspected by Brig-Genl. CARTWRIGHT C.B., C.B. IX Corps	
	31/10/18.		Headquarters R.E. moved from FRESNOY-LE GRAND to BOHAIN. 465 Field Co. & 466 Field Co. moved from FRESNOY-LE GRAND to BOHAIN 468 Field Co R.E. moved from FRESNOY-LE GRAND to BUSIGNY.	

APPX I War Diary

RT ON R.E. WORK DURING OPERATIONS OF 29th SEPTEMBER.

465 Field Co R.E.

In the attack on BELLENGLISE on 29/9/18 the 465 Field Co R.E. was divided into 3 Sections. Both Sections followed 137th Inf Brigade acting as guides to Monmouth carrying parties. 2/Lieut BLACKLOCK took the carrying party to Left Hand front of Brigade and 2/Lieut AINSCOUTH took the carrying party to the Right. They got to the Canal and found Cork Pier Bridges unnecessary. They then repaired 6 Footbridges across the Canal. 20 of their Sappers were then handed over at 12-30 pm to Lieut JAMES, 466 Field Co R.E., and built a Horse Transport Bridge over the damaged dam at G.34.d.6.5. Remaining Sections under Lieut ROME examined dugouts and 100 yards of Tunnel to North of main road through BELLENGLISE, and rendered them safe. They also filled in a few shell holes on the main road through BELLENGLISE.

466 Field Co R.E.

On the night of 28th September the whole dismounted portion of the Company took up their position in the old Front and Support Lines - Nos 1. 2. & 4 Sections with 6th North, 5th & 6th South Staffords Bn Headquarters respectively and No 3 Section, standing by in Reserve for clearing of dugouts. I made my Headquarters with 137 Brigade in Front Line.

Each Section took a portion of tools etc, to help to repair any standing Bridges, and to help to pull the attacking troops over.

The various jumping off lines were taped out between 2-30 am and 4-30 am on the 29th. The 3 Sections went over at Zero, 5-50 pm on 29th - one Section per Battalion - some men with 1st wave and some with 2nd.

On reaching the Canal the Sections assisted the Infantry over by making rough repairs to standing Bridges, pulling them over with rope lines etc. During the crossing Cpl Openshaw bayoneted the two sentries on PONT RIQUEVAL Bridge and led the Infantry over. This Bridge was passable for foot traffic from the first, Sapper GILLHAM was one of the first over. He swam over with a line and then pulled many others across Both these men were hampered by M.G.fire. Cpl Openshaw on his way down to the Canal accounted for one M.G.Nest himself. All Bridges across the Canal were found charged and all charges were withdrawn and the Bridges rendered safe for the following Brigades by 9-0 am.
When the Canal was crossed by the Infantry and they were holding the Blue and Brown Lines, General TOWLER, C.R.A.32nd Division, at about 12 noon told me that he wanted the damaged Bridge, repaired to take Field Guns. This was done with the help of some of the 465 Field Co R.E.

The Bridge was repaired fit for Field Guns at 3-15 pm, and reported as such. On orderly was sent to bring the Artillery over at once.

Lieut FOX with No 3 Section did good work clearing dugouts and withdrawing charges rendering them safe for occupation. This party in the course of their work took over 100 prisoners.

The undermentioned did excellent work and by their example contributed largely to the general success.:-

Lieut F.T.JAMES. 2/Lt T.H.MIDGLEY. Cpl OPENSHAW. Spr GILHAM. 2/Cpl CHAMBERS. L/Cpl BREEZE. Cpl WILLETS. Cpl WITHINGTON. L/Cpl HALIFAX and L/Cpl MACKLEY.

468 Field Co R.E.

Two Sections were detailed to follow in rear of 137th Infantry Brigade and erect Cork Pier Bridges across the St QUENTIN Canal. The material for these Bridges was carried to the waters edge as the Infantry advanced. It was discovered however that the bulk of the Bridges were capable of temporary repair (Watling St Bridge, a stone structure) was badly damaged - temporary repairs were immediately put in hand, and all charges removed (a large number were found) Four wooden Bridges were also quickly repaired. It was not therefore necessary to erect Cork Pier Bridges as it was quicker to get the existing ones repaired.

Two Sections of Sappers were attached to 138th Inf Bde to look for Booby Traps, Water, Roads etc, these Sections were divided into three parties - No 1 - attached to 4th Lincolns.
     No 2 - " " 5th Lincolns.
     No 3 - " "5th Leicesters.

All parties reported back without casualties. Demolition material was carried but not found necessary. No Booby Traps were found.
No 1 Party found two wells at G.35.a.80.80. One in deep dugout was dry. The other in the Village had water which seemed in good condition. Winding tackle and buckets were intact in both cases.
Timber was found at G.35.a.30.80. about 60 ft 12"x 12".
No 2 Party report deep dugouts and tunnel at G.36.a.3.7. containing German Machine Guns, Anti Tank rifles, electric light plant and other stores in parge quantities.
No 3 Party reported 3 wells at MAGNY-le-FOSSE H.25.a.60.40. H.25.a.90.40. and H.25.b.30.40. All these wells contain water which appears to be in good condition.

1st Batt Monmouthshire Regt (Pioneers).

The Battalion arrived at Victoria Cross Roads at G.33.a.35.70. Tools were dumped and they proceeded to carry forward the Cork Pier Bridges, and superstructures, and dump them at Victoria Cross Roads. This was not completed until 5 am as they took at least 6 men to each Pier. The distance to be carried was nearly a mile. They then dug in to get below the ground. At 15 minutes after Zero 2 Companies proceeded to carry the material to the Canal. This was impeeded owing to Dense Fog. Is was impossible to see more than a yard or two. A considerable amount of material was got to the Canal, and carrying continued until 12 noon, when I gave orders for no more to be taken forward, as it was not being used.
At Zero plus 20 minutes C Company proceeded to work on track for Pontoon Wagons. In this case also fog prevented work being expediticusly carried out. The track to the Canal was located and work was carried on. The Track was completed by the time the Pontoon Wagons arrived. The track was in a very bad condition by the Canal. It was impossible to take the track across country as there was a big drop at the Canal Bank. I gave orders for it not to be proceeded with. I saw the O.C. of the Field Co of the 32nd Division and went over the track with him and he was quite satisfied.
At 12 noon I gave the men an hour and a half rest and then told them to proceed with the road East of Canal. These roads, as far as MAGNY LE FOSSE were cleared and made good for Guns and Horse Transport. It was being used by both before 3 pm.

Dear General,

On behalf of the Royal Engineers of the 46th Division I write to thank you very much for your kind letter of congratulations in connection with their share in the operations of the 29th September.

Your appreciation of their work will be a source of encouragement to them and will spur them on to further efforts in all that they may be called upon to do in the future.
They certainly did well and fully upheld the traditions of the Corps.

You will doubtless be pleased to know that Corporal OPENSHAW of the 466th Field Co R.E was one of the first to reach the Canal on the extreme left of the attack.   Three German Pioneers were just about to blow up the brick arch bridge (PONT RIQUEVAL) when Corporal OPENSHAW dashed at them, bayoneted two and took the third prisoner, and thereby saved the bridge which proved to be of the utmost value afterwards.   The prisoner was then made to disclose the demolition charge which was soon extracted.   This same Corporal accounted for a Machine Gun Nest on his way down to the Canal.

The G.O.C is very pleased about it, and is going to give OPENSHAW the D.C.M which he so richly deserves.

No credit whatever belongs to me as all the preparations etc were made by MORSHEAD to whom I am sending your letter.

With renewed thanks,

Yours sincerely

October 2nd 1918.

List of Casualties for period
29th September to 7th October.

Officers.   Other Ranks.

   110   2,500.

APPENDIX II

Copy No

46th DIVISIONAL R.E. ORDER No 68
By Lieut Colonel W.GARFORTH.D.S.O.,E.O.
A/C.R.E.46th DIVISION.

2nd October 1918.

1. The 46th Division will attack tomorrow. (further details will be issued later).

2. The Divisional Engineers will not take part in the attack.

3. 465, 466, and 468 Field Coys R.E. will "Stand To" in present billets from 3 o-clock tomorrow morning, and will be ready to move up if required at five minutes notice, to carry out any engineer work which may be necessary. *(one Bridge Party)*

4. Pontoon Wagons will not be required but Tool Carts should be ready to be moved off at a moments notice from Transport Lines.

5. 468 Field Co will, from 22 o-clock tonight be responsible for the maintainance of all footbridges over ST QUENTIN Canal between BELLENGLISE and PONT RIQUEVAL, until further orders.
   The minimum number of men should be employed in maintaining these bridges - Remainder of 468 Field Co will stand by as per para (3) above.

6. Further instructions will be issued later.

7. ACKNOWLEDGE.

Lieut Colonel,
A/C.R.E.46th Division.

Copy No 1 to 465 Field Co R.E.
     2   466 Field Co R.E.
     3   468 Field Co R.E.
     4   Headquarters "G"
     5   War Diary
     6   File

APPENDIX II

SECRET

ACCOUNT OF THE PART TAKEN
BY THE 46th DIVISION IN THE BATTLE OF
BELLENGLISE ON THE 29th SEPTEMBER, 1918.

46th Division G.114/24.   7th October 1918.

1. <u>General Idea of the Operations</u>.   The general idea of these operations was the breaking of the main HINDENBURG LINE NORTH OF ST. QUENTIN. The special role of the 46th Division being to storm the ST QUENTIN CANAL between BELLENGLISE and RIQUEVAL, and take the villages of BELLENGLISE, LEHAUCOURT, and MAGNY LA FOSSE.

   On the RIGHT of the Division, the 1st Division was to exploit any success gained by working to the EAST, SOUTH of the CANAL, and occupying the high ground about THORIGNY, should the enemy retire from these positions.

   On our LEFT the American Corps were to storm the BELLICOURT defences, and then, turning SOUTH, were to join the 46th Division in the neighbourhood of ETRICOURT.

   The 32nd Division and 2nd Australian Division were to move through the 46th Division, and 30th American Division respectively, after the capture of their final objectives, and seize the general line LE TRONQUOY - LEVERGIES and to the NORTH.

2. <u>General description of the ground on the 46th Division Front.</u>

   The defences in front of the 46th Division were of a very formidable nature, consisting of strong lines WEST of the CANAL, the CANAL itself; with the main HINDENBURG LINE, a strong supporting line and four strongly defended villages to the EAST of it.   The CANAL may be divided into two parts, the SOUTHERN half running practically along the ground level contained little water; but on the other hand, the defences were far stronger than in the NORTHERN part.   The NORTHERN half, where the water was from seven to ten feet deep, ran through a deep cutting with almost perpendicular sides, thirty to fifty feet high.

   The lower ten feet of the CANAL throughout formed a perpendicular obstacle, faced with brick; and both inner and outer banks were strongly wired.

   In BELLENGLISE were the entrances to the famous tunnel which ran from the direction of MAGNY LA FOSSE into this village, and was known to be capable of holding some 2/3,000 men.   The whole area was known to be exceptionally strong in concrete machine gun defences, and was believed by the enemy to be impregnable.

3. <u>Preliminary Arrangements</u>.   The first order for the attack was 46th Division Order 326, issued on the 25th September, and prior to the attack many preliminary arrangements had to be made.   The main difficulty lay in crossing the CANAL, and for this purpose some 3,000 lifebelts were obtained and issued to the storming troops.   On the day prior to the attack, these lifebelts together with light portable rafts, ladders, collapsible boats and heaving lines, were tested on the banks of the SOMME, and it was found that the ordinary lifebelt would easily support a man in fighting order, provided that the weight he was carrying was kept low on his body.

   A preliminary operation with the object of ensuring that there would be little opposition WEST of the CANAL was undertaken by the 138th Infantry Brigade on the 27th September against the trenches in G.28.   These trenches were occupied under a barrage, but on the 28th September severe fighting ensued here, and it was decided that on Y/Z night, our troops should be withdrawn, and formed up WEST, and well clear of any possible enemy opposition.

4. General dispositions of the 46th Division.   The area to be occupied by the 46th Division was divided into two main objectives – the BROWN objective and the GREEN objectives. These were further sub-divided – a BLUE objective included the CANAL and the defences immediately EAST of it, whilst the YELLOW and DOTTED BLUE objectives were inserted between the BROWN and the GREEN on the main tactical features, in order to allow of inter-Brigade "Leap-Frog".

To the 137th Infantry Brigade (Brigadier General J.V.CAMPBELL, VC,CMG,DSO, Coldstream Guards) was entrusted the storming of the CANAL the village of BELLENGLISE, and the capture of the BROWN objective. On this line a halt was made for three hours, in order to allow of the complete mopping up of the area and give time for the 139th Infantry Brigade (Brigadier General J.HARINGTON, DSO) on the RIGHT, and 138th Infantry Brigade (Brigadier General F.G.M.ROWLEY, CMG,DSO) on the LEFT, to pass through and capture the final objective.

To the storming Infantry were allotted a few Sections of Engineers, whilst the remainder of the Royal Engineers and the 1/1st Monmouthshire Regt (Pioneers) followed close in rear with the necessary bridging material.

The Artillery allotted to the Division consisted of one Brigade RHA, and eight Brigades of Field Artillery, whilst a very powerful concentration of Heavy Artillery was arranged by the IX Corps, to deal with the enemy defences and engage his Batteries.

Two additional Machine Gun Battalions, that of the 2nd Life Guards and the 100th Machine Gun Battalion, were also allotted to the Division, and took part in the initial barrage.

Two Companies Mark V Tanks were to cross over the BELLICOURT Tunnel immediately the Americans had captured their first objective, and moving south were to join the Division prior to its advance from the BROWN LINE. One Company was allotted to each of the 139th, and 138th Infantry Brigades.

5. Forming Up.   Forming up was successfully carried out on the night 28th/29th September. 137th Infantry Brigade formed up on a three Battalion front, whilst 139th and 138th Infantry Brigades formed up some distance in rear on a one Battalion front, with orders that their leading Battalion should occupy the trench system on our "jumping off" line, as soon as the 137th Infantry Brigade had left. These Battalions detailed one Company each to follow the 137th Infantry Brigade in order to mop up the area WEST of the CANAL, and the Battalion Commanders were instructed to keep in close touch with the situation and to so handle their Battalions, as to ensure that the 137th Infantry Brigade, having crossed the CANAL, should not be out-fought in the trench system beyond it. The remainder of the 139th and 138th Infantry Brigades were instructed not to move forward pending orders from Divisional Headquarters.

Zero hour was fixed for 5-50 am.

6. The Attack.   The attack was launched at Zero   in a thick mist which rapidly increased to a dense fog as the smoke which had been placed in the barrage and on the flanks began to make itself felt. Under cover of this fog the 137th Infantry Brigade, having stormed the first line trenches, and killed most of the garrison who put up a tough resistance, reached the CANAL well up to time. At the same time, the 1st Division formed a defensive RIGHT flank from our original trenches along the spur towards BELLENGLISE. The RIGHT Battalion (6th Bn South Staffordshire Regt) found little water in the CANAL, and only in few places were they forced to swim. The enemy here at first put up considerable resistance, but, after a number of our men had crossed, surrendered freely, and the Battalion was able to proceed to the BLUE Line and occupy the Tunnel entrances in BELLENGLISE, where some hundreds of prisoners were taken, before they were able to put up any organised resistance.

The centre (5th South Staffordshire Regt) and the LEFT (6th North Staffordshire Regt) found a considerable depth of water in the CANAL. The Officers swimming over first with ropes, were soon joined by the leading lines of their men, and assisted by broken bridges, rafts and boats, the whole force was soon across and dealing with the enemy in strongly held trenches on the EASTERN Bank.
At RIQUEVAL the bridge was found to be intact. The Royal Engineers with some of the storming troops bayonetted the enemy Pioneers who were about to light the fuzes, and withdrew the charges. The saving of this Bridge, due entirely to the rapidity and gallantry of the advance, was of inestimable value, and by it , and the Pontoon Bridges which were later made by the 46th and 32nd Divisional Engineers and Pioneers, the whole of these two Divisions with their Artillery, were later enabled to pass over.

The Infantry rapidly clearing the trenches up to the BLUE Objective, advanced on the BROWN LINE which they reached in scheduled time, capturing on their way a battery of four guns, the gun teams of which were all either killed or captured together with their horses. Owing to the density of the fog, little use could be made of the Divisional Observers' Section. The Divisional Mounted Troop, consisting of men from the D.A.C., and Field Ambulances were, however, sent forward to reconnoitre, and by questioning prisoners and wounded men, were able to send back most valuable information, showing that our Infantry had successfully crossed the CANAL. On this information orders were issued for 139th and 138th Infantry Brigades to push straight across the CANAL up to the barrage, and move directly on the objectives assigned to them.

The leading Battalion of these two Brigades had already pushed forward after the 137th Infantry Brigade, and crossed the CANAL close on their heels. The two Brigades reached the BROWN LINE in excellent time, where they were joined by the two Companies of Tanks, and in spite of the dense fog, the whole were enabled to move forward towards their objective as the barrage lifted.

After passing the YELLOW Objective, the fog having cleared considerably, much inconvenience was caused to the RIGHT Battalion by the enemy occupying the high ground SOUTH of the CANAL. Machine Guns from this direction swept our RIGHT flank continuously and enemy Field Guns firing at point blank range quickly put out of action all six Tanks allotted to 139th Infantry Brigade. This Battery was in its turn put out of action by a party of 139th Infantry Brigade, who with great gallantry crossed the CANAL and shot or bayonetted the gunners. Little Infantry trouble was experienced from SOUTH of the CANAL ; several feeble attempts to counter attack on this flank were made, and one mounted German Officer made three gallant attempts to rally his men;   on the third attempt, both he and his horse were killed, whereupon the enemy immediately retired.

On our LEFT, 138th Infantry Brigade were successfully carrying forward their advance, and at 12-30 pm, we advanced from the YELLOW LINE on to MAGNY LA FOSSE. At this time it was definitely ascertained that the troops on our LEFT, who until now, had been thought to occupy the high ground about NAUROY, had been hung up on their first objective : both flanks of the 46th Division were therefore in the air, and steps were taken to form a LEFT defensive flank, and to hold the bridgeheads along the CANAL on the RIGHT flank. The advance from the YELLOW LINE was slightly delayed by this operation, and the barrage was some distance ahead of the advancing Infantry. In spite of this, our Infantry advanced, and soon caught up the barrage, most ably assisted on our LEFT by the Tanks attached to the 138th Infantry Brigade.

By three pm, the whole of our objectives had been taken, and the 32nd Division, pressing forward, passed through our lines to occupy the RED LINE.   During the later stages of our advance, a number of guns were encountered, giving opportunities for many acts of gallantry on the part of both Officers and men. One battery was seen to be limbering up EAST of our final defensive barrage, and an attempt was made to pass through our barrage and prevent the withdrawal of these guns. Horses and drivers were shot down, and immediately our barrage began to thin, this battery was captured. Several bayonet chargers against the enemy's artillery were made, the crews being killed and the guns captured. The German Artillery men fought with the greatest valour and continued to fire their guns at point blank range up to the last.

During the following night, the Division was continuously in action owing to both flanks being open to the enemy. On the morning of the 30th, the 1st Division on our RIGHT eased the situation by the capture of THORIGNY and TALANA HILL, whilst on the LEFT, the 2nd Australian Division, pushing forward, joined up with our LEFT flank during the day.

7. Work of the Artillery. The preparatory work of the Heavy Artillery cannot be too highly praised, and, it was owing in a great measure to their excellent shooting that the storming of the CANAL with its concrete defences was made possible. The Field Artillery, in spite of the fact that the majority of the guns were in silent positions up to Zero hour, and unable to register, put down one of the finest barrages that the troops have ever advanced under. During the action, the majority of the Field Artillery was moved forward to new positions already selected. These movements were so expediously carried out as to make little appreciable difference in the intensity of the barrage.

8. The work of the Royal Engineers, Machine Gunners, Pioneers and R.A.M.C. was beyond all praise. The first named, besides saving the RIQUEVAL BRIDGE, were able to assist the Infantry in many ways outside their ordinary scope, and incidents of individual gallantry in attacking machine gun nests, etc., were of common occurence.

9. Infantry. As for the Infantry, in addition to the magnificent behaviour of every officer and man, the leadership shown by Regimental Officers and N.C.O's was of a very high nature. The faultless leading of their men across some 5,000 yards of enemy territory in a thick fog, during which some 4,200 prisoners and 70 guns were taken is worthy of the highest traditions of the Service. Their success, and the lightness of their casualties, some 800 in all, is due to this power of leadership and to the fact that not the slightest hesitation was shown throughout the whole engagement.

All ranks were determined to push through to the final objective regardless of the flanks, and right well they carried it out, not only on this occasion but subsequently on the 3rd October.

--- *** ---

Secret.

APPENDIX III

ACCOUNT OF THE PART TAKEN BY THE 46TH DIVISION IN THE BATTLE OF RAMICOURT, ON THE 3rd OCT, 18.

1. At 4.30 pm on the 2nd October, orders were received at a Corps Conference that the 46th Division was to attack and capture the line SEQUEHART (exclusive) - MONTBREHAIN, joining with the 2nd Australian Division, N.W. of the latter place. At the same time, 32nd Division was to attack and capture SEQUEHART.

The area of attack consisted of the BEAUREVOIR - FONSOMME Line, the last defensive position of the enemy in this neighbourhood, and the Villages of RAMICOURT and MONTBREHAIN; whilst on our RIGHT Flank was MANNEQUIN HILL, running in a N.E. direction from SEQUEHART. Little was known about the area to be attacked or about the position of our own troops. For the latter reason, a forming up line was arranged sufficiently far back to ensure that there would be no enemy opposition to our troops forming up for the attack. The 32nd Division, which was holding the line, was asked to withdraw all their troops behind this line.

At 6.5 am, 3rd October, the Division attacked with 137th Inf: Bde on the RIGHT, 139th Inf: Bde on the LEFT, and 138th Inf: Bde to whom was attached the 1/1st Bn, Monmouthshire Regt (Pioneers) in Divisional Reserve.

Three brigades of artillery had to be moved up during the night to positions which it was impossible previously to reconnoitre, but in spite of this fact, the barrage opened well to time, and though slightly more short shooting was reported than usual, it was otherwise everything that could be desired.

Considerable opposition was encountered in the BEAUREVOIR - FONSOMME Line where the enemy fought to the last, some hundreds being killed in the LEFT Brigade Sector alone.

On our RIGHT, the 32nd Division quickly occupied SEQUEHART, but the troops attacking on our LEFT were unable to break through the very strong defences opposed to them.

The 137th Inf: Bde was able to report that it had captured all its objectives up to time. The 139th Inf: Bde, pushing forward to RAMICOURT found its LEFT Flank exposed: two companies were promptly detailed to move through WIANCOURT and form here a defensive flank. After the capture of RAMICOURT, the defence rapidly weakened and this Brigade captured over one thousand prisoners in MONTBREHAIN alone. In both RAMICOURT and MONTBREHAIN, French civilians were found and some seventy of them brought back to our lines. In the latter Village, a battery of field guns was also captured.

Two companies of Tanks, operating with this attack, did excellent work, especially in clearing the outskirts of RAMICOURT. Immediately SOUTH of MONTBREHAIN, one of these Tanks attacked a machine gun nest consisting of sixteen guns and killed the whole of the crews before it was in its turn disabled.

By 10.30 a severe defeat had been inflicted on the enemy and the whole of the objectives of the 46th Division obtained.

The 5th Cavalry Brigade was thereupon directed to move forward and keep in close touch with 46th Division to exploit their success. Unfortunately, this Brigade was a considerable distance to the rear and by the time they arrived in the forward area, the opportunity for using them had passed.

By 1300, the Division was with both flanks exposed and having suffered very severe casualties, was attacked from an EASTERLY direction. At this angle our line was overlooked by the high ground round DOON and MANNEQUIN HILLS, on which the enemy quickly established himself in spite of heavy and continued artillery fire from our guns and by the point blank fire of field guns and machine guns, soon made a gap in our defence immediately SOUTH of MONTBREHAIN.

Our troops in this neighourhood, were slowly pressed back SOUTH WEST of the Village, and a heavy attack commencing shortly afterwards from the NORTH of the village, our troops were withdrawn to a general line EAST of WIANCOURT - RAMICOURT and the Spur in I 13. In the meantime, 138th Inf: Bde had been moved forward

(2).

to occupy the BEAUREVOIR - FONSOMME Line and were placed at the disposal of the Brigades in the line. Later in the day, the Australians on our LEFT were enabled to advance, occupying WIANCOURT and gaining touch with our LEFT NORTH-EAST of that place.

During the afternoon, the enemy developed a very strong counter-attack against our RIGHT Brigade and succeeded in forcing us off the slopes of MANNEQUIN HILL.

5th Cavalry Brigade and the 9th Corps Cyclists, some 150 strong, were ordered to occupy the BEAUREVOIR - FONSOMME Line and were placed under the orders, of the GOC, 137th Inf: Bde. A counter-attack, restored the situation, and the NORTH-WESTERN slopes were again occupied by us. We were, however, unable to retain the summit of the HILL, which was continuously swept by machine gun fire.

During the night 3rd/4th, the 139th Inf: Bde was relieved by the 138th Inf: Bde plus 1/1st Monmouthshire Regt, and the former was withdrawn into divisional reserve. During the whole of the 4th October, the Division retained this line under continuous pressure from the enemy.

On the night 4th/5th October, 2nd Australian Division took over the LEFT Brigade Sector and 3rd Brigade, 1st Division, was placed at the disposal of the GOC, 46th Division, and was used to relieve the 137th Inf: Bde in the RIGHT Sector.

This completed the action so far as troops of the 46th Division were concerned.

The fighting in this action was of the heaviest nature, and our casualties, especially in officers, were heavy, including the loss of Battalion Commanders and one hundred other officers.
five
The captures amounted to some two thousand prisoners and a battery of guns.

Between the 29th of September and the 8th October, the 46th Division has fought two general engagements and, with the exception of a small piece of open country to the SOUTH of JONCOURT, has captured a fortified area between its own front line, WEST of the CANAL, and RAMICOURT, on a front of never less than 4,000 yards.

During these operations, in spite of the fact that both its flanks were continuously in the air, it has captured and maintained all objectives with the exception of the village of MONTBREHAIN, taking 6,000 prisoners, over 70 guns, and machine guns too numerous to count, at a loss to the Division of some Two Thousand, Five Hundred.

A list of casualties for the period 29th September to 7th October is attached.

SECRET   Copy No 6

APP. IV

46th Divisional R.E. Order No 71.
By Lieut Colonel, W.GARFORTH.D.S.O.,M.C.
C.R.E. 46th Division.

16th October 1918.

1. The 46th Division will attack, as part of a Major Operation, the BLUE LINE shown on attached map "A".
   This map also shews :-

   (a) Jumping Off Line - GREEN.
   (b) Divisional Boundaries - BROWN.
   (c) Inter-Brigade Boundary - YELLOW.

   The RED LINE is that held by our troops at present.

   Detail.   The 139th Infantry Brigade will attack on the RIGHT.
             The 138th Infantry Brigade will attack on the LEFT.
             The 137th Infantry Brigade will hold its present line.

   The 6th Division is making a simultaneous attack on our LEFT, and it is expected that the French will attack SOUTH of the FORET D'ANDIGNY on our RIGHT.
   The 1st Division is following the 6th Division and exploiting success to the EASTWARD.

2. O.C.1/1st Monmouthshire Regt (Pioneers) will be ready in present billets, from 08.00 am on "Z" day, to proceed to a rendezvous at D.21.c.0.5., with a view to repairing the road from BOHAIN to ANDIGNY LES FERMES, when the situation permits.

3. O.C.1/1st Monmouthshire Regt (Pioneers) will report at C.R.E:s Headquarters at 08.00 *am* on Z Day

                                        W Garforth
                                        Captain & Adjutant R.E.
                                        46th Division.

Copy No 1 - O.C.1/1st Monmouthshire Regt.
       2 - Headquarters "G"
       3 - O.C.465 Fld Co R.E.
       4 - O.C.466 Fld Co R.E.
       5 - O.C.468 Fld Co R.E.
       6 - File.
       7 - War Diary.

SECRET   APP V
                                                    Copy No 8
            46th Divisional R.E. Order No 70
            By Lieut Colonel, N.HARFORD.D.S.O.,M.C.
                  C.R.E. 46th Division.
            ==================================

Reference Map "A" 1/40,000.   18th October 1918.

1.   The 46th Division will attack, as part of a Major Operation
        the BLUE LINE shown on Map "A".   This Map also shows:-

        (a) Jumping Off Line - GREEN.
        (b) Divisional Boundaries - BROWN.
        (c) Inter-Brigade Boundary - YELLOW.
        The RED LINE is that held by our troops at present.

    Detail.   The 132nd Infantry Brigade will attack on the RIGHT
               The 138th Infantry Brigade will attack on the LEFT.
               The 137th Infantry Brigade will hold its present line.

        The 6th Division is making a simultaneous attack on our LEFT,
        and it is expected that the French will attack SOUTH of the FORET -
        BOANDIGNY on our RIGHT.
        The 1st Division is following the 6th Division and exploiting
        success to the EASTWARD.

2.   The Field Companies will carry out work as follows:-

    (a) 465 Field Co R.E.
        (i) One Officer and 20 O.Rs will be attached to 139th Infantry
            Brigade and will assist in constructing strong points about
            E.13.b.6.0. and RAMICOURT.

        (ii) Mark out Forming Up Line.

    (b) 466 Field Co R.E.
        (i) The cellar of house at D.11.b.5.0. will be strengthened
            and prepared as Brigade Headquarters.

        (ii) Infantry track (to avoid BOHAIN) will be marked out from
             about ~~J.O.~~ D.26.d. via D.22.c. to road in D.11.c.

    (c) 468 Field Co R.E.
        (i) One Officer and 20 O.Rs will be attached to 138th Infantry
            Brigade, and will assist in constructing strong points
            about E.9.c.9.4., and ANDIGNY - LES - FERMES.

        (ii) Place dummy tanks and figures in position WEST of
             BOIS-DE-RIQUEVAL in squares D.24 and D.30.

3.   The 466 Field Co R.E and remainder of 465 and 468 Field Coys
        will be prepared on receipt of orders to repair the road from
        BOHAIN to ANDIGNY-LES-FERMES.

4.   Instructions to amplify the above order have been given to each
        Field Company Commander.

5.   ACKNOWLEDGE.

                                        [signature]
                                        Captain & Adjutant R.E.
                                        46th Division.

Copy No 1 to 465 Fld Co R.E.
       2   466 Fld Co R.E.
       3   468 Fld Co R.E.
       4   Headquarters "Q"
       5   137th Inf Bde.
       6   138th Inf Bde   No 8 File.

OPERATION ORDER
by
C.R.E. 46TH DIVISION.
In accordance with O.O. 108., dated 27/10/1916.

1. The relief of the R.E. of the 46th Division by the R.E. of the 30th Division will be carried out as follows :-

2. One section from each Field Company of the 30th Division will be attached to the respective Field Companies at BIENVILLERS, BERLES and GROSVILLE on the 28th instant.
   The remaining sections of the 30th Division will relieve the respective Companies on the 30th instant.

3. Companies will take their march orders from the Brigades to which they are affiliated.

4. Billets will be arranged for by the Staff Captains of the various Brigades.

5. The R.E. employed on the Divisional Line, under the C.R.E. will be at the disposal of the O.C. Companies after the 28th instant.

6. When on the march Companies will report daily to the Divisional Headquarters R.E. on reaching their destination.

7. Orders for the move of Headquarters, R.E. will be issued later.

Brigadier-General.
C.R.E. 46th Division.

27/10/1916.

HQ Qrs. R.E. 46th Division **WAR DIARY** Reference Maps, France 1/100,000 Page 1
or Sheet 12. VALENCIENNES Army Form C. 2118.
November 1918 **INTELLIGENCE SUMMARY**
(Erase heading not required.)

Place	Date	Hour	Summary of Events and Information	Remarks and references to Appendices
MOLAIN	4.11.18	0800	Advanced Divisional H.Q. opened at MOLAIN	
	4.11.18		Attack by IX Corps on SAMBRE-OISE Canal, 46th Divn in Reserve. See 46th Divisional Order No 73 annexed. One Pontoon Bridge erected between Canal & 466th Field Co. RE and Two by 466th Field Co. RE. cut between LOCK No 1 BOIS L'ABBAYE and CATILLON.) See RE & Pioneer Instructions annexed.	Appendix I Appendix II
ARBRE DE GUISE	5.11.18		Advanced Divisional H.Q. opened at ARBRE de GUISE	
PRISCHES	6.11.18		RE H.Q. opened Companies employed in filling in Road craters on forward roads CATILLON to PRISCHES & bridging streams near PRISCHES	
	9.11.18		Trestle bridge erected by 466th Field Co. over LA PETITE HELPE River at CARTIGNIES by 465th " " over stream between CARTIGNIES & LA BOULOGNE.	
	10.11.18		Lt. Col. MORSHEAD returned from leave in England	
SAINS DU NORD	11.11.18	1518	Divisional H.Q. opened at SAINS du NORD Armistice declared at 1100	
LANDRECIES	14.11.		Div. Hdqrs. moved to LANDRECIES. Field coys moved into Billets in BUSIGNY, PREUX & LANDRECIES. Remainder of month spent in Salvage operations in surrounding country.	

H.T. Morshead
Lt-Col.
C.R.E. 46th Division.

SECRET   COPY NO_____

46th Divisional Engineer Order No 73
By Lieut-Col. W.GARFORTH.D.S.O.,M.C.
Commanding Royal Engineers 46th Division

Operation "P"   2nd.November 1918.

1.   The IX Corps will, at an early date, force the passage of the SAMBRE-OISE Canal, in conjunction with XV French Corps on the Right and XIII British Corps on the left.

2.   The 1st.Division will attack on right and 32nd.Division will attack on left.

3.   The 46th Division will be in Corps Reserve and will be prepared to relieve the 1st.Division after its capture of the final objective, and exploit success.

4.   Bridges of various capacities which will be constructed by IX Corps, 1st.Division and 32nd.Division are shown on Map "P" attached.

5.   In addition to the bridges above, 46th Division will construct three medium pontoon bridges over the canal between M.31.d.4.5. and S.1.d.5.8.. These bridges will only be fit for Infantry, but it is hoped that on Z plus 1 day, they may be fit for Artillery.

6.   At Zero hour the three Field Companies and 1/1st.Monmouthshire Pioneers will be located in Squares W.6.c. and W.6.d. and will be prepared to move off at five minutes notice.

7.   Engineers and Pioneers will be employed as below, and work start at a time to be notified by C.R.E.
   (a) 465th Field Co R.E.   In Reserve.
   (b) 466th Field Co R.E.   Construction of two and maintainence of three pontoon bridges in squares S.1.b.& S.1.d.
   (c) 468th Field Co R.E.   Construction of one medium pontoon bridge in square M.31.d.
   (d) 1/1st.Monmouthshire Pioneers. Construction of approaches to bridges and repairs of roads East of canal.

8.   The detachment of three officers and 80 O.R. 1st.Australian Tunnelling Co, which will search for mines in captured territory, will by Zero be located in W.6.c and will move forward when ordered by C.R.E.

9.   Detailed instructions regarding all work will be issued separately.

10.   Headquarters 46th Division at Zero will be at MOLAIN (W.15.d.9.9.)

11   ACKNOWLEDGE.

                                       Captain & Adjutant R.E.
                                       46th Division.

Copies 1-2-3   Field.Coys.
       4.   Monmouthshire Regt.
       5.   Headquarters "G"
       6.   C.R.E. 1st.Div.
       7.   C.R.E. 32nd.Div.
       8.   1st.Aust.Tunn.Co.
       9   C.E. IX Corps.
       10   War.Diary
       11   File.

46th Division Operation "g"
R.E. and Pioneer Instructions.

Reference Divisional Engineer Order No 73

The following programme of work for Sappers and Pioneers will serve as a guide, for the preparation which Unit Commanders have to make.

1. As banks of canal are reported to be eight feet above water level-they will have to be cut down as low as possible (minus 3 feet), before bridging is started. A party of Pioneers to be detailed for this. Cutting to be at least 8 feet wide at the bottom.

2. A stream reported 8 to 16 feet wide runs West of, and close to bank of canal. This will have to be bridged.

3. Approaches to bridges all have to be cleared, (Hedges cut etc,)

4. Tracks from nearest road, West and East of canal to bridges to be clearly marked with notice boards (for day) and petrol tin lamps (for night),. Notice boards are being prepared for this.

5. Bridge capacity to be marked on notice board at each end of bridge.

6. Six extra pontoons complete with equipment stored at W.S.C., will be available if required.

7. A small party of Pioneers will improve shelter for bridge maintainance detachments - on West bank of Canal.

8. After the three bridges have been completed O.C.466th Field Co. will make approaches to one of the bridges (whichever is most suitable) fit to take horsed transport.

9. Felling axes,(for cutting away felled trees etc) ladders for negotiating canal banks, tracing tapes, for marking approaches, spare timber for odd jobs, picks and shovels, spare lashing, canvas for bridge screens, nails and hammers, mauls and pickets, sandbags, should all be taken to site of bridge.

10. Progress, as well as completion, of bridges to be reported to C.R.E.

11 On completion of his bridge O.C.466th Field Co R.E. will hand it over to O.C.466th Field Co for maintainance, and will then improve Eastern approaches to his bridge.

12. O.C.1st.Monmouthshire Pioneers will attach 100 Pioneers to 466th Fld.Co. and 150 to O.C.466th Fld.Co. for the above work, and these men will be returned to O.C.1/1st.Monmouthshire Regt. (at place arranged by O.C.) as soon as Os.C Field Coys no longer require them.

13. O.C.1st.Monmouthshire Pioneers will be prepared when notified by C.R.E., to send remainder of his Battalion forward to repair main roads running East between the line - CATILLON-M.33.central-M.10.central-and the line S.13.central. (sheet 57 A 1/40,000)

14. The detachment of 1st.Australian Tunnellers (mine searchers) will accompany the Pioneers mentioned in para 13 above.

2/11/18
Lieut-Col.
C.R.E.46th Division

Distribution as D.E.O.73.

WAR DIARY
or
INTELLIGENCE SUMMARY.

Headquarters R.E. 16th Division.

Army Form C. 2118.

Reference Maps. France 1/100,000
Sheet 12 Valenciennes
" 18 St Quentin

Place	Date	Hour	Summary of Events and Information	Remarks and references to Appendices
LANDRECIES	1.12.18		Headquarters R.E. remained at LANDRECIES with 16th Divl. HQ until 12th December. Field Companies being with their respective Brigade Groups at BOUSIES, LANDRECIES & PREUX, employed on salvage of the battlefield within the Divisional Area. On Sunday afternoon H.M. The King passed through LANDRECIES and was met on returning reception from representative groups of men from every unit in the Division.	
PREUX-au-BOIS	12.12.18		On 10th 12th December the three Field Companies & H.Q.R.E. all assembled in PREUX village and remained there throughout the rest of the month, grouped under a Battalion organization. Daily voluntary Classes of instruction for all ranks were instituted in Mathematics, English, French, Book-Keeping, Typewriting, Shorthand, electricity, Building Construction and Motor Driving & repairs, with a view of fitting the men for their return to civil life. Some 200 men availed themselves weekly of the facilities thus afforded. In addition, practical instruction was given to about 75. O.Rs. from all units in the Division in Carpentry, & joinery, Bricklaying, Plating & tiling, Painting & paperhanging. During the month all coal mines from the Divisional R.E. were sent some for demobilization under instructions from the Army Council, thus reducing the strength of the Divisional R.E. by 87. O.Rs.	

J.T. ....
Lt. Col.
C.R.E. 16 Divn.

46th Divisional R.E. Order No 75   Copy No 4
By Lieut Colonel H.T.MORSHEAD, D.S.O.
C.R.E. 46th Division.

8th December 1918.

1. 137th Infantry Brigade (less 466 Field Co R.E) are moving from PREUX to FRESNOY, and Headquarters, 46th Divisional R.E, with 465 and 468 Field Companies R.E, will move from present billets to PREUX in accordance with the attached Movement Table. overleaf.

2. Completion of moves and location of new Headquarters will be reported to this office.

3. My E.124/1 re billetting is cancelled.

    465 and 468 Field Companies will send representatives to meet Lieut PAGE at 466 Field Co Headquarters, PREUX, at 11.00 hours on Monday 9th inst, to arrange for billetting in the new area.

4. ACKNOWLEDGE.

Lieut R.E.
for C.R.E. 46th Division.

8/12/18.

Copy No 1 to 465 Field Co R.E.
     2   466 Field Co R.E.
     3   468 Field Co R.E.
     4   War Diary.
     5   File.

Army Form C. 2118.

H.Q.rs R.E. 46th Division   Rebecca Huts, France 1/1/19
                                Sheet 12 Valenciennes
                                51/1/S. St Quentin

WAR DIARY
or
INTELLIGENCE SUMMARY.
(Erase heading not required.)

Instructions regarding War Diaries and Intelligence Summaries are contained in F. S. Regs., Part II. and the Staff Manual respectively. Title pages will be prepared in manuscript.

January 1919

No. 46

Place	Date	Hour	Summary of Events and Information	Remarks and references to Appendices
PREUX AU BOIS	31.1.19		H.Q.rs R.E. and the 3 Field Companies remained at PREUX AU BOIS throughout the month of January. Classes of instruction have continued daily as last month, but the practical out of doors courses in Lashings, etc., have been considerably hampered by a severe spell of frosty weather which set in on 18th January and continued until the end of the month. During the month 3 Officers and 177 O.R. proceeded on demobilisation - leaving a total of 3 Officers and 263 O.R. demobilised since the armistice. Total Strength of Div.l R.E. on 31.1.19 = 21 Officers and 370 O.R. 410 O.R.	

J.T. Boothroy
Lieut Col
C.R.E. 46th D.

WAR DIARY or **INTELLIGENCE SUMMARY**

Army Form C. 2118

H.d.Qrs. R.E. 46th Division

Reference Maps. France 1/100,000
Sheet 12 Valenciennes
" 18 St Quentin

February 1919

Vol 31

Place	Date	Hour	Summary of Events and Information	Remarks and references to Appendices
PREUX au BOIS	1st to 27th Feb.		Headqrs. R.E. and the 3 Field Companies (chained at PREUX au Bois) during the first 27 days of February. Daily classes of instruction were continued on the same lines as last month. On 28th Feb, the Divisional Engineers marched into new billets at INCHY, on the assembly of the Division near CAUDRY. 120 horses with drivers had to be borrowed from the Divl Artillery to assist in moving the Transport, in replacement of R.E. drivers and horses who had been demobilised.	
INCHY - BEAUMONT	28th Feb.		During the month 2 officers and 76 O.R. were demobilised - making a total of 5 officers and 140 O.R. who have left the Divl R.E. since the commencement of the armistice. Total strength of the Divl R.E. on 28.2.19 = 19 officers and 280 O.R.	

3. 3/19

J.T. [signature]
C.R.E. 46th Divn

[signature]
C.R.E. 46th Divn

CRE 46th Divisional Rachel.

Army Form C. 2118.

WAR DIARY
or
INTELLIGENCE SUMMARY.

Reference Map. FRANCE 1/100,000
Sheet 12. VALENCIENNES

March 1919

Place	Date	Hour	Summary of Events and Information	Remarks and references to Appendices
INCHY-BEAUMONT	1-31/3/19		During the month the Divisional R.E.s were employed in the repair of billets installation of Electric lighting, preparation of New Divisional H.Q. at CAUDRY & other time works of a limited character, Baths &c. Demobilization was proceeded with & by the end of the month the formation had reached "Cadre". All transport was packed at CAUDRY and Divisional arrangements	
	9/3/19		S.E. Col. C. Bradshaw proceeded on 1 months leave to U.K. duties were taken over by Major E.R. Kirkman MG.	
	29/3/19		Capt. F.R. Fox MC. was posted to 237th Field Co. R.E.	
	29/3/19		2/Lieut. L. Edwards & 2/Lieut. H.A.T. Coates were posted to N.O. Army Troops Co.	

H. Cody. Capt. RE
for.

WAR DIARY or INTELLIGENCE SUMMARY

Army Form C. 2118

CRE 46th Divisional Part.

Ref map FRANCE 1/100000 Sheet 12 VALENCIENNES

April 1919

Vol 33

Place	Date	Hour	Summary of Events and Information	Remarks and references to Appendices
INCHY BEAUMONT	April 1st to 30th		During the month the Divisional RE's carried out demolitions of Camps & Divisional RE Workshops — A.O.T.O. to collect demolitions.	
	April 3		R.V. James to F. Corps Sigs	
	4		L./Cpl. Lane to England Div. Sigs	
	8		2 Wards proceeded on leave to join 144 A.T. Co. on return	
	14		Capt. Craig - Adjt. returned from leave & took over from Capt. Daly	
	17		4 horses to CRE CAMBRAI Sub Area	
	20		Major Henderson transferred from 466 Field Coy RE to 466 Field CRE	
	21		2 Boys to 144 OS Co.	
	23		R./Cpl. G.S. Howard returned from leave	
	25		R.E. H.Q. became officials to 466 Div Paint H.Q. and moved from INCHY to CAUDRY	
	27		Major Eveleigh to U.K. for demobilisation	
	28		Cpt. Bennett to No 3 Aux Ref. Co. Staff Sergeant etc.	

Adjt. R. E. 46th Division

Capt.

R.E. H.Q. 46th Div. Parks.   Ennn/10000   Army Form C. 2118.

WAR DIARY
INTELLIGENCE SUMMARY.

Shur M Valenciennes

May 1919.

Wl 34

Place	Date	Hour	Summary of Events and Information	Remarks and references to Appendices
CAUDRY	1st to 30th		Remained attached to Divisional Park H.Q.	
	26.		Lt. Col. H.S. Hooker D.S.O. R.E. left for England to report to India Office.	

G. Page
Capt.
Adjt. R.E. 46th Div.

HQ RE 46th Div Potter

MD RE 46 D

WAR DIARY
or
INTELLIGENCE SUMMARY.
(Erase heading not required.)

JUNE 1919.   Army Form C. 2118.

Place	Date	Hour	Summary of Events and Information	Remarks and references to Appendices
CAUDRY	June 16th		Major Stanham M.C. RE left for U.K. Lieut Cochin of 466 Field C. RE (100 ORs).	
	June 17th		466 Field C. RE left for U.K. (20 ORs). 468 ditto	
	June 22nd		Cadre of 468 Field C. RE left for U.K. (23 ORs) Remaining personnel forming Baggage Guard moved from INCHY to CAUDRY.	
	June 26th		All store of the Field Companies have now from INCHY to Velu Park, CAUDRY.	

Ricyó
Capt + Adjt Recorder
46 Div